Architecture *of* Wales

Architecture *of* Wales

General Editor
Mary Wrenn
Royal Society of Architects in Wales –
Cymdeithas Frenhinol Penseiri yng Nghymru

Series Editors
Oriel Prizeman, Cardiff University
David Thomas, Catalina Architecture
Jonathan Vining

Advisory Panel
Irena Bauman, Director, Bauman Lyons Architects, Leeds
Richard Parnaby, Professor of Architecture, University of Wales Trinity Saint David
Alan Powers, author and architectural historian
Ian Pritchard, Secretary General, Architects Council of Europe (ACE)
Damian Walford Davies, Head of School, Cardiff School of English,
Communication and Philosophy, Cardiff University

RSAW
Architecture.com/wales

Published in cooperation with
The Royal Society of Architects in Wales –
Cymdeithas Frenhinol Penseiri yng Nghymru

Architecture *of* Wales

THE HISTORY AND ARCHITECTURE OF CARDIFF CIVIC CENTRE

Black Gold, White City

John B. Hilling

UNIVERSITY OF WALES PRESS
2016

www.uwp.co.uk

British Library CIP Data
A catalogue record for this book is available from the British Library

ISBN   978-1-78316-842-2
eISBN   978-1-78316-843-9

With thanks to the Royal Commission on the Ancient and Historical Monuments of Wales for supporting the publication of this book. The Royal Commission on the Ancient and Historical Monuments of Wales is the investigation body and national archive for the historic environment of Wales. It has the lead role in ensuring that Wales's archaeological, built and maritime heritage is authoritatively recorded and seeks to promote the understanding and appreciation of this heritage nationally and internationally.

Designed and typeset by Chris Bell, cbdesign
Printed by CPI Antony Rowe, Chippenham, Wiltshire

Contents

Series Editor's Preface   vii

Foreword *Gillian Clarke*   ix

List of Illustrations   xiii

Introduction and Acknowledgements   xvii

Editorial Note   xix

1   A Small, Sleepy Town in the Shadow of a Castle   1

2   Black Gold   13

3   A Gentleman's Park   27

4   A Battle for Sites and Minds   49

5   Negotiations and Diversions   63

6   Plans and Petitions   75

7   A View of the Civic Centre:
Its Layout, Appearance and Open Spaces   89

8   Development of the Civic Centre Before the First World War:
Buildings and Monuments   103

9   Development of the Civic Centre Between the Wars:
Buildings and Monuments   141

10   Development of the Civic Centre After the Second World War:
Buildings and Monuments   155

11   Cardiff's Civic Centre in Context   171

12   Conclusion   187

Brief Biographies of Architects   193

Architectural Glossary   197

Bibliography   201

Index   209

Series Editor's Preface

GIVEN THE CONVENTIONAL image of Wales as a land of song and poetry, architecture and the visual arts can be easily overlooked, a neglected poor relation to the country's seductive musical and literary traditions. Relatively little has been published about the architectural heritage of our nation, despite the fact that buildings and places have been created in Wales that bear comparison with contemporaneous examples elsewhere, produced by architects engaged in the same wider cultural currents and discourse. There are many reasons for this: Wales has so often been judged as being too small, too homely, or simply not distinctive or fashionable enough to attract the sustained attention of architectural critics and historians. Add to this a lack of consistent patronage and a deeply-ingrained Nonconformist tradition that discourages any form of showing off, it is not surprising perhaps that we lack a more complete record of the architectural achievements of past generations.

Of course, the truth is that Wales has a rich built heritage, from the medieval to the modern. Its architectural character is very different from that of the other nations of the British Isles, and it is this very distinctiveness that deserves to be celebrated. The Royal Society of Architects in Wales is delighted to present, with the University of Wales Press, a series of books exploring the architecture of Wales, adding new chapters to the evolving story of the buildings, places and spaces of our 'damp, demanding and obsessively interesting country'.[1]

Mary Wrenn, Director RSAW
The Royal Society of Architects in Wales (RSAW) represents
and supports Chartered Members of the Royal Institute of
British Architects (RIBA) in Wales.

---

[1] Jan Morris, *Wales: Epic Views of a Small Country.*

Foreword

Gillian Clarke

THE POWER OF PUBLIC BUILDINGS and their arrangement to influence the lives of those who live and work among them cannot be exaggerated. We should never underestimate the human need for beautiful spaces, or people's ability to value 'commodity, firmness and delight' in their urban surroundings: the street sweeper, a tramp asleep on a bench beside a statue, the man who prongs litter in the park, the men and women who arrive before dawn to clean a public building, the bin-lorry men at the back doors, students basking on the lawns outside the university, the museum's secretaries and doormen and chattering flocks of children herded by their teachers. All, entering a Civic Centre set among green spaces, gardens and trees, from the terraced streets and farther suburbs of the city where they live, can claim great buildings as their own for a few hours, but they will continue to inhabit them, and be inhabited by them, all of their lives.

By the time I was 10 years old, I was entranced by Cardiff's Civic Centre, its enticing pathways, lawns and trees, its buildings as white as the 'treasure-stones', Penarth alabaster, found on the beach nearby. My favourite stone bear, couchant on the castle wall with his fourteen fellow beasts, was gate-keeper to a land of palaces, gardens, broad avenues, pillars, domes, a dragon, and a clock-tower you could see from miles away. Inside the white palaces were marble halls, curving staircases, statues, patterned tiles, and lofty spaces where I felt part of a fairy story. It was another country, and it was mine.

My reward for being good, while my father checked mail in his office at the BBC in Park Place, was our Saturday visit to the Museum: across the road, past the Gorsedd Gardens, up the wide flight of steps, under the white-pillared portico, and into the glorious lofty space of the hall. I ran to see my favourite treasure: the fox frozen forever in his glass case. A little later, it was the blue lady I most often visited, Renoir's *La Parisienne*, dressed in every blue in the world, the blue of Porthkerry bluebell woods, lapis lazuli, cobalt, indigo and sky.

A recent visit to the gallery reminded me that I know that painting as well as I do, and others in the Davies bequest to the Museum, because I grew up with them. I possessed them. Later, as a new student at the University, at the Freshers' Ball staged in the City Hall, I ran up the staircase into the Marble Hall, past statues of Welsh heroes, to dance to the music of John Dankworth and Cleo Laine.

After the clamour of shops and traffic, once over the canal where boys dived for pennies, something new began. A garden. A rose-coloured road. White stone. Sixty acres where a magic city gleamed among gardens, a perspective of luminous palaces leading through avenues of trees. I possessed it, and it possessed me.

The daily walk to College from Cardiff General Station – I see it as a map – took me up St Mary Street, High Street, past Greyfriars, over the Dock Feeder, up the rose-red avenue of elms, through Alexandra Gardens, over Museum Place, and through the white stone portal into the cool entrance hall of University College. I remember meeting my tutor to discuss my Spenser essay at a window seat in the half-light of the main hall; my Anglo-Saxon seminar in a little room up a narrow stone staircase, coal smoking in the grate; and sitting summer exams as the brass bands of the Miners' Gala Parade passed by every June. In the upstairs gallery of the College library, where I studied for those exams, were little 'rooms', almost enclosed by a pair of bookcase 'walls': the third wall a book-lined walkway, the fourth open to a spacious view from the lofty ceiling to all that was happening on the floor below. I cannot forgive the barbaric destruction of that generous space, and its little rooms-with-a-view, by the insertion of a mezzanine floor. Nor do I forgive those who bulldozed the ruins of Greyfriars. I remember public outrage in the 1970s at a City Council transport department proposal to destroy the animal wall to make room for a highway. Public rage saved it. Even sadder, but nobody's fault, was the loss of the double avenue of elms, planted for the third Marquess of Bute in 1779–80. In my university days they were a green cathedral. I walked that way when they were in full leaf just to see how the giants touched fingers across Edward VII Avenue, or the way their shadows lay on snow. I grieve for them still, long since dead from Dutch elm disease, felled like firewood beside the road.

This book tells the story of Cardiff's Civic Centre in two ways, as a time-line and as a map. The time tells the story from the late eighteenth century to the present day. The map shows the 60 acres (24 hectares) of its architectural plan. At the far north end of Edward VII Avenue and Museum Avenue, Corbett Road draws a line west to east, a conclusion, the end. But it is not, quite. On the far side of Corbett Road, the two avenues of trees and roads continue through Queen Anne Square, separating yet connecting white stone and red brick, civic building and domestic houses. The border is marked by a white stone screen, through which can be seen the lines of the roads and the trees retreating into the distance between the red brick houses of an exclusive little estate. It was designed for the last Marquis by the architect, Howard Williams.

Cardiff's Civic Centre was built from the wealth produced by coal and its transportation from what became the biggest coal dock in the world. My late father-in-law, and his father before him, were miners in Oakdale Colliery, part of the South Wales coalfield. Howard Williams, the architect who designed Queen Anne Square and its screen, was my uncle.

Architect

E. A. Rickards (1872–1920)

Such a tonnage of Portland stone,
shipped to a coal town as the century turned.
Luminous, Jurassic, pure as stacked ice,
and marble from Siena unloaded in the dirt
beside the black, black coal that paid for it.

Oh, to have been there, a hundred years ago,
Law Courts and City Hall complete,
flanking an avenue of sapling elms
among those sixty empty parkland acres,
there at the birth of a city;

to have stood that night with the young architect,
self-taught, flamboyant, garrulous,
in love with high Edwardian Baroque;
to have shared his grand romantic gesture,
bringing a friend to view his work by moonlight,

to see his buildings carved from ice,
the clock tower's pinnacle, the clock
counting its first hours towards us,
when moonlight through long windows of the marble hall
cast pages yet to be written.

Reproduced courtesy of Gillian Clarke and Carcanet Press Ltd.

List of Illustrations

Figures

Fig. 1.1.	Cardiff and the early canals.	7
Fig. 2.1.	Cardiff and the early railways.	15
Fig. 2.2.	Land ownership in Cardiff.	18
Fig. 3.1.	Cathays Park in the eighteenth century.	31
Fig. 3.2.	Cathays Park in the 1820s.	35
Fig. 3.3.	Cathays Park in the 1840s.	38
Fig. 3.4.	Cathays Park in the 1890s.	43
Fig. 4.1.	Central Cardiff, with sites for municipal buildings.	51
Fig. 5.1.	The 1896 Cardiff Exhibition.	65
Fig. 6.1.	Proposed development of Cathays Park.	78
Fig. 8.1.	Development of Cathays Park between 1900 and 1918.	105
Fig. 8.2.	Cardiff City Hall, first floor plan.	109
Fig. 8.3.	Glamorgan County Hall (now Glamorgan Building), ground floor plan.	125
Fig. 8.4.	National Museum of Wales, ground floor plan (1).	129
Fig. 8.5.	National Museum of Wales, ground floor plan (2).	133
Fig. 9.1.	Development of Cathays Park between 1919 and 1940.	143
Fig. 9.2.	Temple of Peace and Health, ground floor plan.	151
Fig. 10.1.	Development of Cathays Park since 1946.	157
Fig. 11.1.	Plan of Saltaire.	173
Fig. 11.2.	Plan of central Birmingham.	174
Fig. 11.3.	Plan of central Liverpool.	174
Fig. 11.4.	Plan of 'Albertopolis', London.	175
Fig. 11.5.	Plan of Marktplatz, Karlsruhe, Germany.	179
Fig. 11.6.	Plan of Konigsplatz Quarter, Munich, Germany.	179
Fig. 11.7.	Plan of Senate Square, Helsinki, Finland.	180
Fig. 11.8.	Plan of Rathauspark on the Ringstrasse, Vienna, Austria.	182

Plates

Pl. 1.	Cardiff in the 17th century.	3
Pl. 2.	The Old Town Hall.	4
Pl. 3.	Cardiff in the late 18th century.	5
Pl. 4.	Dowlais Ironworks.	6
Pl. 5.	Cardiff and the early canals.	8

Pl. 6.   The Pierhead, Cardiff.   10
Pl. 7.   Cardiff and the early railways.   14
Pl. 8.   New Town Hall, St Mary Street.   17
Pl. 9.   Free Library and Art Gallery, Trinity Street.   21
Pl. 10.   Cardiff Castle, from the north east. NPRN: 33   29
Pl. 11.   'A Catalogue of Household Furniture … at Cathayes', 1824.   34
Pl. 12.   Design for the Clock Tower at Cardiff Castle.   39
Pl. 13.   Design for Castle Stables.   40
Pl. 14.   Park House, Park Place.   41
Pl. 15.   Herbert House, Greyfriars Road.   44
Pl. 16.   Aberdare Hall, Corbett Road. NPRN: 17937   46
Pl. 17.   Proposed Municipal Buildings, 1891.   55
Pl. 18.   'The future of Cardiff', 1894.   58
Pl. 19.   Proposed Municipal Buildings, 1895.   60
Pl. 20.   Cardiff Exhibition, 1896.   66
Pl. 21.   Proposed Town Hall, 1897.   71
Pl. 22.   City Hall under construction, c.1903.   81
Pl. 23.   A Vision of the Civic Centre.   86
Pl. 24.   Bird's eye view of Cathays Park from the south. NPRN: 401617   91
Pl. 25.   Aerial view of Queen Alexandra Gardens, 2007.
           NPRN: 421034   97
Pl. 26.   The Gorsedd Gardens. NPRN: 411973   99
Pl. 27.   The Friary Gardens. NPRN: 420855   100
Pl. 28.   Cathays Park from the north-west, 1920. NPRN: 401617   104
Pl. 29.   City Hall, general view. NPRN: 168   107
Pl. 30.   City Hall, south front. NPRN: 168   107
Pl. 31.   City Hall, attic sculpture ('Poetry and Music'). NPRN: 168   108
Pl. 32.   City Hall, H. C Fehr's sculpture. NPRN: 168   108
Pl. 33.   City Hall, the Marble Hall. NPRN: 168   110
Pl. 34.   City Hall, the Council Chamber. NPRN: 168   111
Pl. 35.   City Hall, the Assembly Hall. NPRN: 168   112
Pl. 36.   Law Courts, King Edward VII Avenue. NPRN: 31806   113
Pl. 37.   Law Courts, interior of Courts Hall. NPRN: 31806   113
Pl. 38.   University of Wales Registry. NPRN: 31917   114
Pl. 39.   Gorsedd Circle. NPRN: 301652   116
Pl. 40.   Statue of John Cory. NPRN: 32779   117
Pl. 41.   University College, bird's-eye view of intended building.   118
Pl. 42.   University College, west front. NPRN: 31914   118
Pl. 43.   University College, Great Court. NPRN: 420858   119
Pl. 44.   University College, Drapers' Hall.   120
Pl. 45.   University College, Drapers' Hall, as built. NPRN: 420858   120
Pl. 46.   South African (Boer) War Memorial. NPRN: 32834   122
Pl. 47.   Statue of first Viscount Tredegar. NPRN: 32757   123
Pl. 48.   Statue of Judge Gwilym Williams. NPRN: 32792   123

Pl. 49.   Statue of Lord Aberdare. NPRN: 32791   123
Pl. 50.   Glamorgan Building, east front. NPRN: 31785   124
Pl. 51.   Glamorgan Building, external sculpture. NPRN: 31785   124
Pl. 52.   Glamorgan Building, west front. NPRN: 31785   126
Pl. 53.   Glamorgan Building, Council Chamber. NPRN: 31785   126
Pl. 54.   Proposed Welsh Museum of Natural History,
          Arts & Antiquities.   127
Pl. 55.   National Museum of Wales, competition design.   128
Pl. 56.   National Museum of Wales, south front. NPRN: 167   130
Pl. 57.   National Museum of Wales, attic sculpture. NPRN: 167   131
Pl. 58.   National Museum of Wales, Entrance Hall. NPRN: 167   132
Pl. 59.   Bute Building (former Technical College), east front.
          NPRN: 31905   135
Pl. 60.   Proposed Welsh Insurance Commission.   137
Pl. 61.   Statue of Lord Ninian Crichton-Stuart. NPRN: 32778   142
Pl. 62.   Proposal for National War Memorial.   144
Pl. 63.   National War Memorial. NPRN: 32845   145
Pl. 64.   National War Memorial, interior detail. NPRN: 32845   145
Pl. 65.   Statue of third Marquess of Bute. NPRN: 32774   146
Pl. 66.   Glamorgan Building (Glamorgan County Hall extension).
          NPRN: 420879   147
Pl. 67.   Queen Anne Square Colonnade. NPRN: 420880   148
Pl. 68.   Welsh Government Offices (Welsh Board of Health),
          south front. NPRN: 31921   149
Pl. 69.   Temple of Peace and Health, east front. NPRN: 11820   150
Pl. 70.   Temple of Peace and Health, low-relief sculpture.
          NPRN: 11820   152
Pl. 71.   Temple of Peace and Health, Hall of Nations. NPRN: 11820   153
Pl. 72.   Aerial view of Cathays Park from the north. NPRN: 301652   156
Pl. 73.   Redwood Building, east front. NPRN: 307796   158
Pl. 74.   Statue of David Lloyd George. NPRN: 32780   159
Pl. 75.   Cardiff University, proposed layout of new buildings.   160
Pl. 76.   Cardiff University, Law Building. NPRN: 420881   161
Pl. 77.   Cardiff University, Sir Martin Evans Building. NPRN: 420867   162
Pl. 78.   Cardiff University, Tower Building. NPRN: 420869   162
Pl. 79.   Cardiff University, Life Sciences Building. NPRN: 420868   163
Pl. 80.   Central Police Station, east front. NPRN: 307791   164
Pl. 81.   Welsh Government Offices. NPRN: 420870   165
Pl. 82.   Welsh Government Offices, Entrance Hall.   166
Pl. 83.   City of Cardiff Falklands Conflict Memorial. NPRN: 420871   167
Pl. 84.   Welsh National Falklands Conflict Memorial. NPRN: 420872   168
Pl. 85.   Birmingham Town Hall.   177
Pl. 86.   Dock Office, Barry.   178
Pl. 87.   Senate Square, Helsinki.   181

Plates 24, 26, 27, 29, 34, 50, 63 and 71 are also reproduced in the colour plates section between pages 140–141.

Sites listed are referenced with a National Primary Record Number (NPRN). Further information is available through the Royal Commission's online database *www.coflein.gov.uk*. This can be searched both cartographically and by NPRN, name and other information categories.

The majority of photographs, most of which are by Iain Wright, are kindly supplied for reproduction by the RCAHMW archives (Crown Copyright). The following are generously donated from various sources:

Cardiff Castle: 11, 12, 13.
Cardiff Council Library Service: 2, 3, 17, 18, 19, 21, 23, 60.
Cardiff University: Special Collections and Archives: 41, 44, 75.
© Crown Copyright (2014) Visit Wales: 82.
David Hilling: 7, 86.
John B. Hilling: 15, 87.
Photographs 1, 4, 5, 6, 8, 9, 14, 20, 54 and 62 are reproduced with the permission of the National Museum of Wales; no. 22 is reproduced with the permission of Media Wales Photos; photograph no. 55 is reproduced with the permission of RIBA Library Drawings and Archive Collection; and photograph no. 85 is reproduced with the permission of Historic England Archive.

Introduction
and Acknowledgements

CARDIFF'S MOST OUTSTANDING architectural phenomenon is its justifiably famous Civic Centre in Cathays Park. Indeed, the Civic Centre's creation, and subsequent development during the twentieth century to include some of Wales's principal buildings, is a singular reflection of Cardiff's importance to the nation and architecturally, at least, validates the town's status as city and national capital. How the Civic Centre came about is the subject of this book.

In many ways Cardiff was fortunate to end up with such a fine Civic Centre, as the town was not always seen as a progressive place. In fact, it was little more than a backwater until a canal was constructed to link it with its iron-making hinterland. Even then, it was not until the coming of the railways and the large-scale export of coal – the 'black gold' that filled the coffers of the coal-masters and the Bute estate – that Cardiff began to mushroom in population, importance and wealth, and so became not only Wales's premier town but also the world's greatest coal port. Inevitably, the development brought with it the need for civic institutions and public buildings commensurate with the town's ambitious aspirations. In time this led to the establishment of a Civic Centre in Cathays Park, which was developed over the course of the twentieth century to become 'the finest civic centre in the British Isles', according to John Newman,[1] and one fit for a capital city. Indeed, as a formally planned group of public buildings it is unique in Britain. In order to see anything along similar lines to Cathays Park it would be necessary to go abroad.

The combination of white, Portland stone buildings and green parkland makes Cathays Park unusually attractive – the abundant trees and foliage helping to integrate the various styles of buildings – particularly in spring time when the cherry blossom is out. It is, as I like to think of it, a 'white city', largely built through the wealth that was created by the 'black gold' that poured from the valleys during the nineteenth century. It is, indeed, an extraordinary assemblage of buildings – in effect, a permanent exhibition – illustrating some of the principal architectural styles and tastes of the late nineteenth century and the twentieth century. More than anything, the Civic Centre is a magnificent reminder of the vision of its creators and of the hard-won wealth wrested so painfully from the nearby valleys.

---

1 John Newman, *The Buildings of Wales: Glamorgan*, p. 220.

Surprisingly, only one book has been written about this extraordinary enterprise in architecture and town planning, despite the Civic Centre's renown. This was Edgar Chappell's *Cardiff Civic Centre: A Historical Guide*, a slim volume largely written in 1945. Much has happened in the 70 years since the publication of Chappell's book, and during that period not only has the Civic Centre grown to fill the whole of Cathays Park but also the architectural style of its later buildings has moved further and further away from that of the earlier role models. The time for an update of Chappell's book is long overdue, and in the following pages I have tried to do that by building on his foundations and, at the same time, enlarging the time-scale to include the history of Cathays Park during the nineteenth century and the Civic Centre's development during the whole of the twentieth century.

The first part of this book follows a generally historical approach, outlining Cardiff's phenomenal growth during the nineteenth century – from under 2,000 inhabitants to nearly 170,000 – and exploring how, as it evolved into a major port and the largest town in Wales, the demand for civic and national buildings appropriate to the town's growing position and reputation became insistent and could not be easily brushed aside. Running parallel to Cardiff's meteoric growth is the story of how the fields lying immediately north of the town were transformed into a private park by the fabulously rich Bute family, and of the persistent efforts made by the town's administrators to purchase the same land for their public buildings and future Civic Centre. Chapter 7 takes an overall look at the Civic Centre as it is today, while the following three chapters describe the history and architecture of the individual buildings and monuments that have been erected in Cathays Park over the last century or so. In order to consider the context in which Cardiff's Civic Centre evolved, other formally planned groups of public buildings in Britain and abroad are briefly examined in Chapter 11. Finally, the text concludes with a reflection on how the integrity of Britain's finest Civic Centre can be maintained, and possibly improved, during the coming years.

Accompanying the text are a number of specially drawn maps. They show the early development of canals and railways that led to Cardiff's growth, the strategic importance of the Bute estate, and the way in which Cathays Park has changed and developed over two centuries. In addition, there are comparative plans showing the grouping of public buildings in some other cities, and plans of some of the more accessible public buildings in Cathays Park.

It is impossible to write a work of this nature without considerable help from other people, and I would like to take this opportunity to thank each and every one who has helped in any way. David McLees, Jonathan Vining and Eurwyn William read the full manuscript, and Matthew Williams read the chapter on the Butes and the development of Cathays Park: each made many perceptive comments and gave invaluable suggestions and helpful advice. I am very grateful to Louise Barker and staff at the Royal Commission on the

Ancient and Historic Monuments for Wales (RCAHMW) for making available the majority of the photographs that have been used to illustrate the book, most of which were taken by Iain Wright. At the National Museum of Wales I am grateful for the support and help received from Peter Wakelin, Arabella Calder, Mark Etheridge and Jennifer Evans. At Cardiff University, Peter Keelan and Alison Harvey, both of the Library's Special Collections and Archive, Sarah Nicholas of the Welsh School of Architecture and Jim Atkinson and Richard Frayling of the Estates Department, have each given valuable help in retrieving relevant material for my research, while departmental heads Chris Tweed and Christopher Williams have supported the project. I am grateful to David Lermon, on behalf of the Cardiff Architectural Heritage Society, for financial support towards the purchase of photographs. Others who have helped in various ways are Katrina Coopey and staff at Cardiff Central Library, staff at Glamorgan Archives, Sue Coles of the Welsh Centre for International Affairs, Huw Aled Jones at the Eisteddfod Genedlaethol Cymru, and Simon Unwin. I am greatly indebted to staff at the University of Wales Press for their continued encouragement and for bringing the book to a handsome conclusion. Lastly, but by no means least, I would like to thank my son David for preparing the excellent series of maps and plans from my original sketches and research and for his help with photographic and computer problems, and to my wife Liisa for her continued patience and long-standing support.

Editorial Note

The story of Cathays Park and its Civic Centre covers a period of more than two centuries. During that time there have been many changes, both with regard to the town's administration and the ownership of Cathays Park by the Bute family. It is easy to confuse these changes with events on the ground. I have therefore included the following notes to aid the reader in keeping abreast of the changes.

Cardiff administration

The original Borough of Cardiff was created out of the Norman Lordship of Cardiff about the year 1100. A Royal Charter in 1324 confirmed the various privileges that had been granted by previous Lords, and in 1608 a further Royal Charter declared Cardiff to be a free town and its Burgesses a body corporate. It was not until 1836, however, that the reformed Borough came into existence following the Municipal Corporation Act of the previous year. The Borough was divided into two Wards (North and South), each roughly following the boundaries of the old parishes of St John and St Mary. In 1850 the Borough constituted itself as a Local Board of Health. In 1889 Cardiff became one of the new County Boroughs created under the Local Government Act for that purpose, and in 1905 it was awarded city status. Fifty years later the city was officially recognised as the Capital of Wales.

The Bute succession

I have listed here successive members of the Bute family who had an interest in Cardiff and Cathays Park during the period covered by this book.

Fourth Earl of Bute (from 1792), first Marquess of Bute (from 1796): John Stuart (1744–1814), son of the third Earl of Bute and Mary Wortley Montague. He married Charlotte Jane Windsor (1746–1800) in 1766. When Charlotte's mother, Lady Windsor, died in 1776, Charlotte inherited the wealthy Windsor estate, which included Cardiff Castle and lands around it. After Charlotte's death the first Marquess married Frances Coutts (1773–1832).

Second Marquess of Bute (from 1814): John Crichton Stuart (1793–1848), grandson of the first Marquess of Bute by his first wife. He married, first, Maria North (died 1841) and, secondly, Sophia Hastings (died 1859). He built Cardiff's first dock and became known as the 'creator of modern Cardiff'.

Third Marquess of Bute (from 1848): John Patrick Crichton Stuart (1847–1900), son of the second Marquess by his second wife. He married Gwendolen Howard (died 1932) in 1872. He was responsible for restoring Cardiff Castle and selling Cathays Park to the County Borough of Cardiff.

Fourth Marquess of Bute (from 1900): John Crichton Stuart (1881–1947), son of the third Marquess. He married Augusta Bellingham (1880–1947).

Fifth Marquess of Bute (from 1947): John Crichton Stuart (1907–56), son of the fourth Marquess. He presented Cardiff Castle and the surrounding park to the City of Cardiff in 1947 as a gift.

1

A SMALL, SLEEPY TOWN IN THE SHADOW OF A CASTLE

'CARDIFF LIES LOW', William Gilpin wrote while on a tour of southern Wales during the latter part of the eighteenth century, 'though it is not unpleasantly seated on the land side among woody hills. As we approached, it appeared with more of the furniture of antiquity about it than any town we had seen in Wales . . . From the town and parts adjacent, the windings and approach of the river Taff from the sea, with the full tide, make a grand appearance. This is, on the whole, the finest estuary we have seen in Wales'.[1]

At the beginning of the nineteenth century little had apparently changed and, to the casual observer, Cardiff would seem to be nothing more than a small, sleepy market town in the shadow of a medieval castle. Indeed, there was scarcely anything that might indicate how the place would develop and prosper during the remainder of the century. In fact, any evidence of progress was so unpromising that when the antiquary Benjamin Malkin visited the town in 1803 he observed that 'Cardiff is the capital of Glamorganshire, though far from the first of its towns in extent and population.' Then, in mocking vein, he remarked that 'the requisitions of the Welsh are so moderate, that they consider this as a neat and agreeable place, though it has little contrivance to boast in the arrangement of its streets, little of accommodation or symmetry in the construction of its buildings'.[2]

Nevertheless, despite his snub, Malkin was able to note, in his book *The Scenery, Antiquities and Biography of South Wales*, that there was 'a very good canal, which establishes [Cardiff] as the connecting link between the great iron works of Merthyr Tydvil and the English markets'. The canal and the town's fortunate geographic position even led Malkin to speculate about the town's future. He wrote:

> Cardiff is capable of much greater improvements in a commercial point of view, than are yet contemplated by the inhabitants, notwithstanding the successful example of its neighbours. Pennarth harbour, below the town, is the best and safest in the Bristol Channel . . . When it is considered that by the canal Cardiff might be easily, abundantly, and cheaply supplied with coal from the collieries, and iron from Merthyr Tydvil, for carrying on the hardware manufactories; with tin-plate also from the largest tin mills in the kingdom, on the banks of the canal; with copper and brass by water from Swansea, Neath and other establishments in the western part of the county; it is difficult to ascribe a limit to the commercial capabilities of this place. Cardiff is situated in as plentiful a country as any in the kingdom for all kinds of provisions; and having so good a harbour for the largest shipping, could easily export its produce and manufactures . . . to any part of the world. Cardiff . . . possesses all the advantages of nature that can in this respect be conceived, and those on the largest scale.[3]

Malkin's perceptive views of the town's possible future were, in the end, largely realised, although not entirely in the way that he had envisaged nor during his own lifetime.

When Benjamin Malkin visited Cardiff in 1803, the canal that he had referred to was already 9 years old, and the historic inauguration of the world's first steam railway locomotive a few miles to the north of Cardiff was just a year away. Although the full consequences of these two events could hardly have been envisaged at the time, the opening of the Glamorganshire Canal in 1794 and the trial run of Trevithick's steam locomotive at Penydarren in 1804 were significant occasions signalling, as they did, a period of unprecedented change for Cardiff and the Glamorgan valleys. While it was Trevithick's locomotive that was eventually to have the greatest consequences, initially it was the opening of the Glamorganshire Canal that set in motion Cardiff's extraordinary transition from sleepy market town to capital city.

Cardiff had hardly altered during the two preceding centuries before the coming of the canal and, where there had been change, it had not necessarily been for the better. The town's T-shaped layout, with development blocked off on the north side by the Castle and the Herbert House, was virtually the same as that depicted in 1610 by John Speed in his atlas (Pl. 1). The town consisted of two main streets (Crockerton and High Street/St Mary Street) at right-angles to each other, together with some lesser streets (Church Street, St John Street, Womanby Street) and a number of connecting lanes. Even at this date, there appears to have been a decline from the town's probable thirteenth-century peak of about 2,000 people. Additionally, as Speed recorded, 'as the Taue [Taff] is a friend to the towne, in making a Key [Quay] for arrivage of shipping; so is she a foe to S. Maries Church in the South, with undermining her foundations, and threatning her fall'.[4] During the next half century the population continued to decline, falling to about 1,500 by 1670.[5] A few

Pl. 1. *Cardiff in the 17th century. Model of Cardiff, based on John Speed's map of 1610.*

years later St Mary's Church was roofless and its tower had fallen, leaving the town with only one church.

It was not until 1747 that a new Town Hall (Pl. 2), comprising a council room above a market hall and prison, had been built in the High Street to replace a ruinous medieval Guild Hall, and not until 1774 that a private Act had been passed 'for the paving, cleansing and lighting of the streets of Cardiff'.[6] William Rees noted – and Sandby's 1776 watercolour of Crockerton confirms – that 'even late into the eighteenth century, many burgesses . . . continued to have, on their town plots, cowhouses, stables and pig-sties to house their animals and poultry, the cows passing daily through the streets on their way to and from the town fields' (Pl. 3).[7]

Pl. 2. *The Old Town Hall. The Guild Hall (as it was originally known) was built 1747–53 in the centre of High Street. The statue of the second Marquess of Bute (1793–1848) was erected in front of the Old Town Hall, before being later moved to the end of St Mary Street.*

Progress continued to be slow, however, and another seven years were to pass before any of the old town gates were removed: first, the east and west gates were taken down in 1781, and then the north gate in 1785.[8] Meanwhile the Corporation had repaired and improved the Town Quay mentioned by Speed and, by 1788, there were three private wharves in operation.[9] Together, the wharves dealt with a growing maritime trade much of which was concerned with iron brought down from the ironworks (Cyfarthfa, Dowlais, Penydarren and Plymouth) at Merthyr Tydfil (Pl. 4). But transporting iron from Merthyr was a slow and laborious business, involving either teams of horses or mules along mountain tracks or horse-drawn wagons along a turnpike road in the Taff valley. Soon neither the animals nor the wharves were able to keep pace with the demand for iron exports and so, in 1790, a private Bill was obtained by the ironmasters – with the support of Lord Bute, who owned much of the land in Cardiff through which the canal would pass – that provided 'for making and maintaining a Navigable Canal from Merthyr Tidvile [sic], to and through a Place called The Bank, near the Town of Cardiff'[10] (Fig. 1.1).

Construction of the Glamorganshire Canal began at the Merthyr Tydfil end in August 1790 and work continued more or less steadily until the canal, which was 25 miles (40 km) long, reached the outskirts of Cardiff. From there it passed through lands of the Bute estate (Pl. 5) and along the line of Cardiff Castle's moat – where the towpath was obligingly laid on the bank opposite

Pl. 3. Cardiff in the late 18th century (from a painting by Paul Sandby, 1776). This shows Crokerton (later Queen Street) from the east with its straggling rows of cottages before redevelopment in the nineteenth century. St. John's Church can be seen in the distance.

to that of the castle – through a tunnel under Crockerton and then alongside what remained of the town walls and town ditch until it reached the River Taff. On 10 February, 1794, the canal was finally opened for traffic. John Bird, writing in *The Gentleman's Magazine* reported that 'the canal from Cardiff to Merthir-Tidvil [*sic*] is completed and a fleet of canal boats have arrived at Cardiff laden with the products of the iron-works there, to the great joy of the whole town'.[11] Two years later the canal was extended half a mile downstream to the mouth of the Taff, where a sea-lock was built. Later, a branch of the canal was constructed as far as Aberdare and opened in 1812 to serve the ironworks in that area.

After the coming of the canal all was to change in Cardiff as the town became the outlet for exporting an ever-increasing tonnage of iron that had been processed at various ironworks in the valleys of east Glamorgan. This was soon to result in its becoming Britain's major iron-exporting port. The surge in iron exports was helped by the growing need for weaponry during the Napoleonic Wars (1793–1815). According to *Bird's Directory and Guide to Cardiff* in 1796, 'not less than 8,780 tons of cast and wrought iron of the best manufacture [is] shipped annually for London and other places; the bulk of which is made in Merthyr Tydvil, and which is now brought down from thence by a curious navigable canal'.[12] Although the borough's population had risen again to 1,870 inhabitants by the beginning of the nineteenth

Pl. 4. *Dowlais Ironworks (from a painting by George Childs, 1840). This shows a typical scene at one of the ironworks in the Merthyr Tydfil area, the original source of Cardiff's wealth.*

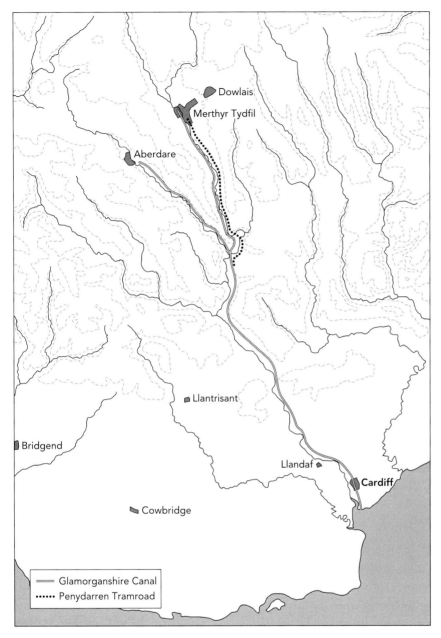

Fig. 1.1. *Cardiff and the early canals. The Glamorganshire Canal was constructed between 1790 and 1794 from Merthyr Tydfil to Cardiff to provide easy access to the sea for the fast growing iron industry; it was later extended to Aberdare. The nearby Penydarren Tramroad became scene of the world's first steam locomotive to run on rails in 1804. Contours are shown at intervals of 500 ft (152 m).*

century, it was still considerably less than either Merthyr Tydfil (7,704 people) or Swansea (6,831 people). Moreover, with only 314 inhabited houses in 1801 there appeared to be fewer households in Cardiff than there had been a 130 years earlier when recorded in the hearth tax roll.[13]

Within a few years of the canal's opening an attempt was made to link Cardiff with Merthyr Tydfil by rail. A Bill for the construction of a tram-road from Cardiff to Carno in the Rhymney Valley, with branches to Merthyr and

Pl. 5. *The Glamorganshire Canal. A quiet scene on the canal at Forest Lock (3 miles [5 km], north of Cathays Park) in the 1930s, by which time traffic was very much reduced (from a photograph by Samuel Coupe Fox).*

Aberdare, was first presented to Parliament as early as 1799 by Samuel Hom-fray of the Penydarren Ironworks.[14] Objections were raised by rival parties and the full scheme was unable go ahead. Instead, a shorter length of tram-road, nearly 10 miles (16 km) long, was laid in 1802 between Penydarren and the canal basin at Navigation, better known now as Abercynon. Hom-fray, keen to be at the forefront of affairs, commissioned Richard Trevithick to build a steam locomotive for the tram-road. The trial run of Trevithick's 'high pressure tram engine' – the world's first steam locomotive to run on rails – took place in February 1804. Hauling a train of wagons with 10 ton of iron and 70 passengers, it made a successful journey down to Abercynon at a rate of 5 miles (8 km) per hour.[15] *The Cambrian* newspaper reported the historic journey, noting: 'It is not doubted but that . . . the machine in the hands of the present proprietors, will be made use of in a thousand instances never yet thought of for an engine.'[16] Unfortunately, the engine's weight broke some of the brittle cast-iron plate rails and the engine was unable to complete the return journey to Merthyr. Two more runs were made with a 10-ton load before the project was abandoned.[17] Even so, the trial had demonstrated the potential for steam locomotive power, a power that was to be successfully used by the Taff Vale Railway, 36 years later.

Although the tram-road had fulfilled its original object of conveying iron to the canal at Abercynon, it was the canal itself that was the means of bringing the raw material down to Cardiff. By 1817, despite a depression following the Napoleonic Wars, almost 30,000 ton of iron a year was exported from Cardiff; by 1830 this had risen to 66,000 ton, and by 1839 to 132,781 ton.[18]

The town's population continued to grow in tandem with the prospering iron trade, gradually gaining momentum from a roughly 3 per cent increase per year during the first decade of the nineteenth century to more than 7 per cent per year by the third decade, until it had reached a total of 6,187 people by 1831. Meanwhile, there had been a development that was to have a crucial and long-lasting effect on the town's later growth. This was the acquisition between 1780 and 1814 of large areas of land in and around the borough by the fourth Earl (later first Marquess) of Bute. Starting from a comparatively small base the Earl had, 'by making substantial purchases of strategic land at Cardiff and within the [south Wales] coalfield . . . considerably enhanced the position of his family in east Glamorgan'.[19] It was this 'enhanced position' that allowed the Butes to dictate the way in which the town would develop over the next century. Resolute land acquisition by the estate naturally created a certain amount of ill-feeling locally. There were even rumours that Lord Bute intended to divert traffic from the turnpike road (to Merthyr Tydfil) in order to bring his Cathays property – or Cathays Park as it would come to be known – into a closer relationship with the Castle estate. But, as often with rumours, there were few grounds with which to substantiate the gossip. It is ironic, nevertheless, 'that the land preservation and wealth that led to the creation of one of the best civic centres in Britain was the consequence of the creation of one of the worst, the scars of industrialisation on the coalfield'.[20]

From the 1820s coal became an increasingly important export (mostly coastwise) from Cardiff, and by 1830 coal exports exceeded iron exports in weight for the first time.[21] Coal, however, being bulkier than iron was less valuable per ton, and it was to be another 20 years or so before the value of coal exported actually exceeded that of iron. The growing use of the canal for transporting iron and coal down to Cardiff soon led to serious congestion at the canal Basin, which was situated between the town and the sea-lock. In order to improve the situation the canal company proposed widening and deepening the Basin, but the proposal came to nothing as it involved land belonging to the second Marquess of Bute, who opposed the scheme, saying that it 'may defeat a very important plan that has been suggested to [me] to improve [my own] property in Cardiff'.[22] Quite what was intended by Bute at this stage is not clear for a number of schemes were in the air, including a canal through Cathays Park (see Chapter 3).

In the end it was a scheme for a new dock that was realised. The project, which had started off in 1828 as a mile-and-a-half long ship canal designed by James Green to be built in the marshlands south of the town, and been

Pl. 6. *The Pierhead,*
Cardiff (from a painting by
Alexander Wilson, 1840).
This scene was painted
shortly after the opening
of the first of the Bute docks
(Bute West Dock) in 1839,
the narrow entrance to
which can be seen in the
centre.

revised by Thomas Telford the following year, received parliamentary approval in 1830.[23] Then, after much discussion of alternatives, an amending Act was obtained in 1834 for a 19-acre (8 ha) dock. This was eventually built between 1837 and 1839 and became known as the Bute West Dock (Pl. 6). Long and narrow, the dock was an ambitious project and probably larger than was strictly necessary at that time. Trade at the new dock was, at first, sluggish as the canal that fed it was unable to deal with the growing levels of iron and coal that required to be transported.[24] It was not until the next great venture – the Taff Vale Railway – had been brought into service that the new dock's prosperity was assured and Cardiff was able to take a lead over other ports in the area. Nevertheless, the initiative of Bute had been crucial in establishing Cardiff as the largest port and town on the south Wales coast; the subsequent history of the town followed on from this.[25]

NOTES

1   William Gilpin, *Observations on the River Wye and Several Parts of South Wales*, p. 84.

2   B. H. Malkin, *The Scenery, Antiquities and Biography of South Wales*, pp. 136–7.

3   Ibid., pp. 144–5.

4   John Speed, *Theatre of Great Britain, Part II: The Principality of Wales* (London, 1676).

5   M. I. Williams, 'Cardiff: Its People and Its Trade, 1660–1720', *Morgannwg*, 7 (1963), p. 79.

6   William Rees, *Cardiff: A History of the City*, pp. 218–19

7   Ibid., p. 209.

8   Ibid., p. 223.

9   Ibid., pp. 229–30.

10   Stephen Rowson and Ian L. Wright, *The Glamorganshire and Aberdare Canals*, vol. 1, p. 19.

11   Ibid., p. 35.

12   Edgar L. Chapell, quoted by, in *History of the Port of Cardiff*, p. 62.

13   Williams, 'Cardiff: Its People and Its Trade, 1660–1720', *Morgannwg*, 7 (1963), p. 81.

14   Stephen K. Jones, *Brunel in South Wales*, vol. 1, p. 41.

15   Ibid., p. 49.

16   *The Cambrian*, 25 Feb. 1804.

17   Jones, *Brunel in South Wales*, vol. 1, pp. 51–3; D. D. and J. M. Gladwin, *The Canals of the Welsh Valleys and Their Tramroads*, p. 63.

18   Rees, *Cardiff*, p. 238.

19   John Davies, *Cardiff and the Marquesses*, p. 40.

20   Wayne K. D. Davies, 'Towns and Villages', in David Thomas (ed.), *Wales: A New Study*, p. 223.

21   John Davies, *Cardiff: A Pocket Guide*, p. 63.

22   Davies, *Cardiff and the Marquesses*, p. 249.

23   Ibid., pp. 249–50.

24   Chapell, *History of the Port of Cardiff*, p. 81.

25   M. J. Daunton, 'Coal to Capital', in *Glamorgan County History*, vol. VI, pp. 206–7.

2

BLACK GOLD

THE IDEA OF LINKING Cardiff and Merthyr Tydfil by rail was not, as we have seen, a new one. However, the railway proposed by three of the Merthyr ironmasters in 1834 – in an effort to overcome the inability of the Glamorganshire Canal to cope with the growing traffic in iron and coal – was on an altogether different scale to the Penydarren Tramroad that had been laid more than 30 years earlier. The Canal Company tried to oppose the scheme, but the railway (now known as The Taff Vale Railway) received Royal Assent in June 1836, though only with the proviso that the maximum speed on the line should be no more than 12 miles (19 km) per hour.[1] The railway, designed by Isambard Kingdom Brunel to run parallel to the Taff river, opened for goods and passenger traffic between Cardiff and Navigation (Abercynon) in October 1840. Six months later it was continued up the valley to Merthyr Tydfil, crossing the Penydarren Tramroad on its way (Pl. 7). Branch lines were later added to Aberdare (1846), Dowlais (1848) and Dinas (1849) (Fig. 2.1).

As with the Bute West Dock, the railway was slow to pick up traffic in its early days. Part of the problem had been the second Marquess of Bute, who had objected to any scheme for the new line to unload its cargoes at anywhere other than his new dock.[2] Eventually agreement was reached between the two parties, although it was not until 1848 that the railway was extended to the Bute West Dock.[3] Soon afterwards, coal exports from Cardiff began to

Pl. 7. Taff Vale Railway and Merthyr Tramroad. Here, near Quaker's Yard (photographed in 1981), Brunel's 1841 viaduct (later widened) carries the Taff Vale Railway over the remains of the tramroad along which the 'world's first steam locomotive to run on rails' hauled a train of wagons between Penydarren and Navigation in 1804.

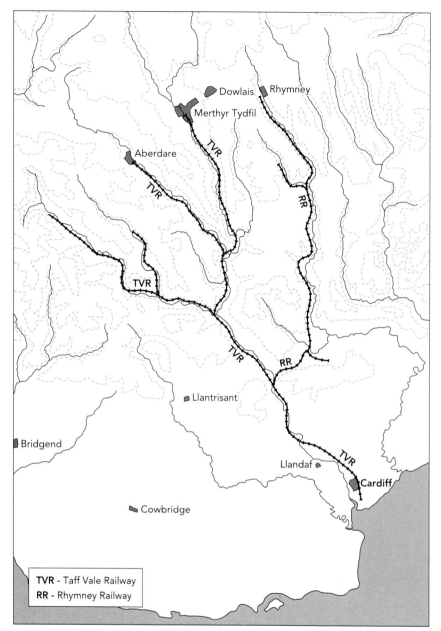

Fig. 2.1. *Cardiff and the early railways. The Taff Valley Railway (the first mainline railway in Wales) was opened between Merthyr Tydfil and Cardiff in 1840–1 with later branch lines to Aberdare and the Rhondda valleys. The Rhymney Railway was built 1854–8 to provide access to the valleys further east. Contours are shown at intervals of 500 ft (152 m).*

take off, rising from a total of 157,733 ton in 1841 to 744,193 ton a decade later.[4] As trade at Bute's new dock began to exceed trade at the canal sea-lock, the Taff Vale Railway became profitable and was soon on its way to becoming one of the most prosperous railways in Britain. During the next decade the Taff Vale Railway Company extended its network into the Rhondda Fawr and Rhondda Fach valleys, opening as far as both Ferndale and Treherbert in 1856. The impact of the railways on the rise of Cardiff's coal trade, and consequent growth, was phenomenal and 'difficult to overestimate'.[5] In 1840 Cardiff lagged well behind both Newport and Swansea in coal exports, but by 1874 the port was exporting three-and-a-half times as much coal as Newport and almost five times as much as Swansea.[6]

Changes in Cardiff began to accelerate following the opening of the new dock and the introduction of railways, so that within a decade the town's population had almost doubled from 11,442 (including Roath and Canton) in 1841 to 20,258 in 1851. During 1848 a competition was held to obtain a comprehensive scheme for draining the town, and in 1849 the river Taff was diverted to allow construction of the South Wales Railway. The railway itself was brought into operation in June 1850 when the first train ran from Cardiff to Swansea. During the following year the railway was extended eastwards to link to Gloucester allowing connections onwards to London.

Meanwhile, the eighteenth-century Town Hall on its island site in High Street was deemed to have outlived its usefulness and a competition was held in 1847 for a building to replace it at a new location in St Mary Street. The competition was won by Horace Jones of London with a design in 'Italian' style. Despite the estimate of cost being almost 50 per cent higher than required in the brief, the scheme went ahead; it was started in 1849 and appears to have been finished in 1851. Alterations were made in 1853 to include a new front elevation with clumsy-looking, Ionic columns, and the second Town Hall (after the Guild Hall) – comprising a large assembly room, police station and magistrates court – was finally opened in June 1854[7] (Pl. 8).

The export of coal, or 'black gold' as it was sardonically known, continued to grow rapidly so that by 1854 foreign exports of the mineral had overtaken coastwise trade. Soon, the value of coal exported from Cardiff would exceed that of iron. Further rapid increases in coal exports were heralded by two developments that took place during the decade. The first of these, the construction of a new dock capable of accommodating the latest ships, was carried out by the Bute trustees on behalf of the third Marquess of Bute who, at the time, was still a minor. The 45-acre (18 ha) Bute East Dock, which ran parallel to the Bute West Dock, was not only considerably larger than the earlier dock but was also deeper and wider making it necessary to build it in three phases, the first part opening in 1855, the second in 1857 and the final part in 1859.[8]

The second development, the Rhymney Railway, was built between 1854 and 1858. It followed the river down from the ironworks at Rhymney – at almost 900 ft (274 m) above sea level – to Caerphilly before crossing over to Taffs Well, from where the company had running powers over the Taff Vale Railway for the last few miles into Cardiff. Five separate coal-mining valleys had now been opened up by railways, which together with the Glamorganshire Canal, converged on Cardiff through the Taff Gorge. However, the arrangement with the Taff Vale Railway was not entirely happy, causing as it

did much traffic congestion and tension between the two railway companies, as well as for the Bute trustees who were heavily involved in the Rhymney Railway. It was not until 1871 that the situation was improved, after the Rhymney Railway had made a direct link with Cardiff and the Bute docks via a costly tunnel driven under Caerphilly Mountain.[9]

The trustees of the Bute estate continued to be a major influence in the development of Cardiff and the neighbouring valleys throughout the nineteenth century. In addition to being heavily involved in the docks and transport Lord Bute, 'as lord of most of the manors of east Glamorgan, owned the minerals not only beneath his freeholds but also beneath the commons within the basin of the Taff', a total of 36,000 acres in all.[10] Already extremely wealthy, the leasing of mineral-bearing land for the extraction of iron and coal made Bute wealthier still. His estate included an immense amount of land in and around Cardiff, so that by the middle of the century the borough was hemmed in on nearly all fronts by Bute land[11] (Fig. 2.2). Virtually the only exception to this encirclement was the land owned by half a dozen much smaller estates to the north-east. As a result of this near total grasp by just one estate it was extremely difficult for any organisation to obtain additional land for the needs of the town or to carry out development of any sort without involving the Butes. What residential development there was in the borough during the 1850s and 1860s was – apart from the creation of Butetown by

Pl. 8. New Town Hall, St Mary Street. A nineteenth-century photograph showing Cardiff's second Town Hall, designed by Horace Jones, and completed in 1854.

Fig. 2.2. *Land ownership in Cardiff. By the middle of the nineteenth century most of the land around Cardiff was owned by the Bute estate making it difficult for the Borough to obtain sites for public recreation, and later for public buildings. (Based on 1844 Tithe Survey.)*

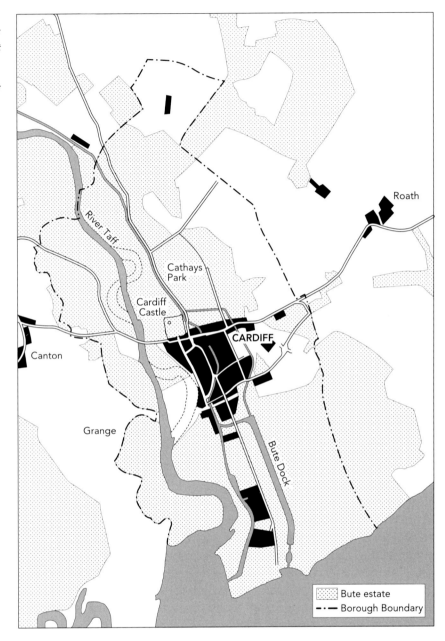

the Bute estate on land south of the town centre – limited to non-Bute land east of Charles Street and at Newtown and Temperance Town (near the main station). Soon there was no further land left to develop and further growth had to take place beyond the borough boundaries at either Roath, Canton or Grangetown.

The issue of land for development was brought to a head in 1858 when the borough tried to obtain urgently needed land for public recreation.

Cathays Park, immediately to the north of Crockerton, was ideally situated for the purpose and, in the first of many attempts, a subcommittee approached the Bute estate with an offer to acquire part of the Park. Unfortunately, the proposal was turned down, the trustee responsible declining to allow 'the sale of any part of the Park to the Corporation for recreation purposes', adding that 'there will be no place for him [Lord Bute] to take a gallop in'.[12] The trustees were not, however, unsympathetic to the need for recreation land – provided it was not on the east bank of the river Taff belonging to the Castle – and in the same year they donated Sophia Gardens, on the west bank, for the town's use as public open space. Yet how far this was a purely philanthropic act is questionable for, meanwhile, the Bute estate had arranged for the park to 'be skirted by a long line of beautiful villa residences which are to be erected between the gardens and a new road intended to be formed and called Cathedral Road'.[13] Clearly, a well-groomed public park between the villas and the river could only help to increase the value of the land.

At the Bute docks, coal exports continued to race ahead, reaching a total of 1,915,120 tons of coal, coke and patent fuel by 1861. During the next 10 years coal exports from the docks averaged 2,220,430 tons per year.[14] Cardiff's population also continued to soar, doubling every 15 years so that by 1861 it had reached 41,422 inhabitants. By 1871 the population had increased still further to 57,363. The town, however, was more dependent than ever on coal for its livelihood and future development.

Cardiff was relatively prosperous by the 1860s and was fast becoming the most dynamic town in southern Wales. As a 'going' place, it had a cultural life of its own. There was at least one theatre (Theatre Royal) in the town, as well as a music hall. In addition, there was an embryonic Free Library as well as a number of literary, scientific and musical societies.[15] The Free Library and Museum, which had been founded in 1862 was, in fact, the first to be established anywhere in Wales under the 1855 Public Libraries Act.[16]

As if to underline the town's growing stature, in 1868 the third Marquess of Bute celebrated his coming of age and began to make his own impact, though not always in the ways desired by others. Theoretically, at least, he was now his own master, although there were financial problems and trustees continued to administer the estate on his behalf.[17] He was, nevertheless, free to do as he liked and he showed his independence by beginning the rebuilding of his feudal castle as a remarkable *tour de force* of 'feudal' Gothic architecture. Two years later, an important and innovative, if temporary, event took place in the town when a Fine Art and Industrial Exhibition was arranged to celebrate the achievements of the borough and the industrial south. It marked 'the first large-scale public venture into the field [of visual culture] in Cardiff'.[18]

A further attempt was made by the borough council in 1873 to acquire Cathays Park as part of an Improvement Bill that was being prepared. Once again the offer was declined as, according to Bute's solicitor, the Park formed part the Castle grounds and could not be sold. He added that 'the terms upon which it was left by the late Marchioness of Bute prevented his [the third Marquess] disposing of it, however otherwise he might consent to it for such a purpose'.[19]

The Marquess of Bute was not in high favour at the time and during the 1874 municipal elections the estate came in for much criticism. David Duncan, editor of the *Cardiff Times*, was particularly aggrieved when a pet scheme for building a new library 'was scuppered at the eleventh hour by the Marquess of Bute's obstruction as landlord of the proposed site'. He wrote that:

> The Marquis [*sic*] of Bute … has shown the most utter disregard for the social and moral well-being of the town from which he derives his boundless wealth. He has ever evinced the most utter lack of sympathy with all municipal progress; has not given the slightest help, either by purse or by counsel, towards improving and beautifying the streets or squares, or public buildings of Cardiff. No commanding municipal structure, no literary or philosophical institutes, no public libraries, no art or science galleries or museums owe their origin to this wealthy peer.[20]

A further dock – the 12-acre (5 ha) Roath Basin – was opened during the same year to cope with the port's growing trade.[21] It had started out as a small tidal harbour before being converted to become the third Bute dock, bringing the total area of docks belonging to the Bute estate to 76 acres (30 ha). But even this amount of dockage was insufficient to surmount the difficulties caused by delays and lack of facilities at the port. To overcome the problems the Bute trustees obtained Parliamentary approval to construct an entirely new dock on a larger scale. A slight depression in the coal trade 2 years later – despite the docks handling well over 3 million ton of coal exports – caused Lord Bute to have second thoughts and the scheme was abandoned temporarily.[22]

As with the docks, the complex of Town Hall, Police Station and Fire Station became increasingly unable to cope with the everyday demands for space made upon them. To overcome this problem, a three-storey extension to designs by James, Seward and Thomas was added at the rear of the group, facing Westgate Street, in 1876–7.[23]

By 1881 Cardiff had grown to become the largest town in Wales, with a population of 82,761 people. At the same time, coal exports at the Bute docks had risen to a staggering 5 million ton a year. It was during this decade that Cardiff grew to a position of pre-eminence as far as the coal trade was concerned, handling 72 per cent of coal exports from southern Wales, 29 per cent of British coal exports and nearly a fifth (18 per cent) of the world's coal exports.[24] It was an extraordinary position at which to arrive after having grown from a small, sleepy market town and fishing port.

Pl. 9. *Free Library and Art Gallery, Trinity Street. A nineteenth-century photograph of the building designed by Edwin Seward and opened in 1882. It was here at the rear of the building that the Science and Art School and the Cardiff Museum were housed.*

A growing sense of pride in the town's leading position led to a second Fine Art and Industrial Exhibition in 1881. This was held at the Drill Hall in Andrew's Lane. The exhibition 'had been organized by Edwin Seward to raise funds to decorate the shell of the new Free Library and Art Gallery'.[25] The Library, which had had a peripatetic existence since its establishment in 1862, was finally given a permanent home in 1882 in a new building in Trinity Street, designed by Seward in competition (Pl. 9). Squeezed in with the library was the Science and Art School and the Cardiff Museum, the collections of which would eventually form the nucleus of acquisitions by the National Museum of Wales in Cathays Park.

During this period all kinds of education began to to be taken seriously and, in 1870, the first elementary school was opened in Cardiff. Secondary education had to wait still longer, for it was not until after the passing of the Welsh Intermediate Education Act in 1889 that the first secondary school was opened. Higher education was more fortunate, and as early as 1881 a meeting was convened to promote the cause of establishing a university in the town. Fund raising began and Lord Bute contributed £10,000, a fifth of the total amount that was being sought. The Council also pledged to give £10,000 towards the cost of a site for the university and its buildings. When, however, enquiries were made to Lord Bute regarding the necessary land it turned out that he, 'was not disposed to give Cardiff Arms Park as a site for a new University College as it was being reserved for recreation, but he was willing to provide a site in the Cathedral Road area, or possibly in the Ten Acre Field, in Roath'.[26] Further complications arose when the Council acquired the Cathedral Road site on behalf of the university college at the same time as Bute proposed a site in Cathays Park for the same purpose. In the end, none of these sites proved to be acceptable.[27] Instead, in 1883, it was decided to establish the University College in the old Cardiff Infirmary in Newport Road, the building having recently been vacated by the hospital.[28]

While discussions were going on regarding a university college site, the Bute estate had begun construction of yet another dock. This, the 33-acre (13 ha) Roath Dock, was built on reclaimed land south of the earliest docks. It was deep enough to cater for the largest ships and, now that local sources of iron ore were worked out, designed to deal with minerals imported from foreign lands for the steelworks at Dowlais. The new dock was opened in 1887. In the same year the Bute docks as a whole were parted from the estate and formed into a separate company, the Bute Docks Company. Though independently managed the new company remained under the chairmanship of the Marquess.[29]

Another attempt was made by the Corporation during the same year to acquire Cathays Park for public use. It was a rather half-hearted attempt, beginning with a proposal in Council to acquire the Park as a memorial to celebrate Queen Victoria's forthcoming jubilee, before being watered down 'to ascertain from the Marquis [sic] of Bute if his Lordship is agreeable to permit the use of the Cathays Park by the public during the summer months'.[30] Clearly anything relating to the Park had become sensitive, the proposer of the request adding that 'he had brought forward the motion believing it had no socialist tendency', and that 'he had no desire to take away from Lord Bute any part of his property, or to encroach upon the rights of his Lordship'. Once again, nothing resulted from the proposal.

In April, 1888, the mayor, aldermen and burgesses petitioned the Local Government Board to award Cardiff with county borough status on the basis that, among other things, it was 'the largest Town and principal Seaport in Wales, with a population of 123,000, which is still rapidly growing', and that it was 'the premier port in Great Britain', outranking, in terms of registered tonnage, both Liverpool and London. The actual tonnage of shipping registered in Cardiff was 4,677,301 ton, compared to 4,622,014 ton in Liverpool and 4,320,304 ton in London.[31] Only New York had a greater number of ships registered in its port. The petition was accepted and a year later Cardiff was duly constituted a county borough, thus retaining its independence instead of being subordinated to the new county councils that were about to come into force.

During 1889 the council resolved to elect, as Mayor of the new county borough, the third Marquess of Bute. It was an unusual thing to have done, since it was rare for members of the aristocracy to be elected to offices of this kind. Bute, nevertheless, felt honoured by the invitation and accepted it with a certain amount of trepidation.[32] Fortunately, the Marquess' year of office went well and did much to heal the troubled relationship that had grown up between the town and the Butes. According to Hannah, 'Bute never seemed to be aware of how much of his wealth he owed to the struggling poor, and to those who worked in the mines', although his 'family had grown rich from the town of Cardiff and their south Wales land'.[33] Yet, it should be remembered that for all his unmindfulness, Bute was generous in supporting local charities, including schools, the Infirmary, the University College, and Catholic causes, as well as by gifts of land.

For some time changes had been taking place in the long-established iron industry at Merthyr Tydfil. Two (Penydarren and Plymouth) of the town's four ironworks had ceased working altogether during the 1870s; the remaining two (Cyfarthfa and Dowlais) had converted from iron-making to making steel.[34] Of these latter, Cyfarthfa was going through a period of difficulties, leaving the works at Dowlais as the main producer of steel in the town. But producing steel required richer ores than were needed to produce iron, necessitating the importation of high grade iron-ore from abroad, and this added significantly to the cost of steel manufacture. Soon the Dowlais company decided to move part of its works to a coastal site to be nearer the point of import. In the event, Merthyr's loss was to be Cardiff's gain as work started on the construction of a new steel-making plant on the East Moors. In 1891 the Cardiff-Dowlais Iron and Steel Works opened with four blast furnaces.[35]

Three years later, in 1894, the centenary of the Glamorganshire Canal was celebrated. During the hundred years since the canal's opening there had been enormous changes, particularly at the canal's lower end; in this time Cardiff had grown from a tiny port-cum-market town, with a limited coastal trade in agricultural products and fewer than 2,000 inhabitants, to become a major administrative centre of about 140,000 people. More than that, it was now an internationally important port with annual coal exports of more than 10 million ton. This total was made up of 7,668,606 ton of coal from the Bute Docks and 2,429,408 ton from the nearby Penarth Dock, which had opened in 1865.[36]

With growth had come additional needs and greater responsibilities. Unfortunately, although the county borough's boundaries had been extended in 1875 to include the nearby settlements of Canton and Roath there was still a dearth of space for development. In particular the Corporation now had a wider administrative remit than ever before and the strip of land between St Mary Street and Westgate Street, where the complex of Town Hall, Justice Courts, Post Office and Fire Station were squashed together, was seriously overcrowded. The Library in Trinity Street remained congested – sharing as it did its premises with the Museum and the Science and Art School – for although a large extension (designed by Edwin Seward) had been added in

1893–96 at the southern end further accommodation was still desperately needed. The newly established University College, too, required space in which to expand out of its cramped quarters in the old Infirmary. There was also a need to build new schools. The question was, how and where could all these competing needs be accommodated?

As far as the existing Town Hall complex was concerned the poor sanitary conditions in the court room had led to criticism and on 6 June 1890, a special committee met to discuss the matter and consider ways in which extra accommodation could be provided. Apart from instructing the borough engineer to 'prepare plans for temporarily improving the sanitary arrangements' little more appears to have been done.[37] Even so, there must have been some effort to improve the situation, for in December 1891 an article in the *Western Mail* referred to the acquisition of land by the Corporation in the vicinity of the Town Hall. The article itself was an attempt to persuade the Corporation to acquire even more land adjoining the Town Hall so that 'municipal buildings worthy of the town' could be built, possibly in the form of an open rectangle with a courtyard in the centre.[38]

The Corporation was still, in the following year, 'considering the urgent need to either enlarge the Town Hall in St Mary Street, or, alternatively, erect an entirely new building'.[39] Evidently a new Town Hall had considerable support for negotiations were begun with Lord Bute during the same year to try, yet again, to acquire Cathays Park for public purposes. Regrettably, there was still some hostility in the town towards the Butes and, partly because of this, 'considerable opposition was offered to the proposed purchase on a variety of grounds'.[40] Among the objections to the purchase of Cathays Park were that the site was too large, that the price was too high, that the restrictions were unfair, and that the removal of the Town Hall from St Mary Street would unfairly affect the interests of ratepayers in the area. So began a dispute over possible sites for urgently needed public buildings, a dispute that came to be known as the 'battle of the sites'.

But before considering the 'battle' in detail, it is time to look more closely at the main site contender, Cathays Park, and discover how it came about and the part played by the Bute family in its evolution.

NOTES

1   Jones, *Brunel in South Wales*, vol. 1, p. 107.
2   Ibid., p. 157.
3   Ibid., p. 175.
4   Rees, *Cardiff*, p. 278.
5   J. H. Morris and L. J. Williams, *The South Wales Coal Industry 1841–1875*, p. 98.
6   Ibid., p. 91.
7   *Builder*, 8 Nov. 1851 and 17 June 1854.
8   Rees, *Cardiff*, p. 272.
9   R. W. Kidner, *The Rhymney Railway*, pp. 13–20.
10 Davies, *Cardiff and the Marquesses*, p. 215.
11 M. J. Daunton, *Coal Metropolis: Cardiff*, map of ownership, pp. 76–7.
12 Edgar L. Chappell, *Cardiff's Civic Centre*, p. 13; Cardiff Central Library (CCL),
    A. A. Pettigrew, *The Public Parks and Recreation Grounds of Cardiff*, vol. 1, p. 130.
13 Daunton, quoted in *Coal Metropolis Cardiff*, p. 80.
14 Davies, *Cardiff: A Pocket Guide*, p. 60.
15 Rees, *Cardiff*, pp. 322–6.
16 M. Evans and O. Fairclough, *National Museum of Wales: A Companion Guide to the National Art Gallery*, p. 9.
17 Davies, *Cardiff and the Marquesses*, p. 73.
18 Peter Lord, *The Visual Culture of Wales: Imaging the Nation*, p. 301.
19 Chappell, *Cardiff's Civic Centre*, p. 13; CCL: Pettigrew, *Public Parks of Cardiff*, vol. 1, pp. 152–65.
20 John Wilson, 'The Chicago of Wales: Cardiff in the Nineteenth Century', *Planet* 115 (1996), p. 21.
21 Rees, *Cardiff*, p. 273.
22 Davies, *Cardiff and the Marquesses*, p. 256.
23 J. H. Matthews, *Cardiff Records*, vol. IV, p. 493; Anon., *Illustrated Guide to Cardiff 1882*, p. 26.
24 Davies, *Cardiff: A Pocket Guide*, p. 64.
25 Peter Lord, *Visual Culture of Wales: Industrial Society*, p. 117.
26 Rees, *Cardiff*, pp. 332–3.
27 'New Municipal Buildings at Cardiff', *Western Mail*, 13 Feb. 1893; CCL: Pettigrew, *Public Parks of Cardiff*, vol. 2, p. 153.
28 Chappell, *Cardiff's Civic Centre*, p. 35.
29 Chappell, *History of the Port of Cardiff*, p. 111.
30 CCL: Pettigrew, *Public Parks of Cardiff*, vol. 2, p. 150.
31 Cardiff Corporation, *Cardiff 1889–1974: The Story of the County Borough*, p. 140.
32 Rosemary Hannah, *The Grand Designer: Third Marquess of Bute*, p. 280.
33 Ibid., p. 253.
34 Laurence Ince, *The South Wales Iron Industry 1750–1885*, pp. 51, 57, 61, 64.
35 Chappell, *History of the Port of Cardiff*, p. 126.
36 Davies, *Cardiff: A Pocket Guide*, p. 68.
37 CCL: Cardiff Corporation, *Proceedings of the Council, 1889–90*, p. 386.
38 CCL: Cardiff Corporation, *Proceedings, 1890–91*, 19, 24 Dec. 1891.
39 CCL: Pettigrew, *Public Parks of Cardiff*, vol. 2, p. 151.
40 Cardiff Corporation, *Cardiff 1889–1974*, pp. 28–30.

3

A GENTLEMAN'S PARK

BEFORE THE ARRIVAL of the Butes the area that later came to be known as Cathays Park belonged to a number of different owners including, at one time, the town's Corporation. The name 'Cathays' was taken from a farmhouse on the site known in 1682 as Cate Hayes and in 1699 as Catt Hays. During the eighteenth century the name was occasionally spelt in different ways – such as Katt Heys, Kate Hays, Gate Hayes and Catt hay – but generally came to be known as Cathays.[1]

Although a number of possible sources for the name have been suggested in the past the most likely origin appears to be Old English or Scandinavian.[2] The latter part of 'Cathays' is, of course, similar to the street in Cardiff known as The Hayes – originally Sokshey – and to the town of Hay (formerly La Haie) in Powys, and is most likely derived from Old English *haga* or Old Norse *hag*, which became *haie* in French. The word originally meant 'a haw or hedge' but eventually came to signify an 'enclosure'. The first part of the name also looks Scandinavian, apparently related to *katt* as found in *Kattegat* (Danish), *Katthavet* (Swedish) and *Katthagen* (a medieval term from a number of north German towns) – each referring to a smaller or outlying place. In the case of Cathays the compound name probably refers to an outlying enclosure, or 'small subsidiary pieces of land held … outside the walls', compared to the Hayes (or Sokshey), which lay within the town walls.[3] The assumption that Cathays – like Womanby (Street) near the original course of the river Taff – is Scandinavian implies an early date, one perhaps going back as far as the eleventh century when Viking raiders may have settled, or raised a trading post, on the banks of the Taff.

The probability that Cathays alludes to an enclosure, or enclosures, suggests that most of the land north of the borough walls was originally waste or common land. This was possibly a continuation of the Little Heath, which (before it, and the Great Heath, were enclosed in 1809) reached all the way from the north-eastern corner of the future park to present-day Albany Road. Such a reading is borne out by George Yates's beautifully drawn map of Glamorgan that was published in 1799, more than three decades before the first Ordnance Survey map of the area.[4] On Yates' map the Little Heath is shown to begin immediately north of Dobbin Pits farm, where the main building of the University now stands. Corroborating this is the fact that some parts of the 'park' still continued to be referred to as 'waste' at the beginning of the nineteenth century.

The Butes' association with Cardiff Castle and their subsequent involvement in the affairs of the town and Cathays Park began with John, Lord Mountstuart (1744–1814), the son and heir to the third Earl of Bute. The Butes were not a particularly wealthy aristocratic family and it was perhaps for that reason that when John married Charlotte Jane, daughter of the second Viscount Windsor, in 1766, it was said that 'the match was made upon prudential considerations only'.[5] The marriage appears to have been successful, nevertheless, resulting as it did in nine offspring, seven sons and two daughters. Charlotte was descended on her grandmother's side from the Herbert family – earls of Pembroke since the fifteenth century – who owned large estates in Wales and elsewhere. When her father died in 1758 without a son and heir, she and her younger sister Alice became co-heiresses. However, as Alice died childless, Charlotte became sole heiress to the Windsor estate, which at that time included Cardiff Castle and the Glamorgan lands of the Herberts as well as property in Durham. When Lady Windsor died in 1776 the estate passed to Charlotte as life tenant, with her husband Lord Mount-stuart enjoying possession *jure uxoris*, i.e. by right of his wife.[6] In the same year Mounstuart was granted the title of Baron Cardiff, and when his father died in 1792 he became the fourth Earl of Bute; four years later his title was upgraded to that of Marquess of Bute.[7]

Despite having come into possession of the Glamorgan estates, including Cardiff Castle (Pl. 10), the first Marquess does not appear to have had a great deal of interest in the management of the same. As John Davies has pointed out, 'his life in the 1760s and 1770s as a man-about-town flirting with politics, his diplomatic career in the 1780s and 1790s, and the ceaseless wandering of his last years can have left little time for the earnest application of estate man-agement'.[8] The administration of the estate during this period seems con-fused, with no one in full-time control as well as some uncertainty as to the exact extent of the estate and the many encroachments on the land by other

Pl. 10. *Cardiff Castle, from the north east. The castle is really three castles in one, with Roman outer walls, a medieval keep surrounded by a circular moat and, on the west wing, a mansion built between the fifteenth and nineteenth centuries. A corner of the Civic Centre can just be seen at the bottom, right-hand corner.* © Crown copyright: RCAHMW.

users.[9] And yet, for all that, there was a positive side to management, for it was during these years that strategic purchases began to be made of land in and around Cardiff and in parts of the coalfield to enlarge and consolidate the estate.

As far as the Cathays Park area is concerned, Lord Bute was already in possession of Cathays House, a farm lying next to the turnpike road (North Road) leading to Merthyr Tydfil. This was, according to A. A. Pettigrew, the last of a family to work for the Butes as gardeners, 'a rambling building of no particular pretension'. In 1786 the house was occupied by Bute's steward, Henry Hollier, and by 1798 it was the home of Thomas Clutterbuck, a tenant of Lord Bute.[10] Further acquisitions took place during this period, the first resulting from an agreement between Lord Bute and Lord Tredegar in 1791 to exchange some of the former's property in the Roath area for some of the latter's property alongside the turnpike road.[11] The land, shown on an extract from the Tredegar Estate map, comprised just over 6 acres (2.5 ha) on the west side of the road, north of the castle, and two irregularly shaped fields of about 4 acres (1.5 ha) lying east of the road between The Friars (also known as White Friars, Greyfriars House, or Herbert House) and Cathays House[12] (Fig. 3.1).

It was at about this time that Bute began negotiating for the purchase of the Friars estate, an immense area of land that included not only the ruins of The Friars and the site of Greyfriars friary but also much of Cardiff as well. Bute's clerk, John Bird, noted in February 1791, 'I am very happy to hear of the purchase of the Friars.'[13] In fact, the purchase was not completed until 1793.[14]

The ongoing acquisitions were enough to provoke rumours, so that Bird was also able to write in 1791: 'it is said that you [Bute] are going to turn the road round Cathays and the Friars'.[15] This has since been interpreted as evidence of Bute's intention to close off part of the turnpike road (North Road) as part of a scheme to consolidate his holdings around the Castle.[16] Whether, however, closing off the turnpike road was ever Bute's intention is questionable for the newly acquired property would, in any case, soon be divided by a major canal. In fact, Bute had already given his support to Richard Crawshay for his Glamorganshire Canal Bill before it went to Parliament in February. Furthermore, Bird, writing in his diary, refers to a meeting in March 1790 in which 'they have settled on having it [the canal] through part of the White Fryers Land, and thence to enter the town ditch at the east Gate'.[17] Clearly, Bute must have been aware of the canal's proposed route even before he exchanged lands with Lord Tredegar.

Soon, Bute was improving some of his land near to the Castle, as Bird was able to record in April, 1799: 'The Plantation on the Hill next the Friars and onwards to Cathays [House] will soon have a very pleasing effect.'[18] This, presumably, refers to the band of trees that bordered the turnpike road, the planting of which may have been suggested by a new interest in Cathays House itself. Nine months later Bute had other things to distract him when his wife Charlotte died on 28 January 1800, at the age of fifty-four. At first

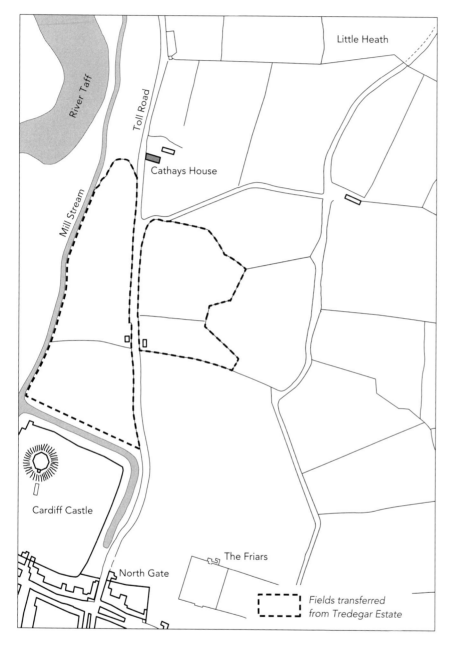

Fig. 3.1. *Cathays Park in the eighteenth century. The exchange of lands on both sids of North Road between Lord Tredegar and Lord Bute in 1791 (shown here by broken lines) marked the beginning of the area to be known later as Cathays Park. The exchange took place before the Glamorganshire Canal had been constructed. (Based on Tredegar Estate map.)*

she was buried in London, but then 9 months later, in an unusual show of affinity with his Welsh base, Bute had her remains brought back to Cardiff to be reinterred in a specially built mausoleum at St Margaret's Church, Roath.[19]

During the interim there appears to have been new interest in Cathays House for, in June 1800, Bird reported that, 'it is said that Mr Clutterbuck leaves Cathays in the course of the year, and that in future when the Marquess of Bute visits Cardiff his residence will be there and not at the Cardiff

Arms as heretofore'.[20] Curiously, the diary note was crossed out later, suggesting that either there had been a change of heart or that Bird had misinterpreted the information. Whatever, it was still a hint of the changes that were to take place later at Cathays, though not for a few years. In fact, the biggest change in 1800 was to be to Bute's own life. Twelve days after reinterring Charlotte at Roath, he married again – this time to Miss Frances Coutts, a young woman who was half his age as well as being the daughter and heiress of Thomas Coutts, the wealthy banker. The partnership is said to have put an end to Bute's financial problems. After the marriage, 'the marquess and his wife wandered from rented house to rented house in England and on the continent'.[21]

While Bute was wandering around Europe, property continued to be added to his Cardiff Castle estate. In 1803 some land was exchanged with the Corporation for parcels of land in the neighbourhood of Greyfriars and the Castle. These included four areas near Cathays House, i.e. 'waste before Cathays' (valued at £90), 'waste behind Cathays' (£68) and '2 fields near Cathays' (£254).[22] Then, a few years later, in 1809, Bute became one of the main beneficiaries (along with the Earl of Windsor and the Borough of Cardiff) of land made available following the enclosure of common land at the Great Heath and Little Heath.[23] As a result of these transactions virtually all the land that would comprise the future Cathays Park seems to have been brought into the hands of the Butes.

A few years later, Cathays House reappears in the picture – almost, it seems, as if by accident – with strange results. With the Castle already reserved for the future use of his grandson and heir, John Crichton Stuart (his father having died in 1794), Bute had to consider another place for his 'second' family to stay when they visited Cardiff. Initially, Cathays' situation was thought to be too 'low lying, and too near the turnpike road and canal' to be regarded as a suitable option. But then, after looking at a number of other sites for building a new house, Bute changed his mind. On 1 March 1812, he came up with a suggestion and wrote to William Mylne saying 'I shall be glad to consult you touching on an alteration I may perhaps make to a small house [i.e. Cathays] in this part of the country, and should wish to see you for the purpose.'[24] Bute had previously used William's better-known father, the architect Robert Mylne (1733–1811), to do alterations for him at his house in Petersham, Surrey, but since Robert had died he now turned to the son for advice. William Mylne (1781–1863) had a mixed practice, mainly connected with engineering works such as water-supply and drainage but also alterations and extensions to country houses.[25]

The consultation with Mylne must have resulted in a decision to build anew on the Cathays site, for a month later Bute wrote again to him confirming that 'The old farm house is down. They have found little timber and what there is, little serviceable.'[26] The letter appears to indicate total demolition of the farm house, but this seems unlikely, bearing in mind that the new house was built, for no obvious reason, hard against the turnpike road. With so much space and money available to the first Marquess, the most likely reason for limiting the new house's position was in order to incorporate some of the walls of the original building within the new structure. Bute may also have been interested in reviving the idea of closing off the turnpike road in order to make it a private right of way.

Although no views, illustrations or plans of the new Cathays House have survived it must have built on a lavish scale. It had a ground floor area of about 800 square metres (8600 sq. ft) and contained thirty-one rooms, many of them with marble fireplaces and richly furnished.[27] In addition, there was a coach house, stables and an ice-house. Construction of the house seems to have taken a long time. Before it could be occupied, Bute fell seriously ill, dying abroad in November 1814. His body was brought back to St Margaret's Church, Roath, for burial in the family mausoleum. Upon the death of the first Marquess of Bute, Cathays House became the property of Frances, his second wife, while Cardiff Castle fell to his grandson, now the second Marquess. Frances, however, seems to have shown little interest in the house and, as far as one can tell, it remained unoccupied.[28]

John Crichton Stuart, the second Marquess of Bute, was just 21 years old when he succeeded to the title. Earlier, he had acquired a severe eye disease that threatened blindness, the prospect of which forced him, for a time, to give up any idea of involving himself in estate management. Instead, he retired to Mount Stuart on the Isle of Bute for the best part of 6 years while his estates in Glamorgan, now looked after by his agent, continued to grow.[29] Despite his affliction, the second Marquess had a deep sense of duty and after 1820 he 'devoted his entire life to estate administration and improvement', spending much of his time travelling around his various estates in Scotland, England and Wales, checking that all was in order.[30] He soon realised 'that his holdings should be to some degree consolidated so that Cardiff could be his principal focus', and, with this aim in mind, began in 1821 trying to sell his large English estate at Luton.[31]

It was during this period, in 1824, that the second Marquess bought Cathays Park, as Cathays House had become known, from Frances, Marchioness of Bute. It is not clear what Bute had had in mind when he bought the house off his step-grandmother, but within a few months he had decided to auction off everything. The 3-day auction for the furniture and other effects took place at the end of June and raised a total of £1,517 (Pl. 11).[32] A few days later the building materials were sold off in lots. The house was demolished and 'the greater part of the materials bought for the manager's house at the Rhymney Iron Works'.[33] This was one of 'three commodious houses' then under construction at the Lawn, Rhymney, for the Directors, General Manager and Works' doctor of the Bute Ironworks.[34] Although some of 'the fine old oak furniture [was] restored to its original place in the Castle, a large portion of the Cathays furniture was also purchased by Mr Forman'. of Penydarren,

Pl. 11. Cathays House catalogue. Frontispiece of 'A Catalogue of Household Furniture' listing the 'Fixtures and other Effects' belonging to Cathays House to be sold in June 1824. This is almost the only evidence there is of the mansion that was built (1812–24) in grand style for the second Marquess of Bute.

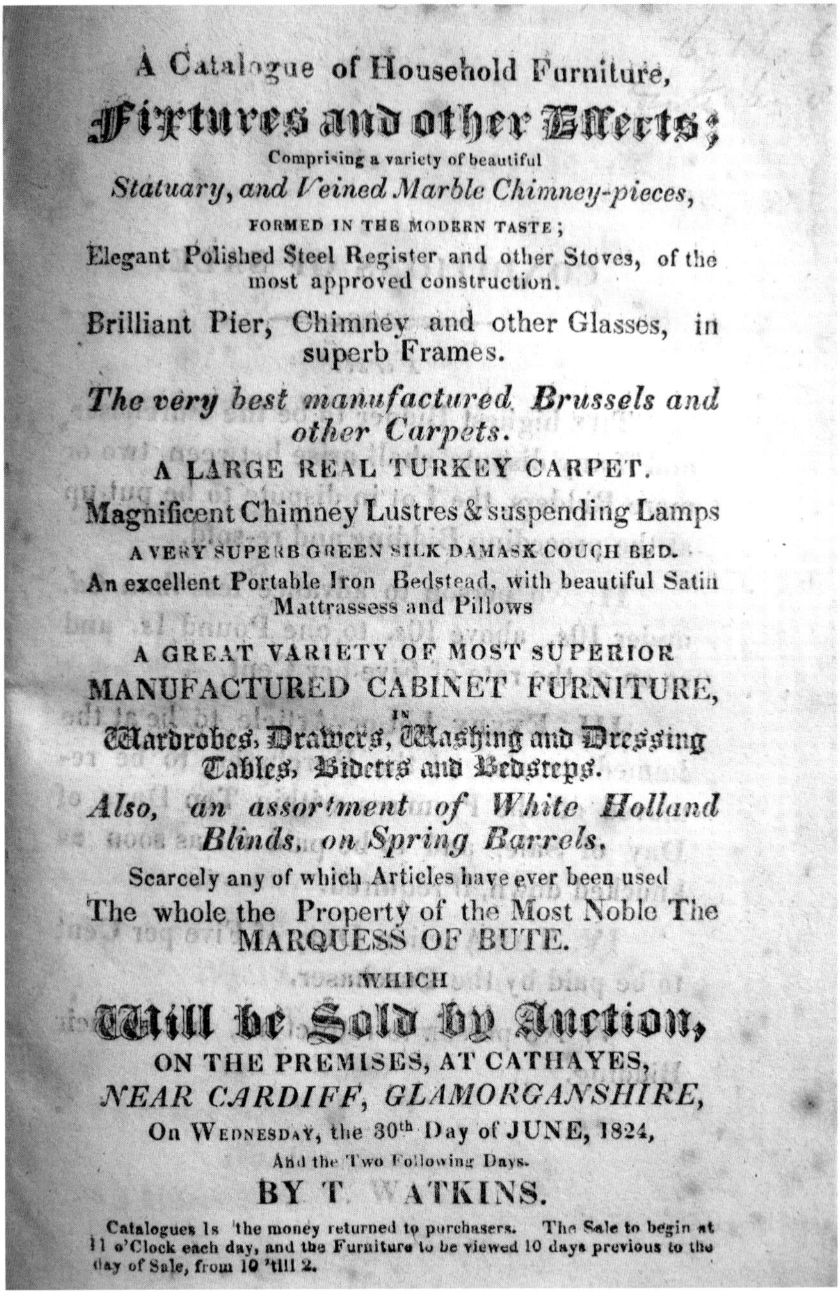

A Catalogue of Household Furniture,

Fixtures and other Effects;

Comprising a variety of beautiful

Statuary, and Veined Marble Chimney-pieces,

FORMED IN THE MODERN TASTE;

Elegant Polished Steel Register and other Stoves, of the most approved construction.

Brilliant Pier, Chimney and other Glasses, in superb Frames.

The very best manufactured Brussels and other Carpets.

A LARGE REAL TURKEY CARPET.

Magnificent Chimney Lustres & suspending Lamps

A VERY SUPERB GREEN SILK DAMASK COUCH BED.

An excellent Portable Iron Bedstead, with beautiful Satin Mattrasses and Pillows

A GREAT VARIETY OF MOST SUPERIOR

MANUFACTURED CABINET FURNITURE,

IN

Wardrobes, Drawers, Washing and Dressing Tables, Bidetts and Bedsteps.

Also, an assortment of White Holland Blinds, on Spring Barrels,

Scarcely any of which Articles have ever been used

The whole the Property of the Most Noble The MARQUESS OF BUTE.

WHICH

Will be Sold by Auction,

ON THE PREMISES, AT CATHAYES, *NEAR CARDIFF, GLAMORGANSHIRE,*

On WEDNESDAY, the 30th Day of JUNE, 1824,

And the Two Following Days.

BY T. WATKINS.

Catalogues 1s the money returned to purchasers. The Sale to begin at 11 o'Clock each day, and the Furniture to be viewed 10 days previous to the day of Sale, from 10 'till 2.

near Merthyr Tydfil.[35] So ended the short life of Cathays House or Park, having lasted barely 10 years.

A few years earlier Bute had been considering schemes that, if carried out, would have profoundly affected Cathays Park. In 1820, for example, a proposal was made 'by the Bute estate to develop a quay further up the river at the Black Weir, to serve that area, but nothing came of it'.[36] Possibly connected with this was a scheme for a proposed new canal that crossed (or maybe joined) the Glamorganshire Canal at Blackweir, and ran across Cathays Park to connect with the Glamorganshire Canal east of the Castle[37] (Fig. 3.2). The scheme also included a new road (alongside the proposed canal), which was intended to replace the turnpike road to Merthyr Tydfil, as well as a new road leading directly to the Castle and one that anticipated the future line of Park Place. How serious these proposals were is open to question; after all, the only record

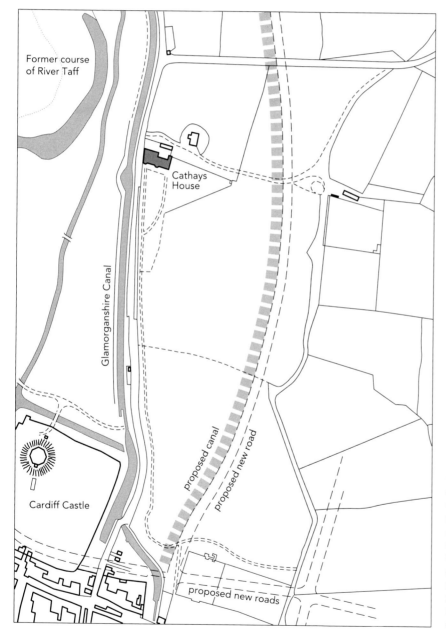

Former course of River Taff

Cathays House

Glamorganshire Canal

proposed canal

proposed new road

Cardiff Castle

proposed new roads

Fig. 3.2. *Cathays Park in the 1820s. By the 1820s Cathays House had been rebuilt in grand style and the Park was almost complete, except on the east side where it followed the line of an old lane. During this period a scheme was proposed for a new canal through the estate together with new roads to provide better access to Cardiff Castle. (Based on unpublished survey.)*

appears to be some pencil sketches on an undated map of the area. The original map shows the new Cathays House, which was probably drawn by David Stewart between 1815 and 1825 when he was employed to survey the Bute estate in Glamorgan. The sketches may represent embryonic ideas that were intended to counter proposals by others that were being bandied about – such as the Glamorganshire Canal Company's proposed purchase in 1822 of 'Bute land in order to improve its facilities',[38] or a scheme by three of the Merthyr ironmasters in 1823 to construct a tramroad west of the Taff to connect with a proposed canal from Canton to the sea, thereby avoiding the Bute Docks.[39]

On the other hand, the pencil sketches (possibly also by Stewart, who advised the Marquess whenever the Glamorganshire Canal Company encroached on his land) may well have represented the beginning of a plan to divert the Glamorganshire Canal and close the turnpike road, thus bringing the western part of Cathays Park (including Cathays House) into a closer relationship with the Castle lands. That this was a serious proposition is suggested by the wording of the lease of 'the walled garden of Cathays' to Robert Short, gardener, on 3 July 1824. The lease specified the use and enjoyment of:

> the rights of way he now has until a new carriage road or way shall be opened from the blind lane to the cross road [later known as Corbett Road] at the north end of Cathays Park after the formation, completion and opening of which the said Robert Short is to use such new road only and cease to use the present roads and ways.[40]

Assuming that the 'new carriage road' refers to the proposed road alongside the new canal and that the 'present roads' includes the turnpike road, then it looks as though the ideas embodied in the pencil sketches were being considered seriously. Fortunately, for Cathays Park and the future Civic Centre, nothing came of the scheme.

In fact, the second Marquess appears to have shown very little real interest in either Cathays Park or Cardiff Castle *per se*, staying only a few weeks a year at the latter and unwilling to spend much money on it.[41] Even so, he was keenly aware of the importance of his Welsh estate and was determined to get the most out of it. In order to do this he kept himself well-informed about Glamorgan affairs and was closely involved in progressive matters across the eastern part of the county. The development in which he was most closely involved, and is best remembered, was the creation of the first Bute dock in 1837–9 (see Chapter 1). It, more than anything else, paved the way, for the phenomenal growth in coal exports and with it Cardiff's own growth. As part of the project a Feeder was constructed during 1835–6 to scour silt from the proposed dock.[42] This involved building a weir across the River Taff, remodelling the brook supplying water to the Castle moat and continuing it in a cut across the lower end of the park – thus severing The Friars from the park – before skirting the eastern side of the town.

Meanwhile, the land with which this book is concerned (i.e. the site of the future Civic Centre) was now nearing its final outline and shape. North Road had always served as its western boundary, while its southern limit was marked by the newly cut Feeder, and its northern limit was determined by the construction of Corbett Road (presumably by the Bute estate) sometime after 1802, according to a map seen by Pettigrew.[43] The eastern boundary was less consistent – at first it took an irregular line formed by a narrow, straggling lane that led to Cathays Nursery and Dobbin Pits Farm; somewhat later, the line followed that of a new road (Park Place) built on a straight line further east, from Crockherbtown (Queen Street) to Cathays Nursery (by then called Park Garden) and the far side of Dobbin Pits Farm, where it finished abruptly. Still later, the construction of the Taff Vale Railway in 1839–40 helped to define the Park's eastern boundary. Both the lower part of Park Place (still uncompleted and undeveloped with houses) and the railway are shown for the first time on the Tithe Survey map of 1844 (Fig. 3.3). Most of the land between these four boundaries – apart from the old garden of Cathays House and smallish fields and strips along the eastern side – was a continuous open space, formally known as Cathays Park, although none of it, except for a plantation bordering North Road, could be regarded as ornamental. It was, perhaps a park in name only, for every part, save for the plantation, was leased or rented out to others, mostly as meadow (about 45 acres – 18 ha) with only very small amounts in use as either arable land or garden.[44]

And so it remained until the sudden death of the second Marquess, the so-called 'creator of modern Cardiff', at Cardiff Castle in March 1848. He was fifty-five and, according to Sir John Guest of Dowlais, 'was at the height of his glory', and 'had been boasting that he would make Cardiff a second Liverpool'.[45] He had, it seemed, been in good health and had brought his 6-month old son and heir with him to Cardiff for the first time.

On the death of the second Marquess, his infant son – John Patrick Crichton Stuart – succeeded to the lordship. Unfortunately, his father had left little in the way of direction for the management of the estate or of instruction for his son's upbringing. During his early years the young Bute spent a good deal of time with his mother at Cardiff Castle. But after she died in 1859 he was no longer able to visit Cardiff. Instead, there were quarrels between his guardians over how and where he should be educated.[46] During Bute's minority, the estate was managed by trustees who successfully reduced the debts on the Glamorgan lands while income from minerals under the same lands grew rapidly.[47] In this way, Bute's wealth, 'which came mainly from south Wales estates', continued to accumulate, so that by his coming-of-age in 1868 he was an extremely wealthy man.[48]

The shy third Marquess was different in almost every way from his dour father. Whereas the second Marquess's religious views had been either Anglican (in England and Wales) or Presbyterian (in Scotland), and he had

Fig. 3.3. *Cathays Park in the 1840s. With the construction of the Dock Feeder (1835), Park Place and the Taff Vale Railway (1839) the boundaries of the Park were more or less complete. (Based on 1844 Tithe Survey.)*

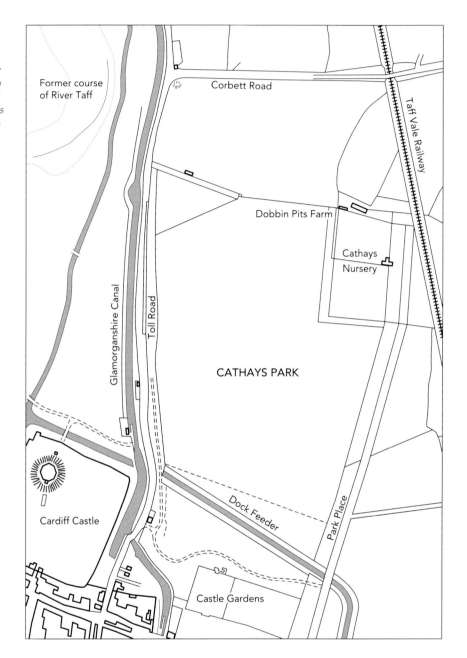

had a deep concern for managing his estate, his son was more interested in what he saw as the healing aspects of religion – converting to Roman Catholicism in 1868, soon after his 21st birthday – medieval architecture and travel than in involving himself in the running of his estate.[49] The third Marquess's romantic passion for architecture had become evident at an early age and in 1865, while still a minor, he commissioned the inimitable medievalist, William Burges, to advise on the restoration and improvement

of Cardiff Castle.[50] Burges reported early the following year with a scheme
that was not so much restoration as a rebuilding in Gothic style. Bute was
delighted and, with unrestricted funds at his disposal, the work of rebuilding began soon after he had attained his majority in 1868. By 1874 the first
part – an extraordinary 45-metre high Clock Tower at the south-west corner
of the castle – had been completed, along with the removal of old houses
adjacent to part of the curtain wall and the creation of a semi-public moat
garden in their place. Work then continued on other parts of the castle in
similar exotic style for the remainder of Bute's life (Pl. 12).

Pl. 12. *Clock Tower, Cardiff
Castle. William Burges's
dramatic design for the
213 ft (65 m) high tower
built at the south-west
corner of the castle.*

While the castle was being rebuilt, Bute was active with building-work elsewhere in the vicinity, as well as in England and Scotland. In the Cardiff area his most ambitious project was the restoration of a ruinous castle, Castell Coch, a few miles north of the town. Burges was again chosen to prepare the designs and he submitted his report at the end of 1872. The restoration was intended to be an eye-catcher that could be seen rising above the Taff valley from the windows of Cardiff Castle and 'integral to the marquess's policy of improvement to Cardiff Castle's great landscaped park'.[51] Construction was delayed, however, partly because of ongoing work at Cardiff Castle and partly because of financial difficulties during the construction of the Roath Basin Dock, 1868–74.[52] When building finally got underway in the autumn of 1875, Bute was able to 'continue work on it from his own pocket' without involving the trustees of his Welsh estate.[53] Castell Coch was completed in 1891, its exterior appearing as a scholarly reconstruction in thirteenth-century style with conical roofs to each of its three towers. The interior, by contrast, was a dazzling High Victorian fantasy, more reminiscent of fairyland than a product of the Middle Ages.

Other buildings involving the Bute estate included three that were close to Cathays Park and erected with 7 years of each other. The first of these, the

Pl. 13. *Castle Stables. William Burges's design for the stable buildings to the north of the castle. The stables were built in two phases, 1872–5 and 1927, and are now incorporated within the Royal Welsh College of Music and Drama.*

Pl. 14. *Park House, Park Place. A nineteenth-century photograph showing the building designed by William Burges soon after completion.*

Castle Stables, is situated across North Road from the park. It was designed by William Burges in 1868–9 in, for him, an unusually sober manner to form, as the *Building News* noted, 'an entire quadrangle entered by gateways on opposite sides; a lean-to roof, on wooden supports, gives shelter cloisterwise all round the interior' (Pl. 13).[54] Half of the Stable block was built in red stone and green slate between 1872 and 1875 and, the other half, in a simplified version, was completed in 1927.[55] The stables later became part of the Royal Welsh College of Music and Drama.

Park House, when first built in 1871–4, stood facing the Stables, on the far side of Park Place. While Bute was not, as far as we know, directly involved with the house, it has a close connection in as much as the architect was Burges again and it was built for John McConnochie, chief engineer to the Bute Docks and a friend of the Marquess. Asymmetrically planned with an arcade of tall, pointed Bath stone arches supported on pink granite columns, the house is a richly neo-Gothic work with a French bias, 'built in [Pennant] stone by workmen from the Bute docks' (Pl. 14).[56] It was later converted to council offices before becoming a club.

Bute was more concerned with the third of the trio, Nazareth House, standing just north of Cathays Park where North Road and Park Place's continuation (Colum Road) meet. During the 1860s and 1870s, Bute con-tinued to make 'necessary visits to Cardiff', for, 'as well as business, he was heavily involved in ecclesiastical matters'.[57] One of these matters was the Poor Sisters of Nazareth, for whom he leased two and a half acres of land, gave £1,000 to launch a building fund in 1873 for an almshouse and school for Catholics, and provided the services of his architect.[58] The architect was the talented John Pritchard of Llandaf, who Bute occasionally used for his ecclesiastical works. Pritchard designed Nazareth House as a two-storey structure, with many gables and dormers, in Early Pointed Gothic. Extensions, including a large chapel, were added later by the Bute estate architect, E. W. M. Corbett. Significantly, the House faced south-east and looked directly across what was then open space towards Cathays Park and the site of the Greyfriars friary.

These topographically related buildings – the Stables, Park House and Nazareth House – taken together with Bute's refusal to countenance the sale of any part of Cathays Park to the Borough in 1873, suggest that the Marquess was indeed concerned with the appearance of the Castle's environment and that he had more than a passing interest in the park and its surroundings. There was, however, some difficulty in reconciling this attitude with the way in which the park was being managed. During council discussions the following year, councillor David Duncan pointed out that 'ever since I have known the town, [Cathays Park] has never been used as part and parcel of the grounds belonging to the Castle, but had always simply been used as grazing ground let out to anyone for that purpose'.[59] If that were the case, it was perhaps natural to ask why then could not the Borough's growing population also benefit from use of the park?

However, changes were soon to be made to the park by Bute himself, altering both its appearance and management. During the winter of 1879–80 the Marquess had a mile-long, four-line avenue of elms planted between Nazareth House at one end and the Herbert House ruins (which had been built in the late sixteenth century on the remains of the late-thirteenth century Greyfriars friary) at the other.[60] The avenue passed through the length of the park, bisecting it longitudinally (Fig. 3.4). A number of old field hedges were removed – presumably at the same time – in order to open up other parts of the park. The avenue – like two similar avenues planted west of the Taff in alignments with the Castle and Llandaf cathedral – had all the appearances of a setting for horse-riding, in which case it was probably planted with Gwendolen, Bute's wife, in mind. Although Bute was not fond of horses or riding, his wife was and 'was an accomplished horsewoman'.[61] Also, to give substance to the theory, it is known that during the summer of 1877 the Butes bought 'a lovely pair of horses' at Cardiff, and that Gwendolen had sent for her ponies and carriage.[62]

The Cathays Park avenue was planned to link visually the two religious sites – one medieval and the other new. However, the site of the Franciscan (Greyfriars) friary was rather vague, having remained largely hidden under the Castle Gardens. Only the ruins of the Elizabethan Herbert

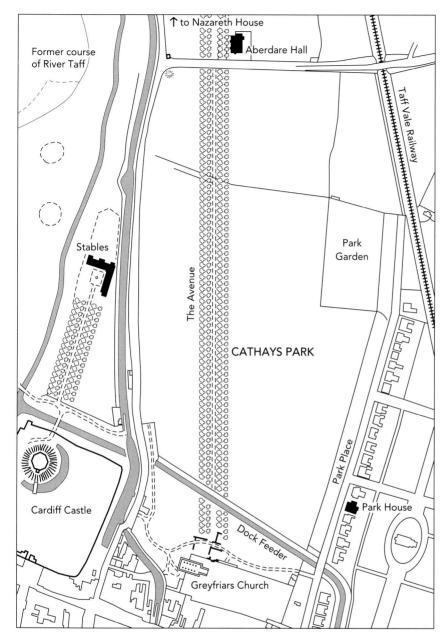

Fig. 3.4. *Cathays Park in the 1890s. The removal of boundary hedges and the planting of the Avenue (1879–80) marked the apogee of the land as a 'gentleman's park'. Nazareth House (1875) – off the map, to the north – and the ruins of Herbert House (on the site of Greyfriars) provided end points to the Avenue, while the Stables (1872–5), Park House (1871–4) and Aberdare Hall (1893–5) were significant buildings at the periphery of the Park. (Based on OS map, 1880–2 edition.)*

House – which had reused some of the friary masonry – gave any indication of its whereabouts. In order to examine what remained below ground the Marquess commissioned Mr C. B. Fowler to excavate the medieval remains of the friary buildings and, as far as possible, restore the plan of the church.[63] This was all part of Bute's overall programme of excavations at the time, which also included the Dominican (Blackfriars) friary in Bute Park and Roman work underlying the Castle's curtain walls. The Greyfriars'

Pl. 15. *Herbert House, Greyfriars Road. Remains of the Elizabethan house and the church (seen in the foreground) of the Dominican friary in 1967. The friary, excavated in 1892–6 and 1925–8, became the focal point of the Marquess of Bute's mile-long avenue.*

excavation, lasting from 1892 to 1896, was successful in revealing in great detail the layout of the six-bay, aisled church, as well as parts of the domestic buildings to the north of it and other remains of Herbert House overlaying the friary cloister (Pl. 15). Bute contemplated building a Roman Catholic cathedral on the remains of the friary church, despite the fact that St David's cathedral (by Pugin & Pugin, 1884–7) in Charles Street was barely a decade old. He had the architects Kempson and Fowler draw up a design for the proposed cathedral in 1897, but the project was later abandoned by the fourth Marquess because of the cost.[64] It should be mentioned in passing that the Greyfriars church was excavated again in 1925–8 by the estate architect J. P. Grant, after which the floor, low walls and column bases were conserved and laid out to public view and enclosed along with the remains of Herbert House. Unfortunately, everything was lost in 1967 when the remains were senselessly destroyed to make way for the multi-storey Pearl House (now Capital Tower); 'a grievous loss', according to John Newman.[65]

Ever since the construction of the Dock Feeder in 1835, the southern 4 acres (1.5 ha) of the original Cathays Park, containing two lodges and some of the remains of the friary, had been separated from the rest of the park. It was natural for Bute to want to reunite the two sections of the park by building a bridge across the Feeder in a similar way to the bridge that he had proposed to unite Cathays Park with the Castle grounds. In the latter case, it had been the excavation of the Castle bank in 1889 prior to the construction of the proposed bridge across North Road that had led to the discovery of Roman walls underlying the Castle's east curtain, and had led to the proposal being abandoned.[66] There were no such problems with the bridge across the Feeder and it was constructed in line with the avenue, thus making it possible to ride or walk all the way from Nazareth House to Greyfriars without hindrance. It is not clear when the footbridge was built, but it was already in place at the end of 1898 when it was used during the handover of keys to the Council (see Chapter 5). The most likely date of construction seems to have been either during the period when Greyfriars was being excavated (i.e. 1892–6) or, perhaps earlier, when the Castle bank was being excavated.

Despite the discovery of Roman remains, Bute was still keen to improve accommodation at the Castle. As late as 1898 he was said to be contemplating adding a new wing containing state apartments for which plans were 'already in course of preparation by Mr Frame'.[67] This news gave rise to speculation, not only that the Marquess and his family might become more frequent visitors to Cardiff but also that the buildings on the north side of Duke Street might be cleared away and so do away with the traffic congestion in the narrow street.

While all this was going on the perimeters of Cathays Park were undergoing change. On the eastern side, Park Place was continued northwards with terraces of red-brick houses trimmed with cream-coloured Bath stone, while, on the northern side, Corbett Road saw the erection of semi-detached villas in Pennant stone and Bath stone trimmings. One building half way along Corbett Road stood out from the rest because of its dignified design and harmonious use of warm red brick and terracotta. This was Aberdare Hall, designed by Herbert Wills, of Hannaford and Wills, and built between 1893 and 1895 as a women's hall of residence for the University College on an acre of land leased from Lord Bute (Pl. 16).[68] A nicely balanced Jacobean composition with triple gables and projecting bays on either side of the entrance, it stands alongside Bute's avenue, making an elegant centrepiece to the northern end of the park.

Pl. 16. *Aberdare Hall, Corbett Road. The women's hall of residence built 1893–5 to designs by Herbert Wills on land leased from the Marquess of Bute.* © Crown copyright: RCAHMW.

With the construction of the Feeder bridge, and the completion of Park Place and Corbett Road, Cathays Park reached its final form of enclosure as a private park. It was an anomaly, however, to have, at the end of the nineteenth century, such an extensive area of open, but still private, green space next-door to the heart of a busy and vibrant town of 150,000 people. It was an anomaly because this was really the only suitable space capable of meeting the town's growing need for land on which to erect much needed public buildings, but land which yet remained unobtainable. It was a situation that could not continue without drastic repercussions and, within just a few years of Cathays Park's flowering as an enclosed private domain, all was to change. But change did not come easily, nor without considerable acrimony and dispute.

NOTES

1   Chappell, *Cardiff's Civic Centre*, p. 3.
2   D. R. Paterson, *Early Cardiff – A Short Account of Its Street-names and Surrounding Place-names*, p. 40.
3   Ibid., p. 41.
4   George Yates, *A Map of the County of Glamorgan; from an Actual Survey*.
5   From a letter by Sir John Pringle to James Boswell, quoted by Davies, in *Cardiff and the Marquesses*, p. 1.
6   Sir John Edward Lloyd and R. T. Jenkins, *The Dictionary of Welsh Biography Down to 1940*, pp. 352, 50–60; Davies, *Cardiff and the Marquesses*, pp. 3–6.
7   Davies, *Cardiff and the Marquesses*, pp. 8–9.
8   Ibid., p. 34.
9   Ibid., pp. 37–8.
10 CCL: Pettigrew, *Public Parks of Cardiff*, vol. 2, p. 173.
11 Rees, *Cardiff*, p. 252.
12 Extract from Tredegar Estate plan, 1764, in Chappell, *Cardiff's Civic Centre*.
13 Hilary M. Thomas (ed.), *Diaries of John Bird, Clerk to the First Marquess of Bute 1790–1803*, p. 70.
14 Davies, *Cardiff and the Marquesses*, p. 41.
15 Thomas, *Diaries of John Bird*, p. 71.
16 CCL: Pettigrew, *Public Parks of Cardiff*, vol. 2, p. 174.
17 Rowson and Wright, *Glamorganshire & Aberdare Canals*, vol. 1, p. 22; Thomas, *Diaries of John Bird*, p. 52.
18 Thomas, *Diaries of John Bird*, p. 113.
19 Newman, *Buildings of Wales: Glamorgan*, p. 297; Diane A. Walker, *A Guide to the Parish Church of St Margaret, Roath*, pp. 10–11.
20 Thomas, *Diaries of John Bird*, p. 122.
21 Davies, *Cardiff and the Marquesses*, p. 10.
22 CCL: *Cardiff Records*, vol. 4, p. 360.
23 John Chapman, *A Guide to Parliamentary Enclosures in Wales*, p. 101.
24 Matthew Williams, '"A Most Magnificent House Near Cardiff": the Mystery of Cathays Park', *Friends* [of National Museum of Wales] *Newsletter and Magazine*, Aug. 2002.
25 Howard Colvin, *A Biographical Dictionary of British Architects 1600–1840*, pp. 577–8.
26 Williams, 'A Most Magnificent House Near Cardiff'.
27 T. A. Atkins, *Catalogue of Household Furniture, Fixture and Other Effects … at Cathayes*.
28 Williams, 'A Most Magnificent House Near Cardiff'.
29 Davies, *Cardiff and the Marquesses*, pp. 14–15, 62.
30 Ibid., p. 17.
31 Simon Green , *Dumfries House*, p. 157.
32 Williams, 'A Most Magnificent House Near Cardiff'; Atkins, *Catalogue of Household Furniture.*
33 Letter, signed Senex, *Cardiff and Merthyr Guardian*, 18t Oct. 1856.
34 Thomas Jones, *Rhymney Memories*, p. 108.
35 Paper read at annual general meeting of South Wales Institute of Engineers, at Swansea, 22 Oct. 1864, quoted in *Cardiff Times*, 28 Oct. 1864.
36 Rees, *Cardiff*, p. 231.
37 National Library of Wales (NJW), Bute A24; GA, DXGC94/4/i–ii.
38 Davies, *Cardiff and the Marquesses*, p. 249.
39 Rowson and Wright, *Glamorganshire and Aberdare Canals*, vol. 2, pp. 246–8.
40 Mount Stuart House, Bute Archives, D213/209 (information from Matthew Williams).
41 Davies, *Cardiff and the Marquesses*, p. 90.

42   Chappell, *History of the Port of Cardiff*, p. 81.
43   CCL: Pettigrew, *Public Parks of Cardiff*, vol. 2, p. 172.
44   CCL: *Tithe Apportionment Award, St John's Parish, Cardiff*, 31 July 1844.
45   Revel Guest and Angela V. John, *Lady Charlotte Guest: An Extraordinary Life*, p. 173.
46   Hannah, *Grand Designer*, p. 3.
47   Hannah, *Grand Designer*, p. 4.
48   Davies, *Cardiff and the Marquesses*, pp. 27, 69–72; Hannah, *Grand Designer*, p. 25.
49   Hannah, *Grand Designer*, pp. 53, 86; J. Davies, *Cardiff and the Marquesses*, pp. 23, 29.
50   Hannah, *Grand Designer*, p. 91.
51   David McLees, *Castell Coch*, p. 20.
52   Davies, *Cardiff and the Marquesses*, pp. 272–5; Hannah, *Grand Designer*, p. 122.
53   McLees, *Castell Coch*, p. 24; Hannah, *Grand Designer*, p. 125.
54   *Building News*, XVIII (1870), p. 387.
55   J. Mordaunt Crook, *William Burges and the High Victorian Dream*, p. 249.
56   Mary Axon, 'Mr McConnochie's House, Cardiff', in J. Mordaunt Crook (ed.), *The Strange Genius of William Burges*, p. 57.
57   Hannah, *Grand Designer*, p. 127.
58   Catholic History Society, *Early History of Nazareth House*, p. 6.
59   CCL: Pettigrew, *Public Parks of Cardiff*, vol. 1, p. 162.
60   Ibid., vol. 2, p. 215.
61   Hannah, *Grand Designer*, p. 114.
62   Ibid., p. 136.
63   Revd J. M. Cronin, *Cardiff Grey Friars*, p. 22.
64   Dennis Morgan, *Memories of Cardiff's Past*, p. 93
65   Newman, *Buildings of Wales: Glamorgan*, p. 181.
66   Chappell, *Cardiff's Civic Centre*, p. 12.
67   *Cardiff Times*, 22 January 1898.
68   Joan N. Harding (ed.), *Aberdare Hall, 1885–1985*, p. 6.

4

A BATTLE FOR
SITES AND MINDS

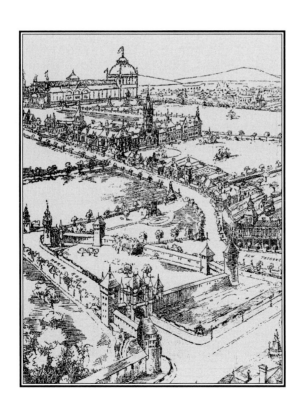

CARDIFF REMAINED ONE of the fastest developing towns in the British Isles during the last decade of the nineteenth century. A total of 128,915 people lived in the borough in 1891 – a remarkable increase of 55 per cent since the previous census 10 years earlier – and there was no sign of any easing in the growth of population. Indeed, by 1901 the population had grown to 164,333 and was still rising. Population growth was, of course, a sign of the prosperity, which brought recognition to the town: with this came additional responsibilities with regard to the people living there, particularly in relation to the provision of public services. It was in this latter area that the borough might be said to be failing, especially in the spheres of education, law and order and general administration. The Council had already decided to build a new town hall and there were many who were keen to see the new University College (1883) in Newport Road expanded. The problem was that there was an absence of suitable land on which to build. By 1892 the matter had become acute and efforts began to be made to tackle the problem.

Apart from rebuilding the Town Hall on its existing site in St Mary Street, there were only two areas of land within a reasonable distance of the town centre that could in any way be considered suitable for the erection of new municipal buildings. These were Cardiff Arms Park on the recently reclaimed land west of Westgate Street, and Cathays Park to the north of the town centre (Fig. 4.1). Both of these sites had their supporters and detractors, and both were owned by the Marquess of Bute. A lively dispute sprang up regarding the merits of each site, with arguments ranging back and fore over their respective advantages and disadvantages and the possibility of purchase. It was a dispute that continued over a number of years with many twists and turns and came to be known locally as 'the battle of the sites'.

The so-called 'battle' could be said to have begun on the 21 April, 1892, when Peter Price (chairman of the Free Library and Museum Committee) wrote to Lord Bute's agent (Sir William T. Lewis) with regard to a possible site for the Cardiff Museum which at that time was sharing premises with the Free Library in Trinity Street. In an audacious and perceptive aside, he added:

> May I also mention another suggestion which is enthusiastically entertained in some quarters, viz, that Lord Bute may be induced to sell the whole or a part of Cathays Park to the Corporation for public uses only. We are sadly in need of land for a new Town Hall, Assize Courts, Municipal Offices, Technical Schools, Intermediate Schools, and a new University College. These could be arranged around a central park. If Lord Bute found it his pleasure to sell this land for a moderate sum (say £100,000), with a right of pre-emption or a proviso that it be devoted exclusively to public purposes such as those indicated above, we could make Cardiff one of the most beautiful towns in the country. The idea of such a disposition of

Cathays Park has taken hold of many minds, and rather paralyses our action as regards the fixing of the proposed new Town Hall and the new University College.[1]

Although Price's original letter refers to the buildings in the Cathays Park idea as being 'enthusiastically entertained in some quarters' it seems that it was he himself who was the instigator and prime mover in the affair.

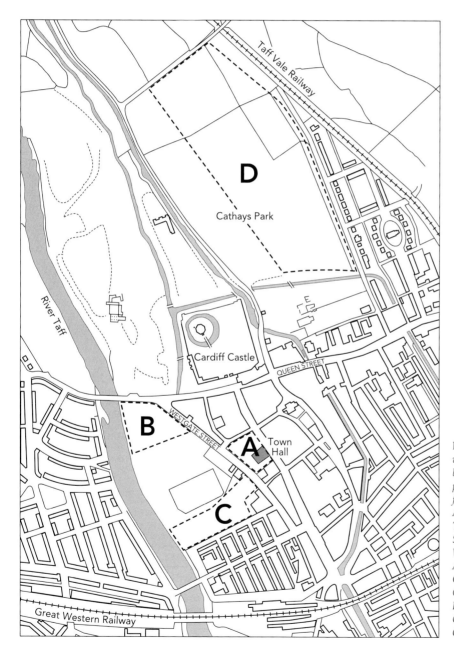

Fig. 4.1. *Central Cardiff, with sites for municipal buildings. The sites proposed at various times for municipal buildings are: A, land around the existing Town Hall, between St Mary Street and Westgate Street; B, Cardiff Arms Park (North); C, Temperance Town or Cardiff Arms Park (South); D, the eastern half of Cathays Park. (Based on OS map, 1901 edition.)*

In addition to being a councillor Peter Price was a leading member of the Cardiff Naturalists Society. Earlier, in 1884, he had had the chance, as the Society's delegate to the British Association for Science annual conference in Canada, to see the latest trends in North American architecture and town planning. He was impressed with what he saw and it could well be that it was these impressions that had influenced his ideas when writing to Bute's agent with regard to the layout of Cathays Park. During the Canadian conference, Price visited Ottawa and was much taken with the Government Buildings (built in Gothic style) there, noting that they 'form an exceedingly handsome group, the House of Commons and the Senate forming a centre block, which is flanked by Government offices on each side'.[2] Later, he visited Toronto and was again moved both by the buildings and the town's enterprise, which:

> throws even Cardiff into the shade. Everything has been accomplished there during the last fifty years. In that time they have built magnificent University buildings [Romanesque style], which are situated in their own extensive grounds, a splendidly fitted Normal School [Gothic style], handsome Courts of Justice [Classical style], and a large public park.[3]

Before returning to Cardiff, Price made his way to Philadelphia, where the principal sights were the uncompleted municipal buildings and the monumental Girard College (Classical). Then on to Washington with its monumental Capitol and White House. He described it 'as the outline of a great city. It is beautifully laid out, but the streets are not yet filled up, and the place has a rather unfinished appearance'.[4] It should be noted here that all the towns visited by Price had been laid out to rigid gridiron plans, and were therefore quite unlike Cardiff's layout at the time.

In due course Sir William Lewis replied to Price's letter, intimating 'that any official proposition made by the Cardiff Corporation for a carefully prepared scheme, will receive his (Lord Bute) best consideration'.[5] The correspondence between Price and Bute's agent was read at a council meeting on 27 June, but, following this, little attempt seems to have been made towards preparing a 'careful scheme'. At the next Council meeting on 11 July, the discussions centred on the amount of money to be offered for a site fronting Westgate Street and Quay Street so that the Town Hall could be either extended or rebuilt. It was agreed that no more than £3,100 should be offered for the land, while Alderman David Jones pointed out that 'there had been suggestions of moving the Town-hall to Cathays Park and Queen-street, but that on the whole would be more costly'.[6] A few days later Price replied in a letter to the *Cardiff Times* saying, 'I venture to prophesy that, before we see a new town-hall built, the rateable value will in the meantime have increased to an extent that will cover the annual cost of the Cathays Park and the buildings on it.'[7]

It was not until the beginning of August that at a meeting of the Council a motion was put to appoint a special committee to consider 'the desirability of initiating negotiations for the purchase of Cathays Park from Lord Bute, and devoting the same principally to the erection of such buildings and institutions of a public character as are or may be required by the authorities'.[8] The motion also included a recommendation to ascertain from other bodies the amount of land they would need, and to consider the value of the existing Town Hall site and the amount asked for alternative sites in Westgate Street and Quay Street. No one seemed to be in a hurry to expedite matters, and on the suggestion of the Mayor the 'matter was left over till after the vacation'.

Numerous letters passed between the town clerk and Bute's agent, Sir William Lewis, during the autumn, culminating in letters dated 2 December and 5 December from Sir William stating that the Marquess was prepared to sell 38 acres (out of a total of 59 acres [24 ha]) of Cathays Park, 'for the purposes of municipal buildings and public recreation ground', for a sum of £120,000, subject to acceptance early in 1893.[9] The area on offer comprised all that part of the park east of the four-line avenue that had been planted in 1879–80, as the Marquess wished to retain the land nearest the Castle for himself. When the Town Hall Subcommittee met on 13th December, concern was expressed regarding the limited access to the 38 acres on offer. This resulted in a decision to appoint a delegation to meet Sir William and to invite representatives of various public bodies in the town to discuss with the committee their requirements.[10] The Town Clerk suggested that various public buildings, such as 'the university college, museum, technical instruction and intermediate schools, public baths, Aberdare Hall, school board offices, offices of the board of guardians &c.' might be located in Cathays Park. It was agreed that the Council 'should approach the other public bodies in the town and ask them to co-operate in the scheme, and then they would be able to ascertain their position'.[11] It looked as if progress was being made, so that Mr Herbert Thompson was, in a lecture entitled 'A Possible Cardiff', able to envisage a future Cathays Park where 'a group of magnificent municipal buildings had been erected'.[12]

But progress was not to be so smooth, after all, for early in 1893 the *Western Mail* ran a series of provocative articles regarding the 'New Municipal Buildings at Cardiff'.[13] There were seventeen articles altogether, written by 'our special correspondent', which, though purporting to be 'the fair and impartial discussion of the *pros* and *cons* of the three alternative [sic] schemes', appear to have been published in order to promote the ideas and views of the newspaper's editor and part owner, Lascelles Carr, on the subject. This becomes clear from some the headlines that peppered the articles: '"Tiger Bay" in Park Place'; 'The Cathays Park Scheme Tabooed'; 'Results of the "Tinkering" policy'; 'Increasing volume of opinion against the Cathays Park scheme'; 'Fickleness of the College authorities'; 'Cardiff Arms Park growing in favour'; and 'The architectural advantages of the Cardiff Arms Park site'.

Nevertheless, for all their evident partiality – bearing in mind Carr's debt to Lord Bute – the articles provide us with an invaluable source of information about the various sites (St Mary Street, Cardiff Arms Park, Cathays Park) and the options involved, as well as about the views of members of the Council who had been approached for their comments.

Beginning with a general introduction the articles went on to reiterate the existing Town Hall situation and to note two schemes (one by the *Western Mail* in 1891) that had been put forward for purchasing additional land and rebuilding on the same site. That was followed by examination of the financial aspects of building at Cathays Park (which would according to the writer, 'involve an enormous outlay, much of which will be thrown away'), an exploration of the University College's problems, and a look at the disadvantages of living opposite public buildings for people in Park Place. After that there were discussions of the views of various aldermen and councillors on the merits of each site.

While all this was being reported to the public at large, the Council received a reply from Sir William with regard to access to Cathays Park from North Road. In his letter he confirmed that Lord Bute had no objection to the corporation constructing a roadway into North Road provided that the road remained open to the Marquess and his tenants. The members of the Town Hall Committee discussed the matter on 6 February 1893 and decided to write to Sir William again, this time to ask for an extension of time in which to consider Bute's offer to sell part of the park.[14]

The next article in the *Western Mail* presented 'readers with a detailed scheme, illustrated with designs and plans, for the erection of a noble pile of buildings' in Cardiff Arms Park, the cost of which would be raised by converting the existing Town Hall site to business use.[15] It was, in fact, Lascelles Carr's own solution – for which he had persuaded Edwin Seward to draw up a schematic plan and elevation – to the ongoing problem of where to put Cardiff's municipal buildings (Pl. 17). On the plan, the Town Hall and municipal offices were shown as being sited at the northern end of the Arms Park, near Canton Bridge and the river Taff, with the main front overlooking the Castle Grounds. The elevation envisaged a heavy Baroque-style building complete with domed turrets, tall chimneys and steeply pitched roofs, with a three-storey main front but side wings of lesser height. Although the scheme as drawn looked somewhat overbearing, it did allow for a sensitive opening up of the river frontage as well as the potential for a handsomely designed group of buildings to stand opposite the Castle Grounds.

Interestingly, one of the reasons that were put forward for siting the Town Hall in the Arms Park was the 'superior commercial instinct of the Post Office authorities, who, in selecting a site [at the lower end of Westgate Street, backing on to the Arms Park] never dreamt of any other centre except in the heart of the town'.[16] This was a reference to the new post office, which, at that time, was still at the drawing-office stage. The post office was designed by

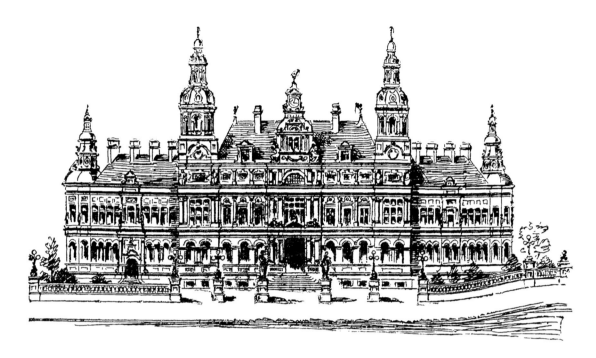

Sir Henry Tanner, the government's chief architect of works, in classical style with elaborate pedimented gables and would be, when completed in 1897, the first large-scale use of spotless white Portland stone in the borough.[17] The County Court Offices were built on an adjoining site a few years later (1904) in similar style and materials. Seen in the light of these innovative government developments, it is easy to see how the borough's councillors might have imagined that Westgate Street was becoming the logical place for all future public buildings.

Pl. 17. *Proposed Municipal Buildings, 1891. An elaborate design by Edwin Seward for new municipal buildings in Cardiff Arms Park, facing across to Bute Park and the castle.*

The Town Hall committee met again on the 20 February 1893, to hear Sir William Lewis's reply (16 February) to their request for an extension of time. He confirmed that although Lord Bute was willing to extend the time limit until 15 March, 'His Lordship is not prepared to sell to the Corporation of Cardiff the whole of the [Cathays] Park free from any restrictions'. Following a discussion, the committee passed a resolution:

> that inasmuch as it is desirable that the projected Town-Hall and Municipal Buildings should be erected as near the centre of the town as possible, Sir W. T. Lewis, on behalf of Lord Bute, be asked to sell to the Corporation about four acres of land forming a part of the Cardiff Arms Park near and adjoining Canton Bridge.

To this was added a rider that Sir William be informed, 'that it had been found impracticable to proceed with the Cathays Park scheme'.[18] The *Western Mail* was quick to point out the committee's volte-face and the `abandonment of the Cathays Park scheme'.[19] A further letter from Sir William Lewis (25 February) regretted his:

> inability to advise the Marquess of Bute to entertain the application of the corporation for the site mentioned (i.e. the northern part of Cardiff Arms Park), but I am prepared to recommend his lordship to sell to the corporation for such purposes what appears to me a more suitable site – i.e. the space between the county club and the proposed new post-office buildings, embracing from one and a half to two acres, and extending from Westgate Street to Park-street.[20]

The suggestion of a fourth site, this time in Temperance Town at the lower end of Cardiff Arms Park, was a surprise move by the Bute estate and it led to the supposition in some quarters that Bute was deliberately putting obstacles in the way of alternative proposals in order that the corporation would eventually come round to seeing Cathays Park as the most suitable site for public buildings.[21] The members of the Town Hall committee declared the site too small for their needs and asked Sir William to reconsider the matter 'or give the committee an opportunity of meeting Lord Bute and himself to discuss it'.[22]

Not to be outdone, the *Western Mail* took Sir William's proposal a stage further by asking Edwin Seward to come up with a scheme for the Temperance Town site. This Seward did on a plan that indicated the Town Hall and municipal offices facing on to the Arms Park with an open square between the building complex and the Taff, all of which showed that twice as much space would be required for the development than had been suggested by Sir William Lewis.[23]

Following a meeting with Bute's agent who, apparently, had not 'drawn a hard and fast line as to the area', the Town Hall committee met again to reconsider the offer. After a heated debate – and facing yet another town hall scheme from the businessmen and traders of Queen Street – the committee gave up the battle for its preferred site at the northern end of the Arms Park, lacking as the *Western Mail* put it the nerve to 'schedule' or compulsorily purchase it. Instead, they decided to go for the Temperance Town site, provided that Lord Bute would be willing to sell the whole stretch of land between the unbuilt post office and the river. This was, of course, much the same scheme as had been envisaged in Seward's plan.[24] There appears to have been little further discussion during the remainder of the year, suggesting that the matter had been, at least temporarily, lain to the rest.

Meanwhile, Lascelles Carr, the *Western Mail* editor, had gone to the United States in 1893 to visit Chicago and see the World's Fair. He was impressed with both the Fair and with Chicago itself, which had been 'burnt to the ground' after a disastrous fire 22 years earlier. He wrote back that the town was now 'a city of palaces – phoenix-like – sprang from its ashes'.[25]

Like Peter Price before him, Carr also visited Philadelphia and was again impressed. 'The public buildings here, though perhaps a little grandiose in style, are worthy, alike in extent and architectural beauty, of a great and free community …What an example for Cardiff – dear, old, Cardiff – the town of my adoption and warmest affection!'[26] On his return to Cardiff, Carr published a pamphlet, *Yankee Land and the Yankees*, in which he extolled, among other things, the virtues of North American architecture. While dwelling on the superb park setting of Philadelphia's Beaux-Arts museum and picture gallery (erected in 1876 for the Philadelphia World's Fair), he had words of advice for the councillors back home. 'Here again,' he wrote (in what appears to have been a change of mind on his part), 'surely, is a hint for Cardiff. Acquire, if it may be done at a reasonable price, a few acres of land in the Cathays Park, and place there our museum and picture gallery, and possibly a palm-house and other horticultural buildings.'[27] He had further advice for the setting of other public buildings:

> Let me say this, that in my opinion the man who at the present crisis in the municipal history of the Welsh Metropolis thwarts the legitimate aspirations of the people for courts of justice and municipal offices worthy of the town – placed on a worthy site, dignified in design, ample in extent, and creditable in execution – is no patriot and no friend of Cardiff.[28]

Although Carr was not a Welshman – he had been born in Yorkshire and had come to Cardiff when the third Marquess of Bute appointed him as the *Western Mail*'s first sub-editor – his comments regarding the 'Welsh Metropolis' fitted in with the mood and aspirations of many in the town who saw Cardiff as not only Wales's leading town but also its natural 'capital'. Another outsider who recognised the town's merits was the United States' consul in Cardiff, the Honourable Anthony Howells. In a letter that he sent back to the States in 1893, he wrote:

> I find this country very progressive and aggressive. So we Americans must not delude ourselves with thinking that Great Britain is at a standstill. This city (Cardiff) is a very stirring place. It is the Chicago of Great Britain, as well as the cosmopolitan town of the island, and now the metropolis of Wales.[29]

The epithet 'Chicago' stuck, as did the feeling for many that Cardiff was the nation's real capital.

However, as Carter has pointed out, 'the title of capital must always go to a city of size *and build* [my italics] that can compare with other capitals and which can carry out effectively the functions which it inherits'.[30] This meant, according to Morley, that 'if Cardiff yearned to be recognised in both Wales and Westminster as the "authentic capital" of Wales then it had to contain the infrastructure typical of a nation's hub'.[31] To do this the town had to have civic and national buildings appropriate to and worthy of the nation. The appetite for such was certainly there, as can be gleaned from the Minutes of the Museum and Art Gallery Committee, where a resolution was recorded (1 December 1893) 'to watch over the interests of Cardiff in respect of the movement for a Welsh national museum'.[32] This was followed, in 1894, by a memorial to the Chancellor of the Exchequer from the Council calling for a 'State supported Museum … on similar lines to the National Museums of Edinburgh and Dublin', and giving reasons why Cardiff, the `premier port of the British Empire', should 'be selected as the actual site'.[33]

One person who had the vision to see Cardiff as it might be in the twentieth century was the architect Edwin Seward. As president of the Cardiff, South Wales and Monmouthshire Architects' Society he gave an address in February 1894, entitled 'The Architectural Growth of Cities, and the Future of Cardiff'. In the address he suggested the transformation of Cardiff's town centre along the lines of 'recent improvements of Paris and Vienna', illustrating his proposals with a vision of wide new thoroughfares and open spaces embellished with fountains and statues. For Cathays Park he proposed a curious Gothicised building 'which may be the location of any or all of the town's institutions now seeking homes' as well as a permanent Peoples' Palace for exhibitions, festivals and eisteddfodau (Pl. 18).[34] Seward pointed out – probably to avoid offending Carr, who had earlier commissioned him to illustrate

Pl. 18. *'The future of Cardiff', 1894. An illustration from Edwin Seward's lecture showing how Cardiff might be developed, with grand new buildings, including a People's Palace, on Cathays Park.*

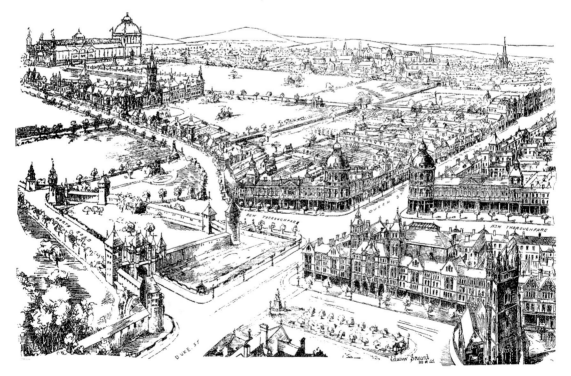

his project for the Arms Park site – that the scheme was intended to illustrate the possibility to 'open up, not one site for public buildings, municipal and otherwise, but more probably one dozen such sites'. Carr gave full publicity to the address in the *Western Mail* and reprinted it in a special pamphlet, thereby implying his approval of Seward's proposals.[35]

Yet, despite the publicity given by Seward's scheme, little serious consideration seems to have been given to the possibility of acquiring Cathays Park for public buildings. Even the new museum and art gallery that the Council had decided to proceed with, following an Act of Parliament (1881) that allowed raising a local rate for such a purpose, was to be denied a site in the park. Instead, Lord Bute offered a plot of land for the building in 1894 in Park Place (where the New Theatre now stands) for £4,000. The site was accepted by the Museum committee and the conveyance of land took place the following year on the 14 January.[36] Now everything seemed to be in place, and Seward was commissioned in May 1895 to design the museum, which he did in a Classical style.[37] Unfortunately, for Seward, other events intervened and in the end his museum was not to be. This must have been very disappointing for Seward for, according to Lord, he had 'identified himself thoroughly with the national cause in Wales'.[38]

Meanwhile, discussions about constructing new municipal buildings continued to rumble on. Early in 1894, the Town Hall Committee resolved that 'the site now occupied by the present Buildings (including the site to be compulsorily acquired) will be sufficient for the purposes, provided the Fire Brigade Station, the Police Station and the Police Courts are removed to another site'.[39] To show that they were in earnest the Committee also decided at the same meeting to launch an architectural competition for the new Town Hall with prizes of £500, £250 and £100. Six months later, the same Committee resolved, in yet another volte-face:

> that the present building be reserved, with improvements, for the assizes with all essential accessories, county court, quarter sessions, and police headquarters, and that a separate structure be provided on a site as near as possible to the present Town-hall for all the necessities of the municipal work of Cardiff.[40]

In October the committee confirmed their intention to adopt the 'St. Mary-street site as the location for the new municipal buildings, all of which should be placed there'.[41] The *Western Mail* was quick to respond, stating that `the proposal to build on the present site is economically unsound'.[42]

And so the matter remained for another year until, in October 1895, the Town Hall committee, much to the *Western Mail* special correspondent's glee, 'abandoned the proposed extension of the present site in St Mary-street, and marvellous to relate, resolved to ask Lord Bute for three or four acres of the Cardiff Arms Park'. Once again, the newspaper persuaded Edwin Seward to

Pl. 19. *Proposed Municipal Buildings, 1895. A further design, this time with an impressive clock tower, by Edwin Seward for municipal buildings at the lower end of Cardiff Arms Park.*

prepare a plan and sketch elevation showing how the three-storey municipal buildings with a tall clock-tower at one end might look (Pl. 19).[43] This was followed up by a visit to the Temperance Town site by the Marquess, along with E. M. Corbett, his architect, Sir William Lewis, and the mayor. Bute pointed out his desire 'to preserve as much open space as possible' and 'inspected the plans in detail, but he gave no inkling as to whether he was in favour of the scheme or otherwise'.[44] Eventually, a reply came from Sir William Lewis indicating that the Marquess was only willing to sell a plot of about half an acre next to the new post office at a cost of over £15,000. This was obviously insufficient and on 16 December a Town Hall Special Committee resolved to ask Lord Bute to reconsider the matter.[45]

It was a disappointing situation: after 4 years of discussions and looking at prospective sites the Town Hall Committee was no further forward than it had been early in 1892. The committee, not surprisingly, appeared to run out of steam and nearly another year was to go by before the question of where to build the new municipal buildings was seriously taken up again. For most of 1896 the overriding consideration for the Council was to be the Cardiff Exhibition.

NOTES

1   CCL: Pettigrew, *Public Parks of Cardiff*, vol. 2, p. 152.
2   Peter Price, 'Notes of a Trip to Canada and the United States with the British Association in 1884', *Cardiff Naturalists' Society Report*, vol. XVII (1895), p. 37.
3   Ibid., p. 38.
4   Ibid., p. 42.
5   CCL: Matthews, *Cardiff Records*, vol. 5, p. 170.
6   CCL: Cardiff Corporation, *Proceedings, 1891–92*, p. 479.
7   *Cardiff Times*, 23 July 1892.
8   CCL: Cardiff Corporation, *Proceedings, 1891–92*, pp. 527–8.
9   CCL: Matthews, *Cardiff Records*, vol. 5, p. 173; *Evening Express*, 14 December 1892.
10   CCL: Cardiff Corporation, *Proceedings, 1892–93*, p. 97.
11   Ibid., p. 45.
12   *Cardiff Times*, 24 December 1892.
13   *Western Mail*, 25 January–17 February 1893.
14   CCL: Cardiff Corporation, *Proceedings, 1892–1893*, pp. 162–3.
15   *Western Mail*, 7 February 1893.
16   Ibid., 3 February 1893.
17   P. Wakelin and R. A. Griffiths, *Hidden Histories: Discovering the Heritage of Wales*, p. 247.
18   CCL: Cardiff Corporation, *Proceedings, 1892–93*, pp. 220–1.
19   *Western Mail*, 21 February 1893.
20   CCL: Cardiff Corporation, *Proceedings, 1892–93*, pp. 270–1.
21   Chappell, *Cardiff's Civic Centre*, p. 15.
22   CCL: Cardiff Corporation, *Proceedings, 1892–93*, p. 271.
23   Ibid., 30 March 1893.
24   Ibid., 25, 26 April, 1893.
25   *Western Mail*, 18 May 1893.
26   Lascelles Carr, *Yankee Land*, p. 30.
27   Ibid.
28   Ibid.
29   *Evening Express*, 15 September 1893.
30   Harold Carter, *The Towns of Wales*, p. 355.
31   Ian Morley, 'Representing a City and Nation: Wales's Matchless Civic Centre', *Welsh History Review*, XXIV (2009), p. 62.
32   Douglas A. Bassett, *The Making of a National Museum*, Part I, p. 12.
33   Ibid., pp. 12–13.
34   *Western Mail*, 21 February 1894.
35   Reprint of Seward's Presidential Address from *Western Mail*, 21, 22, 23 February 1894; John Wilson, 'The Chicago of Wales', *Planet*, 115 (1996), p. 23.
36   *Western Mail*, 7 Apr. 1894; Matthews, Cardiff Records, vol. 5, p. 204.
37   Glamorgan Archives (GA), BC/C/43, part 2 (1895).
38   Lord, *Imaging the Nation*, p. 301.
39   CCL: Cardiff Corporation, *Proceedings, 1893–94*, p. 152.
40   *Western Mail*, 7 June 1894.
41   CCL: Cardiff Corporation, *Proceedings, 1893–94*, p. 651.
42   *Western Mail*, 16 October 1894.
43   Ibid., 3, 14, 17 October 1895.
44   Ibid., 18 Oct. 1895.
45   CCL: Cardiff Corporation, *Proceedings, 1895–96*, p. 103.

5

NEGOTIATIONS
AND DIVERSIONS

T HE CARDIFF EXHIBITION took place in Cathays Park on more or less the same area of ground that Lord Bute had previously offered the corporation for municipal and other public buildings, that is the eastern part of the park between Park Place and the 1879–80 avenue (now King Edward VII Avenue). With this fact in mind it is worth looking at the exhibition in more detail to see how it related to its site.

The 1896 Cardiff Exhibition, or the Cardiff Fine Art, Industrial and Maritime Exhibition to give it its full name, was not the first of Cardiff's art and industry exhibitions, for others had been held in 1870 and 1881 in the Drill Hall behind St Andrew's Church, but it was by far the largest and most successful. It was intended to vie with, or even eclipse, similar exhibitions that had been held in other large towns such as Birmingham (1886), Liverpool (1886), Manchester (1887), Glasgow (1888) and Bristol (1893).[1] Like many in a series of provincial industrial and art exhibitions during the latter half of the 19th century, the Cardiff Exhibition was influenced by the 1851 Great Exhibition that had been held in the Crystal Palace, London, and perhaps also by the World's Fair held in Chicago in 1893.

The movement to hold the exhibition originated with a suggestion by Mr Rose, an electrical engineer at the Cardiff docks, towards the end of 1893.[2] The idea was quickly taken up and a committee formed of public figures, businessmen and industrialists to promote local resources and industries. Early on the question of a site for the exhibition was raised and four different venues were proposed, including Cardiff Arms Park, Sophia Gardens, Grangetown and Cathays Park. While each site had its advocates, the use of three of them would be dependent on Lord Bute's agreement as the landowner. The matter was resolved when, following Bute's offer of 'a site on the south-east corner of Cathays Park', a public meeting was held in February 1894. The meeting decided `in favour of holding the exhibition during the present year on the site in Cathays Park'.[3]

Taking into account the time needed to set up the exhibition, the decision to hold it in 1894 was risky. It could not open until August at the earliest, and thus the lucrative summer months would be missed. The proposed date, together with a proposal to reuse the same pavilion that had been used in the Bristol Exhibition a year earlier, caused much argument, with some favouring speed, some urging caution and economy, while still others maintained that nothing but the best would be 'worthy of the town and Wales'.[4]

In the end, both 1894 and 1895 proved to be too soon. Meanwhile, a guarantee fund had been set up and Edwin Seward appointed as the architect. Arrangements for the exhibition began in earnest early in 1895 and by May Seward's plans for the main building were approved.[5] A contract was let and the buildings began to be erected. Unfortunately, poor weather intervened and the work slowed down, although by early December the main framework was up. From then on 130 men had to work day and night with the aid of electric light to complete the main building and other structures by February.[6] The surrounding grounds were filled with larger exhibits, including a reproduction of Shakespeare's house, an old Dutch house, a coal-mine, a colourful, multi-arched Indian bazaar, an 'Old Welsh Fair', a row of shops under a switch-back railway, and a cycle track. Bordering all this was an artificial boating canal that ended in a lake used for spectacular water displays (Fig. 5.1). To encourage visitors from the Valleys to the exhibition, a specially built branch line of the Taff Vale

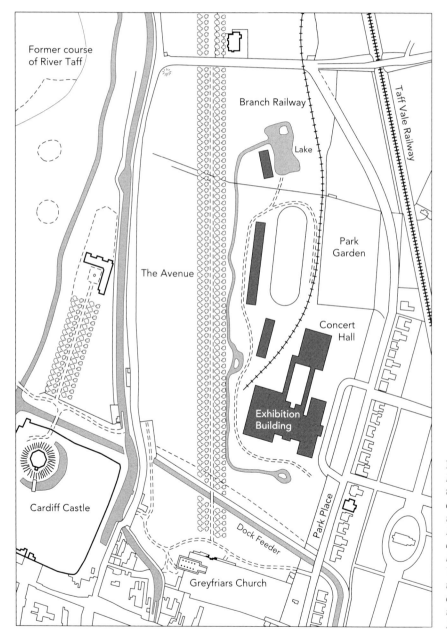

Fig. 5.1. *The 1896 Cardiff Exhibition. Virtually the whole of Cathays Park east of The Avenue was used as a site for the 1896 Exhibition, which included construction of a canal, lake and branch of the Taff Vale Railway as well as numerous buildings. (Based on map in Illustrated Guide to Town and Exhibition, by Revd W. E. Winks.)*

Railway was brought in to the site, from across Corbett Road.[7] When all was ready, the exhibition was opened in grand style on Saturday, 2 May 1896, by Lord Windsor.

From an architectural point of view the principal interest was the main exhibition building designed by Edwin Seward. It was a vast structure, more than 300 ft (91.5 m) wide by 400 ft (122 m) deep, constructed to a tee-shaped plan with additional side wings and linked to a concert hall that had been prefabricated in the nearby suburb of Canton. Visually, the most attractive and solid-looking part of the building was the main front, the remaining areas being of basic warehouse construction, top-lit and unadorned. The main front had originally started off as a fairly plain elevation with a single row of windows and a square tower-like entrance; by the time that Seward had finished adapting and refashioning his design it had become an exotic fantasy in Moorish style. The final result was a colourful façade (two storeys on one side, single storey on the other) that included a central entrance portal with a horseshoe arch under a high onion-shaped dome flanked by towers and oriental cupolas. At either end of the long front there were further eastern-looking towers (Pl. 20).[8]

Though extraordinary by the standards of the contemporary architecture of Cardiff, the exhibition building was, in a manner of speaking, a portend

Pl. 20. *Cardiff Exhibition, 1896. The entrance façade of the main exhibition building facing Park Place. It was designed by Edwin Seward.*

of things to come, both in its scale and in its park-like setting. Now, at least, the town's councillors and citizens could, if they so wished, begin to visualise how Cathays Park might look in the future, lined with public buildings around a central park.

The Cardiff Exhibition closed in November, after having been seen by almost 900,000 people over a period of 6 months. It had been a great popular success, if not a financial one. Now, however, came the job of demolishing all the buildings and associated paraphernalia, including the lake and canal. It was not straightforward and late in January, 1897, the Borough Council was still 'experiencing difficulty in getting the various contractors to clear their structures from Cathays Park'.[9] The ground must have looked more like a building site than a private park, and it is difficult to imagine how Bute – having seen his park disfigured and turned into a busy, public arena – could ever seriously expect it return to a peaceful, pastoral state. It is more likely that the Marquess foresaw that inevitably, one day, despite all the ups and downs, the park, or at least part of it, would come to be developed, either publicly or commercially. It was, after all, a potentially valuable plot of land close to the heart of a vibrant, still growing town.

During the course of the exhibition the Council had given further thought to publicising the merits of Cardiff as a home for other organisations, even though no suitable sites were available at the time. Thus, on 4 September 1896, the Borough Council agreed to appoint a sub-committee to secure the location in Cardiff of the offices of the National [*sic*] University of Wales and the Glamorgan County Council.[10] Swansea was also keen to obtain the University of Wales' offices and offered a site (along with a design by H. W. Wills) for this and a proposed National Welsh Museum, Art Gallery and Record Offices, all grouped around the Free Library in Alexander Road.[11] Exactly what was in the minds of the Cardiff councillors with regard to possible sites for these buildings if they had been secured is unclear, for a few weeks later, on 30 October, the Town Hall Committee decided to ask the Borough Engineer to provide alternative proposals for erecting a new Town Hall on the Temperance Town site and on the existing Town Hall site with the costs and probable income from each.[12]

Then in November came an unorthodox episode reminiscent of Peter Price's action 4 years earlier (see Chapter 4) when Alderman David Jones, on behalf of certain gentlemen concerned with the University College's future, contacted Sir William Lewis unofficially to see whether the Cathays Park negotiations could be reopened. Although at first Sir William was not optimistic about the outcome – noting later that he had been 'obliged to use a good deal of argument to induce his Lordship to favour the idea of rediscussing the matter' – he was successful and the Alderman was informed 'that Lord Bute had signified his assent to the reopening of negotiations'.[13]

Discussions continued on an informal and unofficial basis until the *Western Mail* became aware of what was going on and broke the news. According to the newspaper:

> it is said that the whole of the Cathays Park can be purchased for something like £150,000, or £3,000 per acre, and the idea is that it should be used for the erection of municipal buildings, law courts, the new University College, technical schools, museum, the Welsh University offices and perhaps other requirements.[14]

But then there was a further reversal of opinion by the Town Hall Committee, and on the 6 January 1897, they decided to appoint a subcommittee 'to negotiate with Lord Bute for obtaining the Cathays Park for municipal and other public purposes'.[15] The *South Wales Daily News* was supportive, commenting that 'the idea of acquiring Cathays Park, and placing thereon the public buildings required by the quickly-developing national life of Wales, has seized the local imagination so powerfully that enthusiasm is already enkindled'.[16] Not all were happy, however, and at a public meeting a few days later to consider the best site for a new Town Hall 'the arguments were entirely as between the Temperance Town and St Mary Street sites', with Cathays Park not getting a look in.[17] When the full Council met on 6 January 1897, there was a stormy discussion about possible sites, with Councillor Buist describing the Cathays Park scheme as 'only drawing a red herring across the trail', and Councillor Ramsdale reporting that `he knew there were already three plans prepared for the proposed laying out of Cathays Park, and that it would be built upon whether the Corporation got it or not'.[18] Ramsdale proposed a motion 'that a Sub-Committee be appointed to approach and negotiate with Lord Bute with a view of obtaining the Cathays Park for municipal or other public buildings'.[19] The motion, which had been carefully worded so as not to commit the Town Hall to Cathays Park, was approved.

A week later the *Western Mail* published a plan (prepared by the architects J. P. Jones, Richards and Budgen) depicting a 'proposed lay out of Cathays Park', in which various public buildings were arranged around the perimeter of the Park. Interestingly, the Town Hall was to be sited parallel to the Castle on what was later to become the Friary Gardens with a large public square between it and Queen Street, while new roads crossed Bute Park and Sophia Gardens to link Corbett Road and Nazareth House with Cathedral Road. Surprisingly, the newspaper welcomed the proposal, commenting that 'if the idea shown here can be carried out, possibly with modifications, it would place Cardiff in the unique position of being without comparison to any city in Europe'.[20]

The Council subcommittee met Sir William Lewis on 27 January. At the meeting Sir William was able to confirm 'that Lord Bute was prepared to sell the Park for the sum of £150,000, subject to certain conditions', the exact terms and conditions of which would be forwarded 'to the Town Clerk as early as possible'. The good news seems to have taken everyone by surprise, for 'the price was lower than could have been hoped for, and it had not been anticipated that Lord Bute would agree to the sale of the whole park'.[21] Two days later the *South Wales Daily News* reported that 'the information given us yesterday… has been received in Cardiff with general satisfaction. Everybody who takes any interest in the welfare of the town spoke of the proposal with evident gratification'.[22] The *Western Mail* was less than enthusiastic, saying:

> The purchase of Cathays Park seems a roundabout way of procur-
> ing a Town Hall site. The latter is the only really pressing need for
> the town, and to purchase from fifty to sixty acres for the sake of
> getting four acres is scarcely a method which would commend itself
> to an average business man in the conduct of his own affairs.[23]

On the 24 February the General Purposes Committee 'resolved that a Provisional Agreement be entered into between Lord Bute and the Corporation', for the purchase of Cathays Park at the price of £150,000 for the purposes of municipal buildings, on the understanding that certain trees were to be preserved and that the unused space was to be left open in perpetuity.[24] The idea of acquiring Cathays Park for the county borough's public buildings had, at long last, caught on. Lascelles Carr, the editor of the *Western Mail*, who had softened since his trip to the United States, wrote, 'I think the corporation ought to purchase the Cathays Park, now that they have the opportunity of doing so.' He left the question of choosing a site for the Town Hall to be decided by the public, but added that 'by securing the Cathays Park the town would always have an opportunity of receiving great agricultural shows or of holding exhibitions'.[25]

The General Purposes Committee's resolution was confirmed by the full Council on 8 March 1897, and on 14 April an agreement to purchase was signed by both parties.[26] The agreement was conditional because the Bute estate was entailed and the Marquess could not sell without Parliamentary authority. This meant that the corporation had to bear the cost of obtaining an Act of Parliament.

A few weeks later the *Evening Express* published an unattributed suggestion for a new road – to be known as Victoria Street in honour of Queen Victoria's Jubilee – from the junction of Queen Street with The Friary to Cathays Park.[27] According to the plan, the Town Hall would be placed at the south-eastern corner of Cathays Park and the new street would be lined with shops on both sides. Nothing came of the suggestion that would, in any case, have involved the demolition of St John's School and the remains of Greyfriars Friary.

While the question of the sale of Cathays Park was being discussed in parliament, the Council made a further attempt to secure the University of Wales Registry. On 29 March they sent 'a memorial to the Court of the University of Wales, praying that the Office of the University Registrar be placed at Cardiff', presumably, if they were successful, in Cathays Park. However, when, a month later, it met at Shrewsbury the University Court decided to shelve the question of the Registry's site for a period of five years.[28]

Undaunted, the Town Hall Committee returned to considering the future of their own municipal buildings and, at a meeting on 5 June, resolved to erect a new Town Hall and Law Courts at the south-western corner of Cathays Park.[29] Earlier, on 21 May, a Special Committee of the Council had agreed that a 'Memorial be forwarded to the Prime Minister, praying that the titles of Lord Mayor and City be granted to Cardiff'.[30] The response to the application was disappointing when it was learnt, via the Home Office, that such matters could not be considered in isolation, but 'that the holding of royal events and the awarding of city status were linked'.[31]

Having decided on sites for the Town Hall and Law Courts, preparations were made to hold an architectural competition for the design of the two new buildings. Sir Alfred Waterhouse, architect of Manchester's Town Hall (1868) and London's Natural History Museum (1873), was appointed as the assessor for the competition. By September the Town Clerk was able to report that there had been 80 applications for the competition conditions.[32] On 28 October the Town Hall Committee agreed to recommend the reservation of a site free of charge for a new Cardiff Museum and the sale of a site for the University College, both to be in Cathays Park.[33] As part of the subsequent agreement Lord Bute agreed to buy back the site at the lower end of Park Place (see Chapter 4) that had previously been allocated for the Cardiff Museum.

Everything looked set for the Council to finalise the acquisition of Cathays Park, but incredibly – considering the money already spent by the Council on a Parliamentary Bill and an architectural competition – further opposition to the scheme was raised at the end of 1897. On 30 December it was announced that a Ratepayers' Committee had been formed to oppose the building of a new town hall at Cathays Park. According to a press interview the Committee confirmed that, 'we do not object to the purchase of the Cathays Park for recreation purposes or as a site for educational buildings. Our opposition is exclusively directed against removing the municipal buildings and law courts from the centre of the town'.[34] All of this appears to have been related to an earlier proposal by John Kyte Collett of Penarth – and published in a slim pamphlet – to build new houses south of the Great Western Railway, on the west side of the river, so that the terrace houses in Temperance Town could be demolished in order to make way for a new Town Hall in front of the railway station (Pl. 21).[35] A few days after the formation of the Ratepayers' Committee, at the beginning of January, 1898, the *Evening Express* gave its opinion that to a visitor 'Cardiff is a dirty, overestimated place with two streets and a few shops', particularly when arriving by train, and that therefore 'an imposing, handsome centre of business [i.e. Town Hall], in place of the slums of Temperance-town, [would] be an advantage better than the hiding of a costly new Town-hall in the fields of Cathays Park'.[36] The following week, the

Pl. 21. *Proposed Town Hall, 1897. A design (possibly by John Kyte Collett) for new municipal buildings in Temperance Town, opposite the main railway station.*

Evening Express published a long article on the 'Case against Cathays Park', illustrated with a map showing the distances to alternative sites. Cathays Park was depicted with a 10 acre (4 ha) strip of public buildings along the southern edge, a 14 acre (5.7 ha) park in the centre and the remainder laid out with semi-detached villa residences.[37]

On the 11 January, the ratepayers held an open meeting in the Park Hall (later incorporated in the Park Hotel). The meeting was crowded and, after a long and stormy debate, the Council's policy on Cathays Park was confirmed by an overwhelming majority. Lascelles Carr, however, was not happy and demanded a poll on behalf of the ratepayers. This was agreed, but two weeks' later, after Carr had discovered that the Ratepayers' Committee only wanted to rebuild on the site of the existing Town Hall and not at his preferred site in Temperance Town, Carr withdrew his demand for a poll.[38]

Carr, however, remained antagonistic to what he saw as Bute's influence in the town, despite the setback. On 31 January, he wrote:

> The Cathays Scheme is the result of a long-standing conspiracy between some of the officials of the Corporation and the representatives of the University College. It has been in the air for years, and when the Corporation applied to Lord Bute for land on which to build a Town Hall on the Cardiff Arms Park the extortionate and ridiculous prices asked for one site and then for another were fixed entirely with the object of driving the Corporation to Cathays Park. It all formed part of a policy. With the Bute interest it has always been the Park or nothing.[39]

In truth the probability was, as Chappell has noted:

> that Lord Bute himself was primarily influenced not by financial considerations, but by purely artistic motives, in desiring to reserve Cathays Park as a well-designed Civic Centre. As a trustee for his successor in title he was, however, obliged to demand the full market price of the land. The negotiations on his side were left to that hard-headed business man, Sir W. T. Lewis, who not only executed but largely formulated Bute policy at that period.[40]

Whatever Bute's motives, they resulted in a wonderful opportunity for the borough to redeem itself for past failings and meanness. For, as the mayor, quoting a comment by Sir Alfred Waterhouse regarding Cathays Park, had reminded his audience at the ratepayers' meeting, 'there is no town in the kingdom ever had such an admirable proposal or such a magnificent site for municipal buildings and Law Courts'.[41]

The Cardiff Corporation Act, authorising consent to the purchase of 59 acres of Cathays Park for the sum of £158,500, was passed by Parliament and received the Royal Assent on 25 July 1898.[42] The area included an acre of land on the south side of the Feeder, but excluded an acre at the north-west corner of the park near the site of the former Cathays House. The reason for excluding the latter acre – the 'reserved acre' as it became known – was never made clear, although the *Western Mail* claimed that it was 'to preserve some ruins of historic interest'.[43] The only thing of interest in the reserved acre was an ice-house belonging to Cathays House that had been built in the furthest corner, away from the mansion, in the form of a domed chamber under a turf covered mound. Pettigrew in his monumental survey of Cardiff's parks suggested that 'there can be little doubt that the third Marquis's [*sic*] reason for retaining in his own hands the "one acre reserved" with the "old building" therein, was the preservation of this slight relic of one of his ancestral homes'.[44] Whatever the reason, the ice-house did not remain long, for it was demolished within a couple of years of Bute selling the remainder of the park, leaving behind only a low mound.

On the 14 December, five months after the Act had been passed, the purchase of Cathays Park was completed at the Bute Estate Office when the borough treasurer handed a cheque to Sir William Lewis and he in turn handed the deeds over to the town clerk. Afterwards, all present proceeded to Cathays Park, crossing the footbridge that Bute had had constructed over the Feeder to where the four-line avenue of elms began. At that point, Sir William unlocked the gate and handed over the key to the mayor, who then locked the gate and kept the key. In this way the park become the property of the county borough, placing Cardiff, as the mayor confirmed, 'in the unique position of being the first town in the kingdom which had acquired such a beautiful park whereon all the public institutions of the town could be erected'. It was, he continued, 'a blessing to the present and future generations of the Metropolis of Wales'.[45]

NOTES

1   *Western Mail,* 12, 31 January, 15 February 1894.

2   Ibid., 22 December 1893.

3   Ibid., 31 January, 15 February 1894.

4   Ibid., 23 December 1893, 1 February 1894.

5   Ibid., 21 May 1895.

6   Ibid., 3 December 1895.

7   Revd W. E. Winks, *Cardiff Exhibition, 1896 – Illustrated Guide to the Town and Exhibition,* pp. 3–4.

8   *Evening Express,* 4 May 1896.

9   *Cardiff Times,* 23 January 1897.

10   CCL: Cardiff Corporation, *Proceedings, 1895–96,* p. 869.

11   *Cardiff Times,* 14 November, 1896; British Architect, November 1896.

12   CCL: Cardiff Corporation, *Proceedings, 1895–96,* p. 1009–10.

13   CCL: Pettigrew, *Public Parks of Cardiff,* vol. 2, p. 159; Western Mail, 30 January 1897.

14   Ibid., 11 December 1896.

15   CCL: Cardiff Corporation, *Proceedings, 1896–97,* p. 210.

16   *South Wales Daily News,* 17 December 1896.

17   CCL: Pettigrew, *Public Parks of Cardiff,* vol. 2, p. 162; *Western Mail,* 19 December 1896.

18   *Western Mail,* 7 January 1897.

19   CCL: Cardiff Corporation, *Proceedings, 1896– 97,* p. 210.

20   *Western Mail,* 14 January 1897.

21   CCL: Cardiff Corporation, *Proceedings, 1896–97,* p. 309.

22   *South Wales Daily News,* 29 January 1897.

23   *Western Mail,* 30 January 1897.

24   CCL: Cardiff Corporation, *Proceedings, 1896–97,* pp. 318–19.

25   *Western Mail,* 10 February, 1897.

26   CCL: Cardiff Corporation, *Proceedings, 1896–97,* pp. 753–8.

27   *Evening Express,* 21 May, 1897.

28   CCL: Matthews, *Cardiff Records,* vol. 5, pp. 248, 251.

29   CCL: Cardiff Corporation, *Proceedings, 1896–97,* p. 652.

30   Ibid., p. 603.

31   Morley, 'Representing a City and Nation', p. 60, note 27.

32   CCL: Cardiff Corporation, *Proceedings, 1896–97,* p. 877.

33   Ibid., p. 997.

34   CCL: Pettigrew, *Public Parks of Cardiff,* vol. 2, p. 170.

35   John Kyte Collett, *New Municipal Buildings for Cardiff, a Fresh Scheme by Mr J. K. Collett,* pp. 1–18.

36   *Evening Express,* 4 January 1898.

37   *Evening Express,* 11 January 1898.

38   *Cardiff Times,* 15 January 1898.

39   *Western Mail,* 13 January 1898.

40   Chappell, *Cardiff's Civic Centre,* p. 17.

41   *Cardiff Times,* 15 January 1898.

42   *Western Mail,* 10 February 1897.

43   *Western Mail,* 10 February 1897.

44   CCL: Pettigrew, *Public Parks of Cardiff,* vol. 2, p. 179.

45   *Western Mail,* 15 December 1898.

6

PLANS AND PETITIONS

CATHAYS PARK WAS 'formally declared open to the public as a prome-nade' by the mayor on 29 March 1899, following a council resolution passed in January.[1] The move was evidently a great success, as the *South Wales Daily News* reported in June. 'Sweet are the uses of Cathays Park', its columnist enthused:

> Up to the present the children of Cathays have swarmed there evening by evening. Fond mothers wheel perambulators there, and on one or two evenings a week the Band of the Cardiff Detachment of the 3rd V. B. Welsh Regiment has struck military ardour into the hearts of the frequenters of the park.[2]

A month later, Cathays Park was to be the setting for the National Eisteddfod of Wales. In preparation for the five-day-long Eisteddfod a giant prefabricated, temporary pavilion was erected between the site of the future town hall and the Gorsedd Circle placed near the Feeder. The Gorsedd Circle, arranged as a ring of standing stones with a large, flat-topped stone in the centre, formed the centrepiece for the druidical ceremonies associated with the Eisteddfod, which opened on 18 July.[3]

The use of the park as a recreation ground was to be, of course, only tem-porary, until such time as it was required for the erection of public buildings. Meanwhile, work was progressing on carrying out the requirements of the Act that had been approved in July 1898. The Act confirmed the agreement made in 1897 to acquire Cathays Park and granted the Corporation powers to 'erect and maintain [therein] a town hall, law courts and other munici-pal or public offices or other buildings' and to convey land to the University of Wales, the University College of South Wales and Monmouthshire and the County of Glamorgan to erect their own buildings. In addition, the Act stipulated several matters affecting the future use and arrangement of the park. Among these was a condition that the park should not be used for 'any private dwelling-house hotel restaurant or lodging-house office or place for carrying on any trade profession or business for profit or for manufactur-ing'. With regard to the park's future layout the Act specified that the Corpo-ration should 'maintain in perpetuity' the four-line avenue planted by Lord Bute, construct a new road (Cathays Park Road) – at least 60 ft (18 m) wide – between Park Place and North Road, construct a 'new road and avenue' (Kingsway) between the four-line avenue and the lower end of North Road, preserve in perpetuity the triangular land between these latter roads and the Feeder as a planted open space, and widen North Road.[4]

Although some of the parameters of the park's layout were controlled by the demands of the 1898 Act, the overall road pattern and other details still needed to be worked out. Chappell, writing in 1945–6, was of the opinion that 'a tentative layout had been prepared for the purpose of the negotia-tions', and that the main lines of development had `probably [been] agreed upon with the Bute authorities before the deal was concluded'.[5] Certainly the positions of the Town Hall and Law Courts on the front facing the town centre had been agreed in principle and had been embedded in the conditions of the architectural competition for the two buildings.[6] H. V. Lanchester, of Lanchester, Stewart and Rickards, winners of the competition, had adhered to the agreed locations and included them on a plan he sent to William Harpur, the borough engineer, in January 1898 with suggestions on how to mitigate 'the objections that are being raised to the Cathays Park site for Town-hall, & c'.[7] Interestingly, Lanchester's proposal envisaged continuing Bute's four-line avenue in a straight line across the Feeder as far as Queen Street, where it would connect with Frederick Street and Union Street, the latter widened from 'a back street into an important business thoroughfare'.

While the layout details were being worked out, claims were being made to site various other buildings in the park. On 14 March, 1899, for instance the Council's Parliamentary Subcommittee suggested 'that the Cardiff Corporation should provide a site in the Cathays Park for the said [National] museum'.[8] In the following month the Museum Committee took the matter up and recommended 'that the corporation should contribute towards the maintenance of the national museum'.[9] The point was made during discussion that a National Museum 'would be, if established, a very much larger and better museum than they now had', and would also benefit from a government grant. In the following month the Cardiff Trades' Council decided to ask the town clerk to reserve a site in the park for the erection of a large public hall to be used especially for Friendly Societies and Trades Unions.[10]

When the borough engineer's proposed layout for the park was published in September, the layout was dominated by the roads that had been required by the 1898 Act (Fig. 6.1). Apart from these roads the layout was somewhat different from what turned out to be the final arrangement. Bute's four-line avenue, now referred to as The Avenue, became the main axis of the site and the only through road in a north–south direction. Three roads crossed in an east-west direction: a main road parallel to the Feeder (Cathays Park Road, later to become Boulevard de Nantes), a lesser road passing in front of the designated Town Hall and Law Courts sites (Gorsedd Gardens Road), and an avenue at the upper end of the park (College Road). In addition, Harpur's plan indicated a new road (Kingsway) crossing the Dock Feeder and a widened North Road, the latter necessitating the demolition of the park lodge where Bute's head gardener, Andrew Pettigrew, once lived.

The whole of the western part of the park, between The Avenue and North Road, was allocated for buildings. At the southern end was the Law Courts and behind this were sites reserved for the Board School Offices (1 acre [0.4 ha]), County Offices (1 acre [0.4 ha]), Technical School (3 acres [1.2 ha]), and a Drill Hall (2.5 acres [1 ha]). The eastern part of the park was

Fig. 6.1. *Proposed development of Cathays Park. The layout of the Park for public buildings as proposed by the Borough Engineer in 1899. In addition to the buildings there were to be extensive areas of parkland with fountains, bandstands and an observatory. (Based on Borough Engineer's plan.)*

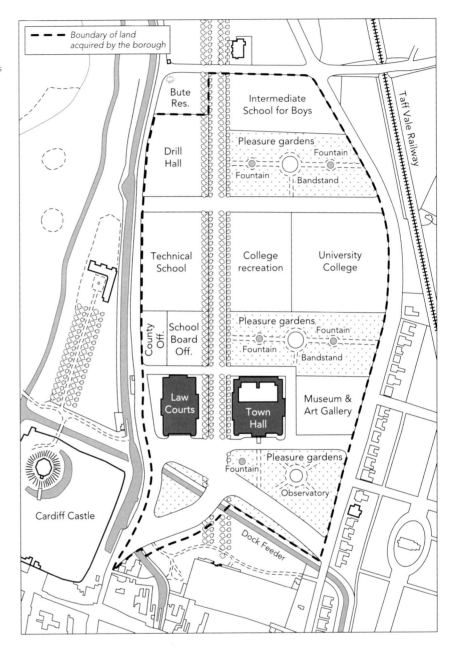

divided into six strips of land, three of which were designated for buildings and three (intervening ones) for ornamental parkland. Immediately to the east of The Avenue would be the Town Hall, with, further east, a site reserved for a Museum and Art Gallery (2 acres [0.8 ha]). The central strip was reserved for the University College (4 acres [1.6 ha] for buildings and 6 acres [2.5 ha] for recreation grounds), and the northernmost strip, next to Corbett Road, for an Intermediate School for Boys (3 acres [1.2 ha]).

Three days after the borough engineer's proposals had been published, the Town Hall Committee met (19 September) with William Harpur to consider the plan. Harpur explained the disposition of parkland, saying that:

> by providing two or three open spaces intervening between the several buildings he believed the whole area would be much more pleasing, and the buildings and trees would show out better than if all the buildings were grouped together and only a single open space of large dimensions was provided.[11]

In the heated discussion that followed, the committee members seemed to be mostly concerned about the large amount of land that had been allocated to the University College. Some felt that it was wrong to give the college 6 acres (2.5 ha) just for recreation purposes when places like Grangetown only had a fraction of that amount of open space for all of its inhabitants. There were also objections to a drill hall being placed in the park, one councillor suggesting that a large public hall could be built there instead. Ironically – in view of the fact that the committee had been set up to sort out the shortage of accommodation in the existing Town Hall – the meeting had to be adjourned before anything was decided owing to the room having been double-booked.[12]

The Town Hall Committee met again on 9 February 1900, to consider the allocation of sites for public institutions. Apart from the fact that the Submarine Miners had not specified the acreage needed for their Drill Hall and parade ground, the requirements were generally in accordance with those shown on the borough engineer's plan.[13] The Committee met for a further meeting in October, 'because various bodies who were wanting sites were looking for replies to their applications'. Once again there was concern regarding the College's requirements. In the end, the Committee resolved that 'five acres be granted to the University College at cost prices' and that `all other applicants for sites (except the Museum, which had already been granted a free site) be notified that they must pay for their sites'.[14]

The decision to reduce, from 10 acres (4 ha) to 5 acres (2 ha), the amount of land allocated for the University College had an immediate effect on the layout of the park. Until then Harpur's proposals had been based on all the land east of The Avenue being divided into horizontal, east–west strips of land. Now, the layout was revised with vertical strips running in a roughly north–south direction, the easternmost strip to be occupied by the museum and university college. A new, private road, capable of being closed when not in use, was to run between the Town Hall and Museum as far as the University College.

Further changes were made in 1902 after the Town Hall Subcommittee had (on 2 October) recommended keeping 'the whole of the central portion of the (Cathays) Park as open space for the use of the public', together with the construction of a 50-foot (15-m) wide road between it and the University College site.[15] The revised layout with public open space between the existing

Avenue and the planned new road (Museum Avenue) was beginning to look remarkably like Peter Price's original vision of public buildings arranged around a central park (see Chapter 4). The final layout of the north-eastern section of Cathays Park was still a matter for the future.

Matters were moving on, however, as far as the Town Hall and Law Courts were concerned. The firm of Lanchester, Stewart and Rickards had won first prize in the architectural competition for the design of the two buildings and now they were confirmed as architects to supervise the work. Tenders had been received in September 1900, for the construction, with the local firm of E. Turner & Sons submitting the lowest offer of £226,288. Subsequently, they were awarded the contract.[16] In October, the third Marquess of Bute died in Scotland at the age of 53. His son John Crichton Stuart, born in 1881, became the new Marquess. Like his father had been, he also was interested in architectural conservation.

A year later, when Cardiff's population had reached 164,333 inhabitants, the 20-year-old fourth Marquess was asked to lay the foundation stone of the Town Hall. This he did on 23 October 1901, before a 'large and distinguished gathering'. After a brief speech by the mayor, the young Lord Bute 'approached the stone. In a few seconds it was adjusted, the powerful crane working with marvellous nicety. His Lordship performed the usual levelling and gave the customary three taps with the mallet before declaring the stone duly and truly laid'.[17] Later, a similar ceremony was carried out at the site of the new Law Courts, this time with the mayor laying the foundation stone and Lord Bute looking on as 'an interested spectator'. Four years were to pass before the new buildings were completed and formally opened (Pl. 22).

While the Town Hall and Law Courts were under construction, the Cardiff Museum project was reassessed in the light of renewed interest in a Welsh National Museum and the possibility of its being approved by the Government.[18] As if in anticipation, the Cardiff Museum Committee resolved to change the name of the Cardiff Museum and Art Gallery to the 'Welsh Museum of Natural History, Arts and Antiquities' in 1901, `to bring the title of the institution into line with the growing national character of its collections'.[19] Then, late in 1902, the Committee recommended spending £25,000 on the building after the Town Clerk had expressed his opinion 'that in view of the hope that the National Museum of Wales could be secured for Cardiff the new building should be of such a character as would be suitable for such a purpose'.[20] It was resolved to ask the architect, Edwin Seward, 'which portions of the building could best be proceeded with for this sum'. Seward came up with a scheme – estimated to cost between £150,000 and £160,000 for the complete building – that closely followed the design of the new Town Hall in scale and style, with a projecting entrance section under a cupola. Although approval was given in February 1905 to proceed with 'the central front and the west wing', nothing happened on the ground, possibly because of the ongoing discussions regarding a National Museum.[21]

Elsewhere in Cathays Park other works were about to begin. Early in 1903 tenders were received for building the two road bridges required for the development of the Civic Centre. The contract for the bridge across the Feeder was won by Charles Davies (£4,035) and that for the bridge connected with widening North Road by E. Turner & Sons (£1,481).[22] As the bridges were being built, work was going ahead widening Park Place as far as the Feeder, widening North Road and constructing Kingsway. The foundation stone of the third public building – the Registry of the University of Wales – was laid in November, 1903.[23] It would be the first building to be completed when it opened a year later, in 1904.

It was to be the following year, however, that proved to be one of the most significant for both Cardiff and its embryonic Civic Centre. The first event of note in 1905 was the anxiously awaited ruling by a committee appointed (by the Privy Council) to decide the location of the National Library and the National Museum. The judgement came in June when the committee, aware that Wales had no capital, decided to disperse the institutions, select-ing Aberystwyth as the site for the new Library and Cardiff as the site for the Museum.[24] Cardiff had petitioned for both institutions, while Aberystwyth – like Caernarfon and Swansea – had sought only one. Although Cardiff, with Cathays Park in mind, had been selected for the Museum, it would be many years before the building became a reality, by which time both the architect and the design had been changed.

Pl. 22. *City Hall under construction. When this photograph was taken in 1903 Cardiff had not been raised to the status of city and the building was still known as the Town Hall.*

Another memorable stone-laying ceremony took place a few weeks later, on the 28 June, when the Prince of Wales, on a two-day visit to Cardiff, laid the foundation stone for the first part of the new University College of South Wales and Monmouthshire.[25] The event took place before a great crowd accommodated on a specially built, semicircular and tiered stand surrounded by a vast area of open space. The University College – again the fruit of an architectural competition – represented, as the fourth public building, a major step forward in the development of the Civic Centre. The following day the Prince was given the Freedom of the Borough at a luncheon given by the Mayor. The Prince's acceptance speech varied according to which newspaper one read: in the *Weekly Mail* he was quoted as having said, '… the honour conferred on me by enrolling me as one of your honorary freemen will link me still closer to the capital and most important town in the Principality'; in the *Western Mail* it was, '… closer to the largest and most important town in the Principality'.[26] Apparently, *The Times*, of London, *had* referred to Cardiff as 'the capital', while the *Cardiff Times* had quoted '… your town, pre-eminent in Wales and one of the greatest commercial ports of the Empire'. However, according to a letter from the Prince's private secretary the Prince did not use the word 'capital'.[27]

Now that the ambitiously conceived Civic Ccentre had become a reality, at least in part, there followed considerable lobbying to raise Cardiff's profile still further by petitioning for the town to be granted city status. It was possible to argue, as Ian Morley has done, that:

> civic design in late Victorian and Edwardian Cardiff should be appreciated as articulating beauty and local accomplishments but also, given the emergence of a new elite, civic ambitions too for it was utilized in the hope that it would help lead to the hugely symbolic diktat declaring city status, an edict that emphasises Cardiff's part in driving Wales away from its agrarian past, and the nation's hitherto identity as being merely an English colony.[28]

The enthusiasm for greater distinction and eminence was no doubt helped by the Prince of Wales's earlier reference to Cardiff's position in Wales, for there were many people who believed that Cardiff ought to be not only a city but also the capital. In fact a petition to be granted city status had been made in 1902 hoping, no doubt, to coincide with the coronation of Edward VII in August of that year. However, nothing had come of the application. Now, soon after the Prince of Wales's visit, the Council petitioned again for city status, this time forwarding a dossier on 3 July to Arthur Balfour, the Prime Minister.[29]

Balfour, however, showed little interest at first, writing to his private secretary, 'that the only possible justification for giving this honour to Cardiff is that it must be regarded as the capital of Wales. And', he added insensitively, 'is there not … a certain absurdity in assuming that Cardiff is to be regarded as the capital of Wales without any ground, as far as I know, based upon history, or general sentiment among the Welsh people?'[30] Balfour changed his mind later, and on 15 October the Mayor was informed by Lord Bute that Cardiff was, after all, about to become a city. This was confirmed on 23 October when, at a specially convened meeting of the Council, the Mayor read a letter from the Home Secretary announcing that the King had been pleased to constitute Cardiff a city with a Lord Mayor at its head.

The news was warmly greeted by the *Western Mail*, which stressed that the new status must carry with it recognition that Wales was a 'nationality' and that `by the King's act the capital has been definitely fixed. Not only does Cardiff take her place in the front rank of the United Kingdom … [but] she is raised to be the appointed leader of the Welsh nation'.[31] The *Cardiff Times* even went as far as to assert that:

> the purchase of the Cathays Park as a site for public buildings and the erection thereon of one of the finest Town Halls and Law Courts … made the claim of Cardiff to the title and the honour of a City imperative, and set up a claim to be the Metropolis of Wales which cannot be withheld.[32]

These sentiments were shared by many in urban Wales (if not in the rural areas) so that the developing Civic Centre became bound up with the notion of both city status and capital status. It would, however, be another fifty years before the latter came to be fully accepted and confirmed.

Work began on the enclosing and laying out of some of the park's open spaces during the autumn of 1905. The area between North Road and Kingsway was handed over to the Parks Department in September, after which the dwarf wall and fence surrounding the site were erected, followed by laying out the space in Dutch style during the winter. To begin with it was known as the Dutch Garden, then the Priory Gardens and later, when the latter title was shown to be inaccurate, the Friary Gardens.[33] The area in front of the National Museum followed a similar pattern. It was named the Gorsedd Gardens after the prehistoric-looking circle of standing stones – originally erected near to the Dock Feeder for the Gorsedd ceremony of the 1899 National Eisteddfod – had been re-erected here owing to its being in the way of the new Cathays Park Road.[34] Both the Friary Gardens and the Gorsedd Gardens were opened to the public in July 1910.[35]

A year after Cardiff had been raised to city status the City Hall (as the Town Hall had now become) and the Law Courts were formally opened on 29 October 1906. Despite miserable, wet weather thousands of people turned out for the opening. A raised platform for attending notables had been set up outside the entrance, and on this dais H.V. Lanchester presented, on behalf of the architects Lanchester and Rickards (Stewart, one of the original partners, having since died), a gold key to Lord Bute. The Marquess then descended from the platform to the entrance, performed the ceremony of opening the gates of the new City Hall and returned to the platform amidst loud cheering. Later, a similar performance was repeated by the Lord Mayor on the steps of the new Law Courts.[36]

With the opening of the City Hall and the Law Courts, Cardiff's infant Civic Centre had entered into a new phase and taken an important step forward. With three buildings completed, a fourth started and a fifth authorised, as well as others in the pipeline, there was every reason to be proud of what had been accomplished and what to expect in the future.

Cardiff, of course, was not alone in trying to express its new-found wealth and importance through architecture. Indeed, a 'common manifestation in Victorian Britain was the erection of large civic buildings, particularly a town hall, which highlighted civic pride and pretension as much as it advertised the taking of local government responsibilities seriously'.[37] One of the differences in Cardiff's case was the sheer scale of the undertaking. Another was the way in which allowance had been made to accommodate a number of other public and national buildings in the same area. The following were not allowed to be built in the park: private dwelling-houses, hotel, restaurant, or lodging-house, office, or any place for carrying on any trade, profession, or business for profit, or any manufacturing or similar process.[38] Fortuitous it may have been to have so much underused land near to the town centre; the decision to use the land wisely, however, was not. It was, as it turned out, a good example of flexible planning within an apparently rigid layout.

In the few years left before the commencement of the First World War, construction work continued in the Park at an almost dizzy pace. The main road layout was completed (apart from the upper end of Museum Avenue) and The Avenue was formally opened by King Edward VII on 13 July 1907, amidst much rejoicing. Now paved and artificially lit, it was immediately renamed King Edward VII Avenue. The main part of the University College, including its superb library, was opened in October, 1909. At the same time, the central garden on to which the college faced was being laid out; at first the garden was known as University Gardens. When it was opened to the public on 27 July, the following year, it was renamed Queen Alexandra Gardens, after the King's wife, as was the Queen Alexandra Dock that the King had opened in 1907.[39]

Cathays Park was soon to become the customary home for national memorials. The most important of the early monuments was the South African War Memorial, erected at the lower end of King Edward VII Avenue in 1909 to commemorate the fallen of the Boer War. Within a few years statues of four illustrious Welsh men were also raised in different parts of the Park.

By now 'public sculpture had become a valued part of public life' in Cardiff. That it was so, is perhaps shown by the interest that was taken in the idea of a national memorial for heroes, a kind of Valhalla ('hall of the slain') known from Scandinavian mythology and found in various memorials that had been erected in German cities. The first suggestion of such a scheme for the 'adornment of the open space in front of the City Hall and Law Courts' seems to have come from a Mr T. H. Thomas in a letter to the Council in March 1908. When asked about his idea, he replied that 'I should like to see a great monumental assemblage to include figures from all the historical ages, to see the space become a sort of Valhalla of the heroes of olden time, place being found in the scheme also of course for memorials of more modern Cardiff.'[40] His aim was to have a plan drawn up so that when statues were erected in future they would be in harmony and conform to an organised scheme. Mr Thomas's suggestion was considered by a Committee, but action was postponed 'till the whole question of the allotment of statuary sites was discussed'.

The idea appears to have gone quiet for a couple of years until it was revived in 1910 in connection with a proposal for a Welsh national memorial to King Edward VII. In this context the 'open space' at the rear of the City Hall – soon to be opened to the public as Queen Alexandra Gardens – 'was seen as "the ideal site for the National Valhalla of Welsh notables"'.[41] The *South Wales Daily News* went as far as to state that:

> It is … fitting that the past should be represented in memorials and statues as the present stands typified in the buildings, and for that reason at various times it has been suggested in our columns that the centre of Cathays Park should be made the site for important monuments.[42]

Later the matter was addressed by Sir Ivor Herbert, MP, at the Cymmrodorion Section of the National Eisteddfod (at Colwyn Bay, 1910) where he suggested that:

> the most suitable memorial … seemed to me to be one which would present to Welshmen and to those who may visit Wales a personal representation of our late King [Edward VII] in close association with a memorial of all the figures of the historic past which forms the background and the inspiration of Welsh nationalism.[43]

As John Wilson commented in *Memorializing History*, 'a Welsh Valhalla in Cardiff would function as the most visible emblem of national identity and pride for visitors and "our own people" alike'.[44] But it was not to be in the form of statuary in the park, but rather became the basis for the pantheon of national heroes set up in the City Hall's Marble Hall in 1916 (see Chapter 8).

As the first part of the University College was being completed, a new building, the Glamorgan County Council offices, was begun on the opposite side of the central garden. This building, one of the finest architecturally in the Park, was completed in 1911. In September of the same year a start was made

Pl. 23. *A Vision of the Civic Centre. This suggested view of the Civic Centre when completed, exhibited at an international planning exhibition in 1912, shows an imagined parliament building on the future site of Welsh Government Offices at the rear of Cathays Park.*

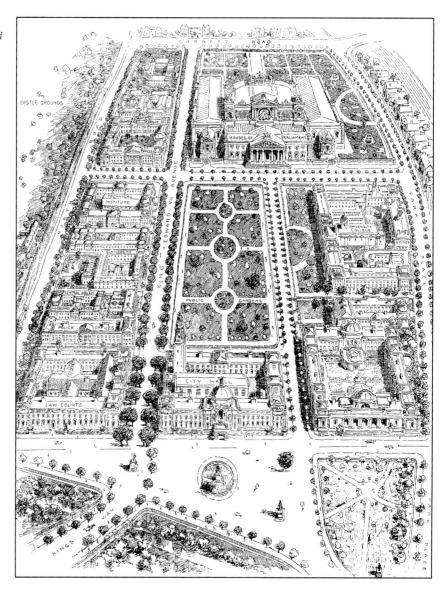

on the construction of the National Museum, ready for a formal stone-laying ceremony by King George V in June 1912. A year later the *Western Mail* produced a supplement that included a 'Bird's Eye View of Cathays Park when completed'. Interestingly, the view (which was also exhibited at the international 'Cities and Town Planning Exhibition' held that year in Ghent, Belgium) showed an imagined Welsh parliament at the rear of the park (Pl. 23), where now stands offices of the Welsh Government, indicating that some form of 'home rule' was, at the time, very much in the minds of many people.[45]

Two more buildings were begun on the western side of the Park: the Technical Institute (later, the Technical College) and the first block of government offices devoted to Welsh interests. The foundation stone of the Technical Institute was laid in April 1914, and the main part of the building was opened in March 1916. At the same time as the Technical Institute was begun, plans were being drawn up for a vast new block of government offices to the north, where now stands the Temple of Peace. The first part of this scheme – the offices of the Welsh Insurance Commission – appears to have been started.[46] Soon, however, the First World War intervened and the scheme was abandoned in 1915.[47]

By the outbreak of the War, the construction of these grand, classically designed, white stone buildings had transformed what hitherto had been a hidden, walled enclave of private affluence into a handsome civic and cultural centre – a 'white city', if you like, conspicuous against the variegated background of an existing, but continually growing city. It was no wonder that Patrick Geddes, the eminent Scottish planner, writing in 1914, was able to claim that Cardiff had risen from a 'mere export-centre of the South Wales coalfield … to deliberate design as regional metropolis; in fact, as the fourth national capital of the British Isles; and one determined to be more complete than Edinburgh or Dublin'.[48] That ambition, he went on, 'is being expressed in the creation of a civic centre far surpassing that of any other British City'. A year later, as if to ensure the Civic Centre's continued importance, the City Council took on Bute's gardener, A. A. Pettigrew, as Head Gardener for the Corporation. Later, Pettigrew was to write a history of Cardiff's parks.

In the period between the First and Second World Wars additional white buildings were erected, including the Welsh National War Memorial, the optimistically titled Temple of Peace and Health, and the long-awaited block of government offices, known as the Welsh Board of Health and built facing College Road rather than King Edward VII Avenue. Further additions were made to the National Museum and the University College as a well as a major extension to the Glamorgan County Hall. By 1939 the *Picture Post* was able to claim that Cardiff `has the finest civic centre in the country … [a] group of civic buildings … which invite comparison with any similar group in the world'.[49]

After a prolonged hiatus caused by the Second World War development of the Civic Centre continued with mixed results in the areas of culture and government. Both the National Museum and the University College were finally completed, although with significant changes to the original conceptions for these buildings. Expansion of the university entailed development of the sports field known as the Ranch to the north of the main building, culminating in an explosion of new structures that have not always been in keeping with the architectural and planning philosophy of the Civic Centre's initiators. Perhaps more in keeping with that philosophy, although on an unexpectedly large scale, is the Welsh Government Office, which was erected at the rear of the old Welsh Board of Health Office on the last available expanse of vacant land in Cathays Park.

NOTES

1   CCL: Cardiff Corporation, *Proceedings, Nov. 1898–May 1899*, p. 501.
2   *South Wales Daily News*, 19 June 1899.
3   *Western Mail*, 4, 19 July 1899.
4   *Cardiff Corporation Act, 1898*, pp. 9–10, 39–42.
5   Chappell, *Cardiff's Civic Centre*, pp. 17–18.
6   R. Gradige, 'Tour of Cardiff Civic Centre', p. 14.
7   *Evening Express*, 10 January 1898.
8   CCL: Cardiff. Corporation, *Proceedings, Nov. 1898–May 1899*, p. 501.
9   *Western Mail*, 29 April 1899.
10 *Evening Express*, 12 May 1899.
11 CCL: Cardiff Corporation, *Proceedings, May 1899–Nov. 1899*, p. 483.
12 *Western Mail*, 20 September 1899.
13 *Cardiff Times*, 10 February 1900.
14 CCL: Cardiff Corporation, *Proceedings, May 1900–Nov. 1900*, p. 452.
15 CCL: Cardiff Corporation, *Proceedings, May 1902–Nov. 1902*, p. 385.
16 *Western Mail*, 19 September 1900.
17 *Cardiff Times*, 26 October 1901.
18 Bassett, *The Making of a National Museum*, Part I, pp. 9–10.
19 Evans and Fairclough, *National Museum of Wales: National Art Gallery*, p. 10.
20 *Cardiff Times*, 13 December 1902.
21 Ibid., 4 February 1905.
22 CCL: Cardiff Corporation, *Proceedings, Nov. 1902–May 1903*.
23 *Weekly Mail*, 21 November 1903.
24 E. W. Edwards, 'Cardiff Becomes a City', in *Morgannwg*, IX (1965), p. 82; *Cardiff Times*, 17 June 1905.
25 *Cardiff Times*, 1 July 1905.
26 *Weekly Mail*, 1 July 1905; *Western Mail*, 30 June 1905.
27 *Western Mail*, 1 July 1905.
28 Morley, 'Representing a City and Nation', p. 61.
29 Edwards, 'Cardiff Becomes a City', p. 84.
30 Ibid., pp. 84–5.
31 *Western Mail*, 23 October 1905.
32 *Cardiff Times*, 28 October 1905.
33 CCL: Pettigrew, *Public Parks of Cardiff*, vol. 5, p. 4.
34 *Cardiff Times*, 25 March 1905.
35 CCL: Pettigrew, *Public Parks of Cardiff*, vol. 5, pp. 4, 7.
36 *Cardiff Times*, 3 November 1906; *Weekly Mail*, 3 November 1906.
37 Morley, 'Representing a City and Nation', p. 64.
38 Cardiff Corporation, *Cathays Park: Conditions as to Grants of Land*, p. 1.
39 CCL: Pettigrew, *Public Parks of Cardiff*, vol. 5, p. 10.
40 *Cardiff Times*, 7 March 1908.
41 Wilson, *Memorializing History*, p. 11.
42 *South Wales Daily News*, 8 and 9 July 1910.
43 Wilson, *Memorializing History*, pp. 11–12.
44 Ibid., p. 12.
45 *Western Mail Industrial Supplement*, 11 June 1913.
46 Chappell, *Cardiff's Civic Centre*, p. 49.
47 *Western Mail*, 16 July 1915.
48 Patrick Geddes, *Cities in Evolution: An Introduction to the Town Planning Movement and the Study of Civics*, p. 275.
49 *Picture Post*, 18 March 1939, p. 21.

7

A VIEW OF THE CIVIC CENTRE:

ITS LAYOUT, APPEARANCE AND OPEN SPACES

'A VAST URBAN SPACE stretched before me towards distant domed buildings. They were white. Unreal to my northern eyes they shimmered in the glow of late summer. The impact of that magical first impression is indelible … All these noble buildings shone in mellow harmonies of white.'[1] With these lines Professor Dewi-Prys Thomas recalled his first impression of Cardiff's Civic Centre when he visited Cathays Park in September 1934. Seventeen years later I, too, had much the same impression when I saw the Civic Centre for the first time; it had, by then, gained two additional gleaming white buildings. Today, more than 60 years later, the Civic Centre still brings forth the same kind of admiration from newcomers although changes have taken place as new buildings have been added, and alterations have been made to roads and landscape. It is, after all, a special kind of place with its own particular environment. Even when viewed from a short distance away, the group of white buildings appears as a visual entity, something that exists in its own right, distinct from its surroundings.

Now, as if to emphasise the Civic Centre's insularity, a busy dual carriageway (Boulevard de Nantes) runs along much of its southern boundary, separating the civic group from the older mercantile core of the town. Visually, the links between the two areas are minimal: thus, busy shoppers in the town centre are hardly aware that a world-class Civic Centre exists nearby. Similarly, little of the town centre – except the upper parts of the parish church tower (from the corner of the law courts) and more recent multi-storey towers of commerce – can be seen from the Civic Centre. This separateness underlines the fact that the Civic Centre is not the hub of the city but constitutes instead a world of its own, apparently unhindered by the pace and restlessness that inevitably permeates large city centres.

As a visual entity, the Civic Centre – a particular combination of regular arrangement, distinctive buildings and greenery – is now largely complete. It is a self-contained district, one of those parts of Cardiff that is immediately recognisable as having a common, identifying character. The aim of this chapter is to consider that character and discuss the fundamental features – layout, appearance and landscape – that are inherent in the composition of the Civic Centre and cause it to be something more than the sum of its parts.

Seen from above – say a bird's-eye view from the south – Cathays Park appears as a roughly rectangular tract of land with the outer edges to the left and right curving in towards the northern horizon (Pl. 24). Two ruler-straight avenues, running south to north (and crossed at intervals by lesser roads), divide the area into three, roughly equal, expanses, each occupied by independent white buildings or green parkland. It is clear from this view that the Civic Centre's layout follows a formal pattern, a pattern that appears to be based on Beaux-Arts ideals of axiality and symmetry. I say 'appears', for though the ideals garnered from the École des Beaux-Arts were certainly at work here, so was an existing underlying pattern that derived directly from

the Butes' earlier ownership of the land. Seen from above, the regularity of the Civic Centre's layout is emphasised by a rectangular ornamental park at its centre and by two wedge-shaped gardens at the southern end, the latter forming, as it were, green `cordons sanitaires' between the civic enclave and the town centre. To the west the strip of trees that follows the former line of the Glamorganshire Canal forms a further soft edge – albeit a soft edge that has been recently eroded by extensions to the Royal Welsh College of Music and Drama – creating a border zone between the civic enclave and the enormous green space of Bute Park that extends from nearby Cardiff Castle to the vicinity of Llandaf Cathedral two miles away.

Although geometric formality is at the heart of the Civic Centre's layout and is fundamental to an understanding of its nature, the formality is not as orthodox as at first it might seem. This, of course, adds to the sense of variety and expression found in the Civic Centre despite its overt orderliness and Classicism. For a start, of the two avenues that divide the site from end to end, one is longer, wider and clearly more substantial than the other. King Edward VII Avenue, the wider of the two thoroughfares, follows the four-line avenue of trees that was planted by Lord Bute between Greyfriars and Nazareth House during the winter of 1879–80: it extends all the way from Kingsway (or, at least did so before Boulevard de Nantes was constructed in the 1970s) to a colonnade at the northernmost end of Cathays Park. On the far side of the colonnade the avenue continues as Queen Anne Square and beyond

Pl. 24. *Cathays Park from the south. A bird's-eye view from the top of the Capital Tower (built on the site of Greyfriars friary). It shows the avenue (now King Edward VII Avenue) planted in 1879–80 by the Marquess of Bute to link the Greyfriars' site to Nazareth House (seen at the furthest end) and now forming the main spine of the Civic Centre.*
© Crown copyright: RCAHMW.

to Nazareth House. Museum Avenue – the lesser highway – started off life in dribs and drabs, first as a narrow access lane between the City Hall and the National Museum, then extended and widened to serve the University College, and finally continued northwards through land that was originally intended as a pleasure garden and a site for an intermediate school.

And, just as there are two main roads running through the Civic Centre, so there are two main axes: one vehicular and the other visual. While King Edward VII Avenue can be said to form the primary movement axis, an imaginary line running more or less through the centres of the City Hall, Queen Alexandra Gardens, National War Memorial and the Welsh Government offices forms an equally significant visual axis. Here the geometry of the layout comes into play, with the War Memorial at the centre surrounded by a rectilinear park, which in turn is surrounded by a larger rectangle of buildings of similar, if not exactly the same, height. It is this hypothetical line between the buildings that, in conjunction with the generally classical style, height and whiteness of the buildings, held the Civic Centre together visually as a unified composition, at least until the latter part of the twentieth century. Unfortunately, the harmony of composition was rudely interrupted by the erection of a group of undesirably high, ill-fitting university buildings at the north-eastern corner of the Park in the 1960s.

An unorthodox feature of the Civic Centre's layout is its ambivalence with regard to a sense of direction. As a result of the way in which the buildings are disposed, the Civic Centre appears to face two contradictory directions – inwards and outwards. This is partly due to the changes that were later made to the layout proposed by the borough engineer in 1899 (see Chapter 6). As originally proposed and as built, the City Hall occupies the central position on the southern front, facing outwards across ornamental gardens, the Boulevard de Nantes and the Dock Feeder towards a largely unseen town centre. At first glance, the stylistically similar Law Courts also appears to face southwards, whereas in reality it actually faces the side entrance and tower of the City Hall. Later, the National Museum joined the City Hall in facing southwards and outwards. The National Museum is physically closer to the City Hall than is the Law Courts, and together they put on a brave front – as though leaders of the pack – demanding attention by virtue of their formality and grandiose architecture. Behind these three edifices the majority of buildings face inwards towards the Alexandra Gardens, and thus across the central open space towards each other.

The common, identifying character of the Civic Centre is the appearance of its buildings. This appearance is partly derived from the nature of the buildings, which being erected for public use differ from those to the immediate east and north, which were generally built for residential and domestic use. The intrinsic difference between the two is enhanced by the colour and materials used for the Civic Centre buildings as well as by the architectural style employed.

The facing material used for the Civic Centre buildings is generally Portland stone, which being white in colour and smooth in texture is entirely different from the grey-brown Pennant sandstone or red brick used for the nearby residential buildings. The Portland stone gives the Civic Centre its outwardly distinctive character, to which only the rough stone curtain walls of Cardiff's Roman fort-cum-castle – seen diagonally opposite the south-west corner of Cathays Park – offer any significant visual competition. Surprisingly, the use of Portland stone was not made mandatory from the start. No mention was made, for instance, in the 1897 competition conditions issued to competing architects of what materials were to be used for the construction of the Town Hall and Law Courts other than that terracotta was to be excluded.[2] Even 4 years later, when the design of the Town Hall and Law Courts had been approved and construction begun, the conditions for any new development in Cathays Park only stipulated that 'all buildings will be required to be [built] of free stone or granite'.[3] Nothing at all about colour or Portland stone!

It is not clear how or when it became the norm to use Portland stone for all buildings in the Civic Centre. Ian Morley proposed that the form of the University College, 'similar to that of the law courts and the city hall, suggests that a systemized approach of the type promoted in the US was evident'.[4] In this assertion he was presumably referring to the City Beautiful Movement that had appeared in the United States during the late 1890s. While the Movement had been stimulated by the pristinely white buildings seen at the 1893 Chicago World Fair, it took time to gather momentum and was not formulated into words until 1903, when Charles Mulford Robinson's book *Modern Civic Art or the City Made Beautiful* was published. How long it took for those ideals to cross the Atlantic and take root in Britain is difficult to say, but Pevsner, referring to 'the movement for the erection of monumental Civic Centres in the United States', noted that the movement only 'conquered England [*sic*] after 1900'.[5]

Already, before 1900, Portland stone had been included in the winning design for the town (later city) hall and law courts, although there had been no imperative to do so. Its use from then on seems to have been made on an *ad hoc* basis until sufficient buildings had been erected with Portland stone façades for it to be recognised as the only suitable facing material. The first building to use it after the City Hall and Law Courts was the University of Wales Registry, erected at the rear of the Law Courts at the same time as the latter was being built. It is noteworthy that in donating the site to the University of Wales the Corporation made it clear that the design of the Registry had to be approved by the donor, although there is no mention of what materials were to be used.[6] The next building to use Portland stone was the University College. Here the requirements issued to architects had, according to J. M. Freeman, been specific in 'that all external elevations of the new college should be faced with Portland stone … and that the heights of the plinths and cornices on the college's main façades should be the same as those of the nearby city hall'.[7] Yet, for all that , the four invited architects came up with different suggestions: two recommended Portland stone; one recommended Doulting stone (light brown in colour) with thick Precelly [*sic*] slates for roofs; and one recommended brick with stone (unspecified) facing.[8]

Five years later, the conditions issued in July 1908 for the architectural competition for the design of Glamorgan County Hall were curiously tentative, stating only that 'the material of which the front is to be constructed must be suitable stone to correspond with the City buildings and the Registry of the University of Wales adjoining'.[9] As the *Builder* commented, as 'all of these are faced with Portland stone … it is therefore practically essential that at least the front … should be of Portland stone'.[10] Requirements for the National Museum were somewhat clearer, the result of conditions that had been laid down by the Corporation in February 1909, which stipulated, among other things, that 'the South main wall of the new building shall not project beyond the front main wall of the City Hall', and that the `outer main walls to be of best Portland stone'.[11]

Perhaps it should be mentioned here that though Portland stone dominates the façades of every building in the Civic Centre, it is not the only stone that has been used in the Park. The external steps before entrances are usually made of gritstone or granite, while Portland Roach has been used extensively in the lower areas of the Welsh Government Offices extension and a rugged, rock-faced Pennant stone used for the sides of the University of Wales Registry. In addition, a variety of different stones has been selected for the memorials and statues.[12]

Important to the Civic Centre's sense of distinctiveness was the early adoption of Classicism as a generic architectural style, in contrast to the surrounding buildings, which were mostly built in some manner of domestic Gothic or even Jacobean, as at Aberdare Hall. There is, however, nothing in the record to suggest that a 'systemised approach' was ever involved in ensuring that all the buildings in the Civic Centre would be classical.

Looking back, it may seem natural that the style employed in the design of the City Hall and Law Courts would create a precedent and that once this had been established all later buildings would follow in like manner. Yet this was not always the case in other towns in Britain where, over time as fashions changed, public buildings were often erected in a variety of styles. During the nineteenth and early twentieth centuries public buildings were usually designed in variations of one or other of the two main styles: either classical, with symmetrical elevations derived from ancient Greek and Roman architecture based on column and lintel (i.e. post and beam) construction, or some kind of Gothic based on the pointed arches and vaulting used in medieval – particularly religious – architecture. Less common was Romanesque based on round arches and heavy walls (again inspired by ancient Roman buildings), and Byzantine associated with Orthodox Christianity. Fashions changed throughout the period, with the result that townscapes were usually a mixture of architectural styles, often in close proximity to each other. True, there have been occasional cases where concerted attempts were made to adopt kindred styles, such as in the centres of Birmingham and Liverpool (see Chapter 11). Nowhere, however, has it been so consistently realised as in Cardiff's Civic Centre where the dominant style has been classical, or classically derived.

That this was the case owes much to the fact that the initial buildings – the City Hall and Law Courts – were designed in a classical manner:

> They more than any other drew the attention of architects to the potentialities of Baroque …The logical and spacious plan, inspired by the axial planning taught by the École des Beaux Arts in Paris, was combined with an exuberant and asymmetrically placed tower which satisfied the English [sic] demand for Picturesque effects.[13]

Later buildings tended to veer away from Neo-Baroque, but were still essentially classical, including the colonnade of coupled Doric columns erected at the entrance to Queen Anne Square in the mid-1930s. Thus, 'the final result is not unlike an exhibition of the period: a series of grandiose buildings, laid out on a formal grid'.[14] Certainly, the adoption of Classicism in its various guises in Cathays Park has enabled the Civic Centre to enjoy a degree of harmony and connectivity that would have been impossible had each building been designed in entirely different styles.

So what is classical architecture? According to the architectural historian Sir John Summerson:

> classical architecture is only recognizable as such when it contains some allusion, however slight, however vestigial, to the antique "orders". Such an allusion may be no more than some groove or projection which suggests the idea of a cornice or even a disposition of windows which suggests the ratio of pedestal to column, column to entablature.[15]

Here an 'order' refers to an assemblage comprising a column, capital and entablature (see Architectural Glossary). Other common attributes of classical architecture include symmetry, axiality, horizontality, triangular pediments at the ends of buildings and over entrances and windows, and the platform (stylobate) on which a portico or colonnade stands.

There have, of course, been changes in architectural direction during the life of the Civic Centre, but, generally speaking, these have stayed within the line of European Classicism that included Beaux-Arts, Neo-Baroque, Neo-Greek and Neo-Renaissance variations as well as the so-called 'new tradition' of stripped down classicism. Even during the later phases of construction, after the Second World War, many of the designs still alluded – in their columns or horizontal banding – to Classical features such as the 'orders' or plinths and entablatures, providing, in the words of Summerson, a 'residual feeling for classical rhythm and proportions [that] merges with Modernist sensibility'.[16]

The third ingredient in the make-up of the Civic Centre is its landscape, and here, as has been pointed out, 'the quality of space between noble buildings was as important as the quality of the buildings themselves'.[17] The landscape that we see today is partly due to the efforts of the third Marquess of Bute. Though limited in extent, they were of fundamental importance in establishing the character of the Civic Centre. First, he was responsible for planting the double avenue of elms that would later determine the line of King Edward VII Avenue. Secondly, Bute stipulated – as a condition of the sale of land to the Corporation – that the avenue should be preserved, that the triangular plot of land that later became Friary Gardens should never be built upon and that the land between the new east–west road and the north bank of the Dock Feeder should be planted with trees. These conditions were later incorporated in the 1898 Act of Parliament confirming the agreement to acquire Cathays Park.[18]

Apart from those areas noted above, the remaining landscape is all of the twentieth century. There are two components to be considered here: roads and public gardens. With regard to the roads, the precedent set by Bute for planting an avenue of trees was followed for most of the internal carriageways in the Civic Centre with the exception of City Hall Road at the rear of the City Hall and Law Courts that, as a result, looks a bit forlorn. The single avenue of trees along Museum Avenue are mostly limes, as are those also in King Edward VII Avenue after the original elms succumbed to old age and Dutch elm disease in the 1970s. The eastern and western perimeters of Cathays Park are for the most part lined with trees, many of which are mature and probably date from the nineteenth century. They form enclosing elements to the Park, although this feeling of enclosure tends to peter out at the north-eastern corner where later university buildings come uncomfortably close to Park Place and trees are, consequently, fewer. The south side of Corbett Road, at the northern perimeter of the Civic Centre, has also been planted with trees. They are of mixed species (lime, Norway maple, birch, plane and conifers) and were planted rather irregularly, so that the feeling of enclosure to this part of the site is less obvious.[19]

There are four public gardens in Cathays Park, as well as a number of smaller areas of private greenery. The public gardens are Queen Alexandra Gardens, Gorsedd Gardens, City Hall Lawn and Friary Gardens. Between them they contain five war memorials and many commemorative statues, including a number by Cardiff's own well-known sculptor Sir William Goscombe John (1860–1952).

Queen Alexandra Gardens, or Alexandra Gardens as they are often referred to, is central to the Civic Centre, both in a physical and an environmental sense. Without this charming and well-mannered area of cultivated ground at the heart of Cathays Park the Civic Centre would have an entirely different atmosphere. For many it is an oasis in an urban world of offices and public buildings. The Gardens can be said to have begun life in October 1902, when it was decided to retain the central area as public open space (see Chapter 6). At first it was left as rough grass and little was done to enhance the area until, in January 1909, two alternative designs for laying out the Gardens were submitted to the Council by the Parks Superintendent.[20] The first design – with formal lawns, island beds, specimen trees and an elaborate fountain at the centre – was approved, less the proposed fountain. Laying out the ground began the following month using unemployed labour, and continued rapidly. On 26 July 1910, the Property Committee recommended 'that the gardens hitherto named University Gardens be named Queen Alexandra Gardens'; on the following day the Gardens were formally opened to the public.[21]

The Queen Alexandra Gardens follow a geometric design with the two main footpaths (north–south and east–west) forming central axes that divide the grounds into quarters (Pl. 25). The quarters are further subdivided by secondary east–west footpaths, and the whole surrounded by a perimeter

Pl. 25. *Queen Alexandra Gardens. Seen from the air the formal layout of the Gardens is very clear. The Welsh National War Memorial, although not originally planned for this site, provides an eye-catching feature at the centre.*
© Crown copyright: RCAHMW.

footpath, a wide shrub border and a beech hedge, the original boundary railings having been removed during the Second World War. Each, except one, of the rectangular grassed areas between the paths has a circular planted bed at its centre. There are also circular flower beds where the secondary footpaths intersect and an extra large circular area at the centre where the main footpaths cross, this having originally been intended for the abandoned fountain. Later, in 1926, the larger circle became the site for the Welsh National War Memorial, which now forms such an imposing structure at the centre of the Gardens.

After the memorial's completion, the designer (Sir J. Ninian Comper) was asked by the Parks Committee for his views on its setting. His answer was that he considered the general setting to be appropriate, but 'suggested beds of deep red china roses around the outside of the path circling the memorial' and also that the acacias lining the approach footpaths be 'replaced with trees of a more columnar shape, such as cypresses'.[22] The changes were approved and the paths were accordingly lined with cherry trees and lawson cypresses. During the time since the Second World War the Gardens have become something of a sanctuary for commemorative memorabilia: in addition to the National War Memorial and the nineteenth-century statue of the first Lord Aberdare, five other memorials (including two for the Falklands Islands Conflict) have been erected there between 1983 and 2007.

The ornamental garden south of the National Museum, named the Gorsedd Gardens after the ring of standing stones – the Gorsedd Circle – re-erected there in 1905 (see Chapter 8), was initiated during the autumn of 1905 when the area was handed over to the Parks Department for development and maintenance.[23] Development continued during the following year, but the opening to the public was delayed until July 1910, owing to the high cost of maintenance.[24] The Gardens, sometimes referred to in its early years as the Druidical Gardens, are laid out with winding paths radiating from the circle of stones, and informal lawns, specimen trees and shrub borders (Pl. 26). The northern side has a yew hedge and iron railings backed by a row of cherry trees. The eastern side is bounded by an earthen bank, a leftover from the original enclosure of Cathays Park, with lime trees growing along the bank and pines at the north-east and south-east corners.[25] Part of this bank was cut through in 2004 when a new access was formed to the gardens from Park Place. Within the Gardens are statues of David Lloyd George, politician, Lord Ninian Crichton-Stuart, soldier, and John Cory, coal owner and philanthropist. There is also a wooden, chalet-type hut of panelled construction, now used as a refreshment bar. Although of unknown date, it has been listed Grade II for its group value, and may be one of the caretaker's shelters referred to in a 1938 'Inventory of Park Buildings and Equipment'.

The City Hall Lawn began as a Green Circle and was originally separated from the Gorsedd Gardens by a road. By 1912 the circular lawn had become

fenced with granite posts and heavy chains[26] that, seeming to represent the spokes of a wheel, later became the ideal place for a plaque to the memory of the First World War 2/7th (Cyclists) Battalion of the Welch Regiment (later refixed to a pillar in front of the City Hall). During the mid-1970s, as Cathays Park Road was transformed into a dual carriageway and renamed Boulevard de Nantes, the Green Circle – which by then had become a semicircle – was enlarged to provide a triangular green space extending from the Gorsedd Gardens to King Edward VII Avenue. It includes a single equestrian statue (the first Viscount Tredegar) at the south-east corner, and a plain, rectangular pool incorporating fountains in front of the City Hall that was constructed to commemorate the investiture of the Prince of Wales in 1969. The southern end of King Edward VII Avenue now terminates – following construction of Boulevard de Nantes – in a roundabout around the South African (Boer) War Memorial, the most distinguished of all the sculptures in Cathays Park and the first war memorial to be erected there, in 1909.

The delightful Friary Gardens, south of the Boulevard de Nantes and now completely cut off from the rest of Cathays Park, owes its fortunate existence to Lord Bute's insistence that the plot be protected from building development. The Gardens include, at the northern end, part of the Dock Feeder which is flanked by deciduous trees. The larger, southern part, was first enclosed by a low stone wall and iron fence in the autumn of 1905. The slightly sunk

Pl. 27. *The Friary Gardens. Formally laid out in Dutch style, these Gardens provide not only a visual entrance to the Civic Centre but also, with its statue of the third Marquess of Bute, recognition of the man who laid down the ground rules for development of Cathays Park.*
© Crown copyright: RCAHMW.

interior was laid out in formal Dutch style during the winter of 1905–1906 with a triangular parterre of box-edged beds surrounded by a gravel footpath and further box-edging[27] (Pl. 27). Midway along the northern footpath is a large statue of the third Marquess of Bute and beyond that a grass strip with shaped bay trees. The Gardens were opened to the public in July 1910. Originally known as the Dutch Garden, the Gardens were renamed the Priory Gardens in 1923 and later, when it was discovered in 1929 that Priory was an inaccurate description, to the present name.[28]

Another public open space, known as the Crown Gardens, existed for a time at the rear of the Welsh Board of Health. It was laid out by the Cardiff Parks Department following a request by the Ministry of Works and opened in 1951, presumably to coincide with the Festival of Britain celebrations of that year. It was mainly grassed with edge borders and, in the middle, a large rectangular flower bed approached by diagonal footpaths. It survived until 1972 when it made way for the Crown Building extension (later the Welsh Government offices), which covered virtually the whole site.

In addition to the above public open spaces, there are significant areas of greenery in front of the main building of the University and behind the Temple of Peace, where there is a small garden of remembrance. Larger than either of these is the broad strip of land that lies between the northern and of the National Museum and the southern wing of the University's main building. This was occupied in the 1930s and 1940s by tennis courts and a putting green; by 1950 the putting green had been replaced by a nursery.[29] The northern half was later grassed over and randomly planted with trees of various species. The southern part, which had originally been intended for completion of the National Museum, was given over in the 1960s for University temporary accommodation (see Chapter 10); later still, it was developed as a visitor car park for the museum.

The Civic Centre has been dismissively likened to 'buildings in parkland, not a concentrated urban precinct'.[30] That may well be, but one can argue that the Civic Centre was never intended to be anything other than a park-like precinct in which major public buildings could be seen together. In this respect, the abundant trees and foliage might be considered essential tools in helping to integrate the Park's various buildings within an overall scheme. Certainly, the overall effect of enclosure softened by planting evokes a real feeling of 'place', and in this sense the Civic Centre can be regarded as a considerable success.

NOTES

1   Dewi-Prys Thomas, 'A Quiet Dignity … William Caroe and the Visual Presence', in Gwyn Jones and Michael Quinn (eds), *Fountains of Praise: University College, Cardiff, 1883–1983*, p. 54.
2   Cardiff Corporation, *New Town Hall and Law Courts: Conditions and Instructions for Competing Architects*, p. 1.
3   Cardiff Corporation, *Cathays Park: Conditions as to Grants of Land*, p. 1.
4   Morley, 'Representing a City and Nation', p. 72.
5   Niklaus Pevsner, *Pioneers of Modern Design*, p. 139.
6   *Cardiff Times*, 10 January 1903.
7   J. M. Freeman, *W. D. Caroe: His Architectural Achievements*, p. 209.
8   University College of South Wales, *New Buildings – Explanatory Statements by the Competing Architects Regarding the Plans Forwarded by Them*, various pages.
9   Glamorgan County Council, *Proposed New County Hall and Offices at Cardiff – Conditions and Instructions for Competing Architects*, p. 3.
10   *Builder*, vol. 95, 25 July 1908, p. 97.
11   National Museum of Wales (NMW), *Minutes of General Purposes & Building Committee*, 9 February 1909, p. 83.
12   John W. Perkins, *The Building Stones of Cardiff – Geological Trail Guides*, pp. 69–74.
13   David Watkin, *English Architecture: A Concise History*, p. 180.
14   Gradidge, 'Tour of Cardiff Civic Centre', p. 1.
15   John Summerson, *The Classical Language of Architecture*, p. 9.
16   Ibid., p. 121.
17   Thomas, 'A Quiet Dignity …', p. 55.
18   *Cardiff Corporation Act, 1898*, The First Schedule, clauses 6, 7 and 11.
19   Jonathan Vining, *Cathays Park: A Landscape Analysis of Cardiff's Civic Centre*, pp. 37–40.
20   CCL: Pettigrew, *Public Parks of Cardiff*, vol. 5, p. 8.
21   Ibid., p. 10.
22   Cadw, *Register of Landscapes, Parks and Gardens of Special Historic Interest in Wales: Glamorgan*, p. 54.
23   CCL: Pettigrew, *Public Parks of Cardiff*, vol. 5, p. 6.
24   Ibid., p. 7.
25   Cadw, *Register of Landscapes*, p. 54.
26   CCL: Pettigrew, *Public Parks of Cardiff*, vol. 5, p. 13.
27   Ibid., p. 4.
28   Ibid., p. 4.
29   *www.cardiffparks.org.uk/cathays/info/gamessection.shtml*; RAF aerial photograph 540/378 frame 0093, 13 July 1950; 1: 2,500 scale Ordnance Survey maps 1941–2 and 1952–4.
30   Carter, H., *Towns of Wales*, p. 262.

8

DEVELOPMENT OF THE CIVIC CENTRE BEFORE THE FIRST WORLD WAR:
BUILDINGS AND MONUMENTS

THE FIRST PERIOD of Civic Centre development in Cathays Park lasted almost two decades, from 1897 to 1915. It was a period that coincided with one of continued growth for Cardiff, during which coal exports from the Bute Docks soared to well over 10 million ton a year, the world's first £1 million cheque is said to have been signed on the floor of the town's Coal and Shipping Exchange and the population of the borough and its nearby suburbs (Ely, Llandaf, and Maendy) reached 200,000 inhabitants for the first time. It was a period during which the borough was raised to city status, and the corporation sought by various means to enhance its position as the leading town in Wales and thus the natural location for the principality's national institutions.

Pl. 28. *Cathays Park from the north-west. This aerial view, taken in 1920, highlights the buildings erected in the Civic Centre's first phase of development.*
© Crown copyright: RCAHMW.

This was a period of exceptional local and national optimism, which manifested itself in a display of building activity in Cathays Park – one new public building begun every 2 years – which was never to be repeated (Pl. 28). Eight new building projects were started in all, thereby laying down the future shape and character of the Civic Centre for the next 60 years (Fig. 8.1).

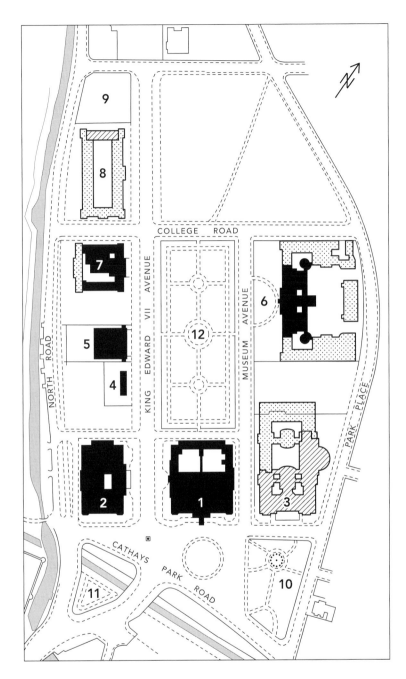

Fig. 8.1. *Development of Cathays Park between 1900 and 1918. Buildings constructed and opened before 1918 are shown solid black; buildings started but not completed before 1918 are shown with diagonal hatching; buildings planned but not started before 1918 are shown stippled. Numbers are as follows: 1, City Hall; 2, Law Courts; 3, National Museum of Wales; 4, University of Wales Registry; 5, Glamorgan County Hall (now Glamorgan Building); 6, University College; 7, Technical College; 8, Welsh Insurance Commission; 9, Bute Reservation; 10, Gorsedd Gardens; 11, Friary Gardens; 12, Queen Alexandra Gardens. (Based on O. S. map, 1920 edition.)*

Appropriately, construction of the first white buildings in Cathays Park – the Town Hall and Law Courts – began during the opening year of the twentieth century. An architectural competition for the design of the two buildings had been held as far back as 1897, a year before Cathays Park came into the possession of the Corporation. The conditions, which stipulated a maximum of £125,000 to be spent on the Town Hall and £75,000 on the Law Courts, were very precise with regard to the siting of the two buildings but mentioned nothing about their height or the external materials to be used except that terracotta would *not* be allowed. There were 56 entries in the prestigious competition and the first prize of £500 was won by Lanchester, Stewart and Rickards, of London. It was fortunate that this firm should be chosen to be the architects of the first two buildings, for not only did they set the trend for architectural classicism in Cathays Park but they also did much to change the face of public architecture in Britain during the early years of the twentieth century, establishing 'a kind of Edwardian Baroque that was not easily surpassed for swagger and sumptuousness in the early years of the century'.[1] For all that, the Baroque style soon began to look dated and was not adopted for any of the other buildings in Cathays Park apart from the Town Hall and Law Courts. Edwin Rickards has usually been given the credit for the design of this pair of buildings,[2] but it is probable that all three partners were involved.[3]

Delays occurred when it was discovered that the competition requirements for the Town Hall were inadequate and the building needed to be widened by two bays.[4] The local firm of E. Turner & Sons, of Penarth, was appointed contractors for the project in September 1900, and construction work began soon afterwards. Ceremonial foundation stones were laid by the fourth Marquess of Bute on 23 October 1901, and the two buildings were completed during 1905. The formal openings took place in October the following year, by which time the town had become a city by royal proclamation and the Town Hall was now a City Hall.

City Hall

This building occupies a dominant position at the centre of the southern group of buildings, a position admirably suited to show off its richly Baroque design. The original competition designs had envisaged a less decorative appearance, but before it was built Rickards had time to work over all the elevations and redesign the dome and tower to produce a bold, imaginative and superbly detailed building, heavily influenced by the Austrian Baroque but with overtones of French Baroque.

From the outside, the City Hall is a largish, two-storey building with corner pavilions and an elaborate, projecting centre section to the main front and a prominent, eye-catching clock tower above the west front (Pl. 29). Though each elevation is treated differently, all four are faced in Portland stone and each is symmetrical in appearance. The palatial main (south) front is dominated by the central projecting section with its imposing dome over the Council Chamber and a lavishly treated *porte-cochère* leading to the main entrance (Pl. 30). A large, round-headed window lights the Council Chamber inside, above which rises an angular drum supporting the graceful, lead-covered dome that, in turn, carries a decorative lantern surmounted by a splendid cast-lead dragon (by H. C. Fehr) with rearing head and snarling tongue. In this way, and unusually for British town halls,

Pl. 29. (left) *City Hall, by Lanchester, Stewart & Rickards, 1901–5: main (south) front, with the clock tower rising up at the rear.*
© Crown copyright: RCAHMW.

Pl. 30. (below) *City Hall, main entrance and dome over Council Chamber.*
© Crown copyright: RCAHMW.

the key position of the Council Chamber in the affairs of the city was signalled. The wings on either side of the central section have tall round-headed windows to the ground floor, and rectangular windows to the first floor with swags and cartouches between the windows. The corner pavilions are treated as angled bays with sculptural groups at parapet level in front of rectangular attic storeys. The sculptural group on the left represents 'Poetry and Music' (by Paul Montford) (Pl. 31), that on the right 'Unity and Patriotism' (by Henry Poole).

The west front facing the Law Courts is treated in a simpler manner, although even here the bays centred around the secondary entrance are highlighted by rusticated stonework. An extraordinary, 200ft (60 m) high clock tower rises above and behind the secondary entrance to form a flamboyant and dramatic landmark that acts as a focal point, visually uniting the two buildings as part of an overall design. The lower half of the tower is severely plain and slab-like, before suddenly erupting into a series of columns, volutes and a sculpture representing the four winds (by H. C. Fehr), all topped by a 'wedding-cake'

Pl. 31. (right) *City Hall, attic sculpture, 'Poetry and Music' by Paul Montford.*
© Crown copyright: RCAHMW.

Pl. 32. (below) *City Hall, H. C. Fehr's sculpture above the dome.*
© Crown copyright: RCAHMW.

dome (Pl. 32). A 'most subtle and brilliant design' according to Gradidge,[5] it is, in both its originality and the splendid way in which it rises above its surroundings, one of the most successful Neo-Baroque towers in Britain. The east front facing the National Museum is a diluted version of the south and west fronts, with tall round-headed lower windows and rectangular upper windows and again a wide, seven-bay, projecting centre section. The north front is simpler still with only rectangular windows and a narrow, single bay, projection in the centre.

The interior of the City Hall – 'a sequence of brilliantly managed spatial contrasts'[6] – is, if anything, even more sumptuous and striking than the exterior (Fig. 8.2). From the main entrance a short flight of steps leads into a spacious but rather austere entrance hall faced in Bath stone, with doors at the far end giving access to the Rates Hall. Unusually there are two grand, richly balustraded staircases – one on either side of the axial entrance hall – giving access to the main civic areas on the first floor. The first of these public spaces is the Marble Hall, an impressive

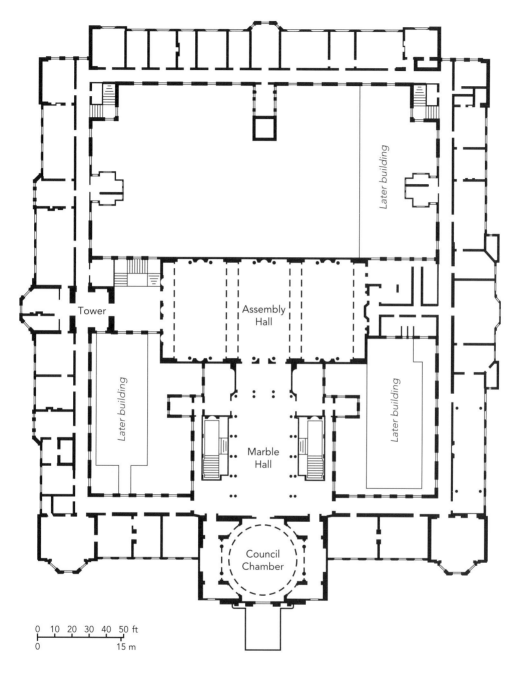

Tower

Assembly
Hall

Later building

Later building

Later building

Marble
Hall

Council
Chamber

0 10 20 30 40 50 ft
0   15 m

reception area, lined on both sides by pairs of colourful Doric columns carved from veined, yellow Siena marble (Pl. 33). A memorable collection of eleven life-sized statues (carved from Serravezza marble) forming a pantheon of national heroes (and one heroine) is arranged on the main landing and the stair heads. Although the original design had allowed for statues in this area – indeed, stone bases were actually built – the cost of carrying

Fig. 8.2. *Cardiff City Hall, first floor plan. This includes the two bays added (after the competition) to the width of the building.*

Pl. 33. *City Hall, interior of Marble Hall.*
© Crown copyright: RCAHMW.

out the work proved to be prohibitive and it was not until the coal owner D. A. Thomas (later Lord Rhondda) offered to pay for the statues that they were eventually commissioned.[7] The collection of statues was unveiled by David Lloyd George in October 1916. Round-headed windows overlooking each staircase incorporate stained glass by A. Garth Jones.

The eleven statues (with their sculptors) are as follows: Dewi Sant – St David (Sir W. Goscombe John); Hywel Dda (F. W. Pomeroy); Buddug – Boadicea (J. Harvard Thomas); Llewelyn, last Prince of Wales (Henry Pegram); Harri Tudur – Henry VII (Ernest G. Gillick); Bishop Morgan (T. J. Clapperton); William Williams Pantycelyn (Leonard. S. Merrifield); Dafydd ap Gwilym (W. Wheatley Wagstaff); Giraldus Cambrenis (Henry Poole); Owain Glyndŵr (Alfred Turner); Sir Thomas Picton (T. Mewburn Crook).

On either side of the Marble Hall doors lead to corridors that continue around the building, giving access to committee rooms and offices. Many paintings acquired by and bequeathed to the city line the corridors. The Council Chamber, situated at the southern end of the Marble Hall, is unusual both for its key position in the building and for its circular layout (Pl. 34). The coffered dome above the Chamber is carried on a drum pierced by circular windows and wide, semicircular arches (some of which are blocked) supported by pairs of Ionic columns with marble shafts and bronze, swagged capitals. A magnificent bronze chandelier, designed by Rickards, hangs from the centre of the dome. The large round-headed window on the south side has further stained glass by A. Garth Jones. The seating is divided into four quadrants with the Lord Mayor's seat in the east quadrant, facing a public viewing balcony opposite. The lower part of the Chamber is clad in carefully detailed wood panelling.

The circular seating arrangement is rare among British town halls, if not unique, for, as Cunningham in his wide-ranging survey of town halls built between 1820 and 1914 has pointed out, 'the special arrangement of the [council chamber] seating, usually semicircular, was hardly ever made the basis for the formal expression of the room as part of the whole conception'.[8] The nearest precedent for external and internal conspicuousness seems to have been the Irish House of Commons in the original Parliament (1729–39) in Dublin. But even there the chamber was octagonal in plan and the original seating arrangement appears (from a painting) to have been semicircular. Also common to British town halls was the Westminster type of seating layout where parallel rows of seats face each other, thus favouring adversarial debate. Elsewhere in Europe and the United States of America the semicircular or horseshoe-shaped debating chamber, designed to encourage consensus, was more usual. However, even where circular rooms were occasionally used for debating the seating layout was usually in the form of forward-facing rows, as in a lecture room.

North of the Marble Hall and entered by triple sets of doors is the Assembly Hall, located in the centre of the building and at right angles to its main axis (Pl. 35). This is another dramatic space, with a vast segmental, tunnel-vault ceiling subdivided into three bays by broad, decorative plaster bands. The ceiling and bands were elaborately modelled by G. P. Bankart in a style that Newman likens to the plasterwork of early eighteenth-century

Pl. 34. *City Hall, interior of Council Chamber showing chandelier by E. A. Rickards.*
© Crown copyright: RCAHMW.

Pl. 35. *City Hall, interior of Assembly Hall.*
© Crown copyright: RCAHMW.

Austrian and south German churches.[9] Each bay has semicircular openings for high-level windows, below which stand pairs of Ionic columns. The highlights of the Hall, as in the Council Chamber, are Rickards's enormous bronze chandeliers, one of which hangs from the centre of each bay.

Law Courts

While clearly from the same architectural stable as the City Hall, the Law Courts is a sufficiently different building to stand on its own in a balanced and related composition. Where the City Hall is square on plan, the Law Courts is rectangular with its main entrance on the long, east front, facing the City Hall's secondary entrance and clock tower. The short, south elevation, with its corner pavilions and round-headed lower windows, is very similar to that of the City Hall but without the central section. Again, the corner pavilions have sculptural groups set against attic storeys – that on the left representing 'Science and Education' (by Donald McGill) and the one on the right representing 'Commerce and Industry' (by Paul Montford). The relative importance of the east front is made clear by a wide flight of external steps leading up to the slightly projecting centre section with its twin loggias flanking the entrance (Royal Coat of Arms above by Albert Hodge) and twin, cupola-topped turrets (Pl. 36). Despite the Doric columns to the loggias, paired colonnettes in the turrets and dragon-topped bronze lampstands to the steps, the limited provision of windows – particularly on the ground floor – ensures that this front retains a grave appearance in keeping with a need to stress its 'serious rather than celebratory function'.[10] The north front, also with a projecting centre section, continues the lines of the main elevation but in a simpler style. The west front, again symmetrical with projecting centre section incorporating the entrance to the old Magistrates' Courts, is single storey only with stepped roof planes behind. It is attractive, but seems curiously incomplete, as though waiting for an additional storey to be added.

Inside, a central lobby gives access, via flights of steps on either side, to a spacious and dignified Court Hall lined with Bath stone (Pl. 37). Loggias giving access to the courts at either end of the

Pl. 36. (right) *Law Courts, by Lanchester, Stewart & Rickards, 1901–5: main (east) front facing King Edward VII Avenue.* © Crown copyright: RCAHMW.

Pl. 37. (below) *Law Courts, interior of Courts Hall.* © Crown copyright: RCAHMW.

Hall have screens of widely spaced Ionic columns. The Hall is lit by high-level, semicircular windows, and covered by a three-bay, segmental ceiling crowned with saucer domes and divided by coffered bands. An entablature with a leafy cornice is carried all around at high level and the delightful light fittings by Rickards survive. Though less decorative than the City Hall's Assembly Hall, the Courts Hall is perhaps a more pleasing space. The two original courts – formerly Crown and Nisi Prius – have enriched plaster ceilings, oak wall panelling and are lit by high, semicircular windows. A doorway inserted in the rear wall of the Courts Hall now gives access to a new court constructed in what was originally an open area. The former magistrates' courts and police areas are on a lower floor at the rear of the building have been much altered.

University of Wales Registry

The next building to be erected in Cathays Park was the University of Wales' Registry, sited to the north of the Law Courts and facing King Edward VII Avenue. The Corporation had tried to secure the location of the far-flung university's administrative office ever since 1896, but it was not until November 1902 that an agreement was reached.[11] In January 1903, the Corporation gifted the site to the University along with '£6,000 to be devoted to the erection and fitting up of a registry in accordance with designs approved by the Corporation'.[12] Designs for the new Registry were invited from Harold Hughes, of Bangor, and Herbert W. Wills, of Swansea. Wills was chosen as the architect in March 1903. A building contract was signed in September, and the foundation stone was laid in November 1903. The building was completed the following year and became the first building to be opened in the Civic Centre. Small – the first phase was only three-bays deep – and unpretentious, it is a pleasant building in English Renaissance mode and worthy of its place in the Park (Pl. 38).

Pl. 38. *University of Wales Registry, by Herbert W. Wills, 1903–4: main front facing King Edward VII Avenue.*
© Crown copyright: RCAHMW.

Though appearing more like a single-storey classical villa than an office block it is actually three storeys, with the lowest floor cleverly hidden behind a rusticated plinth and the attic floor screened behind small circular windows in the parapet, leaving the *piano nobile* to be expressed by tall, rectangular windows. The centre, three-bay section is slightly recessed and has a wide, segmental pediment above the entrance and paired Ionic columns to either side. The dragon-topped metal posts (modelled by Goscombe John) in front add a nice touch of Welshness.

The first phase contained little more than two rooms on the ground floor with a flat above, and soon this became inadequate. In 1921 Wills was asked to design an extension at the rear, but his scheme for a two-storey block around a rectangular courtyard, though approved by the City, was apparently never carried out. Instead, a larger extension, designed by T. Alwyn Lloyd, was built in two phases, 1933 and 1939.[13] Externally, the extension is a straightforward design with two floors of tall windows set in rock-faced Pennant stone walls, all set back slightly from the earlier phase. The inside is more interesting; it is entered from the original entrance hall through an opening between Doric columns and down steps to a corridor that curves around a U-shaped courtyard accessible by further steps.

Gorsedd Circle

As construction of the Civic Centre progressed, so Cathays Park also became the home for various forms of memorabilia. The first of these was the seemingly ancient *Cylch yr Orsedd* – Gorsedd, or Throne, Circle – after which the Gorsedd Gardens were named. The Gorsedd Circle comprised two concentric circles of stones with a seven-ton flat-topped rock (*Maen Llog*, or Logan Stone) at the centre – from which, after a flourish of trumpets, the Archdruid conducted the proceedings – and two portal, or entrance, stones, that to the right pointing to sunrise at midsummer and that to the left directed to the midwinter sunrise (Pl. 39). Initially, in 1898, the stones were erected near the Dock Feeder as the centrepiece for a dignified and impressive ceremony – the *gorsedd* – to proclaim in advance the National Eisteddfod that was due to be held in Cardiff the following July.[14] Although the first recorded eisteddfod – or gathering of bards and musicians – had been held as far back as 1176 by the Lord Rhys in Cardigan Castle, it was not until 1819 that the ceremony of the 'Gorsedd of the Bards of the Isle of Britain' became a regular feature of regional *eisteddfodau* and, after 1860, of national *eisteddfodau*.[15] Due to its location close to the site of the City Hall, the Gorsedd Circle was taken down after the 1899 Eisteddfod and re-erected in front of the site allocated for National Museum in February 1905. Unfortunately, the two portal stones have been removed since the 1930s and the central *Maen Llog* needlessly replaced by a coniferous tree. Now, only the outer circle of twelve red pillars of Radyr breccia, together with the barely visible inner circle (*Meini Gwynion*) of recumbent slabs of white alabaster from

near Penarth, remain. The *Maen y Cyfamod* or Covenant Stone (where the Herald Bard stood), easily recognisable from its greater height, occupies a prominent position facing due east in the outer circle.

Statue of John Cory

The first statue to be erected in the Civic Centre was that of John Cory (1828–1910), in 1906, in a position south of the Gorsedd Circle (Pl. 40). Cory was a colliery owner, philanthropist and supporter of the Temperance Movement and the Salvation Army, and the statue – modelled by Sir William Goscombe John in bronze and mounted high on an ornate Portland stone pedestal – shows him with a Bible in one hand and a doffed hat in the other.

University College

At the same time as the Registry was being built, plans were afoot to expand the University College of South Wales and Monmouthshire. The College had been established in 1883 at the old Infirmary on Newport Road, but within a decade it became apparent that additional premises would soon be required. An appeal for funds for building a new college was launched in February 1896, and by mid-1904 more than £75,000 had been donated.[16] Various sites were considered as a location for the new college, and among these the favourite was Cathays Park. It was not until 1900, however, after the Corporation had granted the University College 5 acres (2 ha) of land north of the National Museum site – the College had asked for 10 acres (4 ha) – that an agreement was made. The College authorities decided to go for a limited architectural competition with a prize of 300 guineas and invited 'four distinguished Architects to submit plans'.[17] It seems, however, that the competition conditions were unclear in some respects for not only did the competing architects offer different types of stone facing (see Chapter 7) but they also raised the question of 'whether the main frontage of the building was to be towards the Avenue or Park Place'.[18] The assessor, Sir Rowand Anderson, reported in September 1903 and his recommendation to award the prize to W. D. Caroe was approved.[19] The cost for the whole building was estimated to be £234,000.[20] Bearing in mind the amount of money available, it was decided to build part of the building (administration, arts and library) as a first phase at a cost of £106,000.[21] The foundation stone was laid by the Prince of Wales on 28 June 1905, and the first phase of the College was formally opened on 14 October 1909 by the Earl of Plymouth. Three years later, on 26 June 1912, the Viriamu Jones Laboratory, at the north-west corner, was opened by King George V, leaving more than half of the proposed building still to be completed.

Pl. 40. *John Cory (1828–1910), by William Goscombe John, 1906.*
© Crown copyright: RCAHMW.

Caroe planned the University College as a rectangular building around a large internal quadrangle, with a library block penetrating and dominating the west side of the quadrangle and a free-standing Great Hall closing the east side (Pl. 41). Taking more than fifty years to complete, the College underwent a watering down of architectural detail in the later years and the eventual abandonment of the Great Hall as originally proposed. The first portion to be completed was the long, 47-bay west range set back from Museum Avenue behind a deep lawn (Pl. 42). This follows the design of the competition entry and is generally of an English Renaissance character,[22] though Caroe himself had been brought up within the tradition of the Gothic Revival. The result is a strange mix of shapes, levels and surface decoration that somehow manages to hang together but, at the same time, reveals a stylistic insecurity – 'a classic

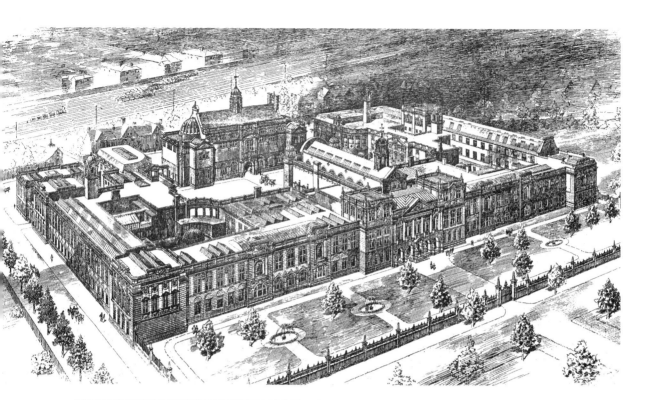

example of a "Goth" unhappily handling classical form', according to Gradige.[23] Caroe, however, said that he once

> had in mind the many delightful classical and semi-classical examples in both our ancient Universities, and endeavoured to give a flavour to the building which, while being distinctly modern and of its time, is intended to recall some of the feeling which is so characteristic of that typically British, and at the same time scholarly, architectural development.[24]

The five-bay central part of the façade with its heavily dentilled pediment is not unlike James Gibbs's Senate House at Cambridge, except that the columns here are Ionic instead of Corinthian and the windows below the entablature are circular instead of round-headed. Below the *piano nobile* there is a rusticated arcade with coupled pilasters and a curved hood supported on banded columns over the entrance. Behind the central section rises a second, but steeper dentilled pediment above a round-headed window lighting the library. Three-storey, castle-like towers flank the central section, with two-storey façades continuing beyond for another fourteen bays (with varying types of ground floor windows) to north and south before coming to stop in four bay, slightly higher end pavilions, each again with different window patterns. The rear of this range, seen from the quadranguler Great Court, appears more organised and restful (Pl. 43). A three-storey central block, highlighted by a Venetian window lighting the Drapers' Library, thrusts forward boldly from lower, bridge sections on either side that, in turn, link to six-bay units with tall

Pl. 41. (opposite, top) *University College of South Wales and Monmouthshire (now Cardiff University), by W. D. Caroe, 1905–30: bird's-eye view showing proposed layout with a Great Hall at the rear.*

Pl. 42. (opposite, bottom) *University College, main (west) front facing Museum Avenue.* © Crown copyright: RCAHMW.

Pl. 43. (below) *University College, Great Court with, in centre, projecting wing of Draper's Library.* © Crown copyright: RCAHMW.

Pl. 44. (right) *University College, architect's drawing showing interior of Drapers' Library as intended and as built.*

Pl. 45. (below) *University College, interior of Drapers' Hall after insertion of mezzanine floor in 1977.*
© Crown copyright: RCAHMW.

mullioned windows over arcaded loggias. Convex quadrants with columned upper floors at each angle of the quadrangle screen light wells or circular toilet areas, and three-bay pedimented projections at the centre of the north and south wings add further interest.

Inside, behind the entrance lobby there is a spacious hall with views through to the small courtyards on either side, all of which are subdivided by multiple and single Ionic columns. Vaulted, tunnel-like corridors on either side of this hall lead to offices, laboratories and cloak rooms. To the left is a staircase rising around an open well, with a ceiling of small saucer domes – two of which are glazed to provide top light – and walls lined with panels of pinkish alabaster from Penarth. A broad landing on the first floor surrounds another top-lit open well and gives access to the Council Chamber on one side and the Drapers' Library on the other side. The Council Chamber is a fine room with a slightly curved ceiling, full-height wall panelling, a carved fireplace and a heavy, central pendant light. The most exciting interior space is the Library, which was paid for by the Drapers' Company of London and inspired by the early-eighteenth century library at Trinity College, Dublin. Once a majestic and lofty hall with many side-bays and galleries inserted between the arcade piers (Pl. 44), it was cut down in size in 1977 when a mezzanine was inserted to provide additional floor space (Pl. 45). The upper part incorporating a fine, tunnel vaulted and coffered ceiling pierced by semicircular side windows with a huge Venetian window at the east end – all reminiscent, in mood if not detail, of C. R. Cockerell's University Library at Cambridge (now the library of Gonville and Caius College) – still remains an impressive space.

As with the other buildings in the Civic Centre no construction work was carried out on the University College during the First World War. After the war work was restarted on the north wing; on completion this was opened by the Prince of Wales in May 1930. The south wing had to wait until after the Second World War before being erected. The architect for this was W. D. Caroe's son, Alban Caroe (1904–91) who, working to a more stringent budget produced, in 1954, a pared-down version of his father's original design. A further tightening of the belt owing to expansion of the University College elsewhere led to the abandonment of the Great Hall that had been intended as a grand closure to the quadrangle on the Park Place side. The awkward gap was partly alleviated by completing the unfinished north and south wings with a pair of three-storey return blocks designed by Alban Caroe. These were formally opened by the Duke of Edinburgh, Chancellor of the University of Wales, in July 1962.

Boer War Memorial

The splendid Boer War Memorial was erected at the southern end of King Edward VII Avenue in 1909 in 'memory of the Welshmen who fell in South Africa, 1899–1902', and paid for by public subscription raised the previous year

(Pl. 46). Modelled in dark bronze by Albert Toft, it is raised on a high Portland stone pedestal that, in turn, sits on a stepped plinth with globular lamps at the four corners. The composition is crowned by a beautiful winged angel of Peace bearing an olive branch. Below are seated figures representing War (male, with shield and sword) and Grief (female, with harp and wreath). Nearly two hundred names of the fallen are inscribed on the pedestal. Later, the memorial was moved slightly to its present roundabout position as part of works involved with constructing Boulevard de Nantes.

Statue of Viscount Tredegar

The splendid equestrian statue of Godfrey Charles Morgan (1831–1913), 1st Viscount Tredegar was also erected in 1909 on what is now the City Hall Green. The bronze statue (Pl. 47) is by Goscombe John. Viscount Tredegar was one of the heroes of 'the noble six hundred' who took part in the Charge of the Light Brigade at Balaclava (1854) during the Crimean War. The pedestal incorporates bronze relief panels showing scenes from the famous charge. Tredegar later became Member of Parliament for Brecknock.

Pl. 46. (above) *South African (Boer) War Memorial, by Albert Toft, 1909.*
© Crown copyright: RCAHMW.

Pl. 47. (right) *First Viscount Tredegar (Godfrey Charles Morgan, 1831–1913), by William Goscombe John, 1909.*
© Crown copyright: RCAHMW.

Pl. 48. (opposite page, top) *Judge Gwilym Williams (1839–1906), by William Goscombe John, 1910.*
© Crown copyright: RCAHMW.

Pl. 49. (opposite page, bottom) *Lord Aberdare (Henry Austin Bruce, 1815–95), by Herbert Hampton, 1898.*
© Crown copyright: RCAHMW.

Statue of Judge Williams

Goscombe John was also the sculptor (1910) of the portly figure of Judge Gwilym Williams (1839–1906), standing in confident pose dressed in gown and wig alongside the south front of the Law Courts (Pl. 48). Born in Aberdare, he was said to be 'a terror to malefactors', and was an 'ardent and patriotic Welshman' as well as being a wealthy landowner.[25]

Statue of Lord Aberdare

The last monument to be erected in the Civic Centre before the First World War was the statue of the 1st Lord Aberdare (Henry Austin Bruce, 1815–95) (Pl. 49). Lord Aberdare was one of the pioneers of 'the movement for the provision of university education in Wales' and was elected first president of the University College and the first chancellor of the University of Wales.[26] The bronze sculpture, by Herbert Hampton, was originally made in 1898 and stood for many years in Howard Gardens, off Newport Road, before being moved in 1914 to its present position in Queen Alexandra Gardens facing, appropriately, the University College.

Glamorgan Building
(former Glamorgan County Hall)

The next institution to be considered is the Glamorgan Building (now part of Cardiff University), which was erected as the Glamorgan County Hall on a site immediately north of the University of Wales Registry. The Glamorgan County Council was established in 1889 and at first the departments were distributed around the county in different towns with council meetings taking place alternately in Neath and Pontypridd. A number of plans were drawn up for erecting a single county hall in places such as Bridgend, Llandaf, Merthyr Tydfil, Neath and Pontypridd before deciding to accept Cardiff Corporation's offer of a site in Cathays Park.[27] At first the Corporation had offered a site of an acre facing North Road before agreeing to the present, somewhat larger site facing King Edward VII Avenue. Glamorgan County Council invited designs for a

new county hall and offices in an open architectural competition in July 1908, with prizes of 100 guineas, 50 guineas and 30 guineas. Altogether there were 190 entries, from which Vincent Harris, along with his colleague Thomas Moodie, was chosen for the new building. The total cost of the building was not to exceed £45,000 for work above the basement, the lower floor being the responsibility of the Council. Construction began in 1909, and the building

Pl. 50. (above) *Glamorgan County Hall (now Glamorgan Building), by Vincent Harris & Thomas Moodie, 1909–11: main (east) front facing King Edward VII Avenue.*
© Crown copyright: RCAHMW.

Pl. 51. (right) *Glamorgan County Hall, external sculpture, 'Neptune in a chariot' by Albert Hodge.*
© Crown copyright: RCAHMW.

was completed in 1911 and formally opened in 1912. After the demise of the Glamorgan County Council and its successor the Mid-Glamorgan County Council, the building was acquired by Cardiff University in 1997 to become the Cardiff School of Social Studies.

The completed building by Harris is a remarkable tour-de-force, though it varies in a number of respects from the prize-winning entry. The Greco-Roman main front is said to have been influenced by George Basevi's Fitzwilliam Museum (of 1834–45) in Cambridge.[28] However, without that building's projecting portico and pediment, the Glamorgan Building looks quite different and less pretentious. It is one of the finest buildings in the Civic Centre and stands comparison with other buildings of its type and period (Pl. 50). The graceful and tightly organised main front is raised on a stylobate of triple-height steps (though single height in the centre) flanked by low podiums on which sit splendidly bold, sculptured groups by Albert Hodge symbolising Navigation, represented by Neptune (right), and Mining represented by Minerva (left) (Pl. 51). The façade is monumental in scale with five central bays set back behind a portico of coupled, giant and fluted Corinthian columns set between outer pavilions, all crowned by a continuous entablature with a heavily dentilled cornice. The end pavilions project further forward than originally planned and are enriched with flat, fluted pilasters instead of round columns. The attic storey is again different from the competition design, with a stone balustrade fronting the recessed centre section and plain extensions to the end pavilions instead of sculpture. Single-storey, balustraded arches at each end of the main front lead into rear service areas.

The side elevations are comparatively simple with arched windows at ground level, two floors of rectangular windows below the continuous cornice and one row of smaller windows above. The rear front facing North Road is similar to the sides except that it has an elaborate, overhanging balcony supported on paired stone brackets to the main floor and tall, slim chimneys protruding above the slate roof, all of which gives it the feeling of an Italian palazzo (Pl. 52). The façade is flanked by arched side entries, this time under curved walls ending in sculpture-topped piers by Alfred Hodge.

Internally, a half flight of steps leads from the sombre entrance hall – clad in stone with a coffered ceiling and Doric pilasters – to the mezzanine level (Fig. 8.3).

Fig. 8.3. *Glamorgan County Hall (now Glamorgan Building), ground floor plan.*

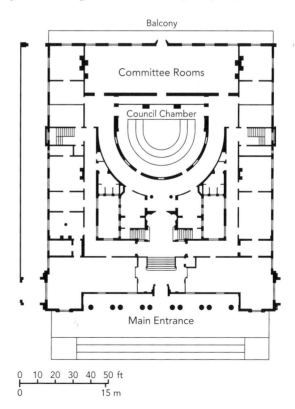

Balcony

Committee Rooms

Council Chamber

Main Entrance

0 10 20 30 40 50 ft

0   15 m

Pl. 52. (right) *Glamorgan County Hall, west front facing North Road.*
© Crown copyright: RCAHMW.

Pl. 53. (below) *Glamorgan County Hall, interior of Council Chamber.*
© Crown copyright: RCAHMW.

Here, there is with a cross-passage and, on either side, stone stairs rising to an upper hall lit by arched and iron-grilled windows. Beyond the cross-passage an apse gives access, past Doric columns and a stone-lined semicircular top-lit corridor, to the Council Chamber. The D-shaped Council Chamber is an impressive space with ash-lared walls and a near hemispherical ceiling lit on three sides by high-level semicircular windows (Pl. 53). Originally it was intended to be panelled and lined with Corinthian pilasters, but when built it was altered to the present 'very French-influenced design'.[29] The door-height stone wall behind the dais hides a communication passage and supports two giant, stone sculptures by Alfred Hodge – on the left of a bard reading a book and on the right a druid playing a harp. To the rear of the Council Chamber is a suite of oak-panelled committee rooms. They have deeply moulded plaster ceilings, heavy stone chimneypieces and tall windows opening onto the cantilevered balcony that overlooks North Road. All the furniture, in both Council Chamber and committee rooms, was designed by Harris.

National Museum of Wales

Originally a site had been reserved for a new Municipal Museum in Park Place (where the New Theatre now stands) and the local architect Edwin Seward had been appointed in May 1895 to design it. Later, when in 1897 it had become clear that Cardiff Corporation would purchase Cathays Park, a site at the south-east corner of the Park was approved for the museum and Seward, who had previously designed Cardiff's Free Library and Art Gallery in Trinity Street, was asked to draw up designs to suit the new site. Soon, John Ward, the Curator of the museum, was making the point 'that these proposed buildings will probably become the National Museum of Wales'.[30] In 1902 Seward was asked to prepare further plans, this time for a Welsh Museum of Natural History, Arts and Antiquities, on an appropriately grand scale. The design included an eclectic classical-style, two-storey main front with a projecting centre section – incorporating an entrance under three arches supported on stumpy columns – and corner pavilions (Pl. 54).[31] The plans 'were finally approved by the Building Committee on 1 February 1905, and Seward was instructed to complete them and prepare quantities'.[32] Then in June that year the Privy Council eventually decided that the proposed National Museum should be based in Cardiff and nearly two years later, on 19 March 1907, a Charter of Incorporation brought the museum into theoretical being.[33] This was to be the cue for the Corporation – which had done so much to encourage the establishment of a National Museum by a gift of land, donation of the contents of its Municipal Museum and by the proceeds from a halfpenny rate – to hand over all liabilities, including that 'in respect of Mr Seward's services'.[34] Unfortunately for Edwin Seward this was the end of his involvement in the project. Apparently, his plans for the 'Welsh Museum' were considered by the Museum Council in November 1908, but to no avail.[35] Seward felt cheated and brought a case – heard in the High Court in December, 1910 – against the Corporation for loss of fees and 'damages for breach of contract'.[36]

Pl. 54. Design for proposed Welsh Museum of Natural History, Arts & Antiquities, by Edwin Seward, 1902 (from an old photograph).

A director was appointed to the National Museum on 1 March 1909, and soon afterwards he submitted a report on the accommodation needed for the museum. The Museum Council then decided 'to put the design of the new building to an open competition rather than invite one architectural practice'.[37] The competition conditions were issued in September for 'a new Museum at a cost for the completed building of £250,000, inclusive of carving but exclusive of decorative sculpture': it was suggested 'that about one-third of the building will be erected in the first instance'.[38] The conditions made it clear that it would be 'desirable that externally the Museum building should be designed in harmony with these buildings [City Hall and Law Courts], that, so far as possible, it may be in sympathy with the general scheme adopted'. A total of 130 entries were received in the competition. The assessors gave their report on 10 March 1910, and recommended the London firm of Dunbar Smith and Cecil Brewer for the first prize (Pl. 55), with T. L. Vesper, Henry T. Hare, and D. Milne and J. P. Hepburn, all of London, as the three runners up.[39] Edwin Seward does not appear to have entered the competition; intriguingly, Milne & Hepburn's bore a noticeable similarity to Seward's earlier design for the 'Welsh Museum'.

The winning design by Smith and Brewer was in the form of a long, hollow rectangle, with a spacious, domed entrance hall on the short, south side, and behind this a large interior garden court containing two, multi-facetted pavilions (Fig. 8.4). The public galleries were grouped on two floors facing onto the inner court with the reserve collections parallel to the galleries but arranged along the outer walls. Following the competition the Museum Council invited Dr F. A. Bather – an internationally recognised museum expert – to comment on the proposals. One of his main criticisms was that the plan's symmetry (resulting, of course, from the competition requirement to harmonise with the City Hall) 'militates against that flexibility which is so necessary in all museums buildings'.[40] Others were that the central courtyard was too restricted in size and, most importantly, that the lighting of the entrance hall would be inadequate. Little could be done about the plan's symmetry,

Pl. 55. *National Museum of Wales, competition design by Smith & Brewer, 1910.*

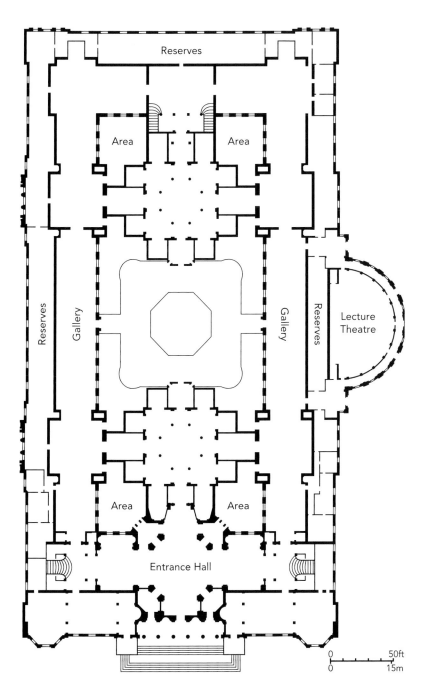

Fig. 8.4. *National Museum of Wales, ground floor plan (1). The winning competition design showing the proposed layout of south front, entrance hall and courtyard pavilions before significant alterations were made following criticism.*

but discussions with the architects led to a major rethink with regard to the entrance hall resulting in an increase in height of the dome from 83 ft (25 m) to 99 ft (30 m), the omission of a floor over the public area and opening up of the side halls. Externally, the southern elevation was restyled with a wider, more empathetic entrance colonnade with paired columns, and the two pavilions within the central courtyard were given sleeker profiles while the garden itself was simplified.

Building began in September 1911, with a contract for constructing foundations and a basement over part of the site. King George V laid the formal foundation stone the following June, and the initial contract was completed on 17 October 1913. A further contract for the first phase of the superstructure was let and construction began early in 1914.[41] Then, as the effects of disruption owing to the First World War began to take their toll, work slowed down until eventually it came to a stop during 1916.

Construction work on the museum's superstructure was restarted in 1918. Conditions remained generally difficult but, by October 1922, the southern section and part of the west wing had been completed and fitting out had advanced sufficiently to open the western half of the entrance hall and nearby galleries to the public.[42] Four and half years later, on 21 April 1927, the sections of the building that had been completed were officially opened by King George V. However, the museum was still, in the words of one commentator, 'little more than a noble entrance hall flanked by a few galleries'.[43] It was not until 1932 – when the eastern wing, along with its protruding lecture theatre, was completed – that it could be said that roughly half of the original conception had been realised. By then one of the architects, Cecil Brewer, had been dead for 14 years while the other, Dunbar Smith, had only a year of life left. When he, too, died in 1933, his ashes were placed in an urn and buried within the walls of the Museum.

Pl. 56. *National Museum of Wales, by Smith & Brewer, 1911–32: main (south) front facing the Gorsedd Gardens.*
© Crown copyright: RCAHMW.

Although it was intended that the Museum should be 'designed to be in harmony' with the City Hall and Law Courts, that did not mean that it needed to slavishly copy the style of those buildings. In fact, the calmer architectural style of the Museum – apparently influenced by the Neo-Classic work of McKim, Mead and White in the United States – indicated a cooling-off of affection for the Baroque of the City Hall's designers. This became even more apparent when the Museum, after undergoing considerable design changes to accommodate a larger and higher entrance hall, was actually built. The result is an impressive, well-groomed smoother-looking building than the City Hall; its presence 'a statement of civic and national pride' for Rhiannon Mason.[44] For Purchon, writing in 1923, 'whether seen in the morning … in the evening … or in the dusk … the new building impresses one with its rare and haunting beauty'.[45]

The majestic, sphinx-like south front facing the Gorsedd Gardens is approached by a broad, double flight of granite steps at the top of which a five-bay loggia of paired Doric columns (not single as in the competition entry) gives access to the entrance (Pl. 56). On either side of the loggia are three-bay, rusticated sections (again quite different from the original design), the centre bay of each incorporating recessed columns and projecting slightly outwards and more emphatically upwards to support sculptural groups set against an attic storey. The sculpture groups were carried out during 1914 and 1915. Those on the south represent 'Prehistoric' and 'Classic' periods, by Gilbert Bayes, and 'Medieval' and 'Modern' periods, by Richard L. Garbe. To the west are 'Mining' and 'Shipping', by Thomas. J. Clapperton, and on the east are 'Learning', by Clapperton, 'Music', by David Evans, and 'Art', by Bertram Pegram (Pl. 57). The attic storey above and behind the entrance loggia provides a plain base for a square drum with facetted corners that rises up to support a large, lead-covered dome over the central hall. This is adorned with dragons and lions sculpted by Bertram Pegram and pierced by a semicircular window (as at the City Hall). The long west and east wings continue northwards with rows of tall (apparently single-storey) windows, any potential for monotony being obviated by a slightly protruding three-bay sections with recessed columns and attic sculpture on the west front and by the bulging, curved shape of the lecture theatre on the east wing.

Pl. 57. *National Museum of Wales, attic sculpture, 'Art' by Bertram Pegram, 1914–15.*
© Crown copyright: RCAHMW.

The Neo-Classical idiom is carried confidently through to the interior. Here, a large entrance hall extending almost the full width of the southern section forms the main architectural focus of attention. As originally conceived the hall was to be only single storey in height with a flattish saucer dome, but following Dr Bather's intervention it was redesigned on an imposing and lavish scale with shining columns of polished Mazzano marble (Pl. 58). The octagonal centre part of the hall rises up three storeys to a great dome with semicircular windows, the light from which casts a slightly pinkish glow on everything below. On either side of the octagon the hall narrows and is ringed by encircling balconies and bridges at first-floor level, the latter supported on Ionic columns. Broad staircases of Comblanchion marble under shallow saucer domes at either end of the hall lead to

Pl. 58. *National Museum of Wales, interior of Entrance Hall.*
© Crown copyright: RCAHMW.

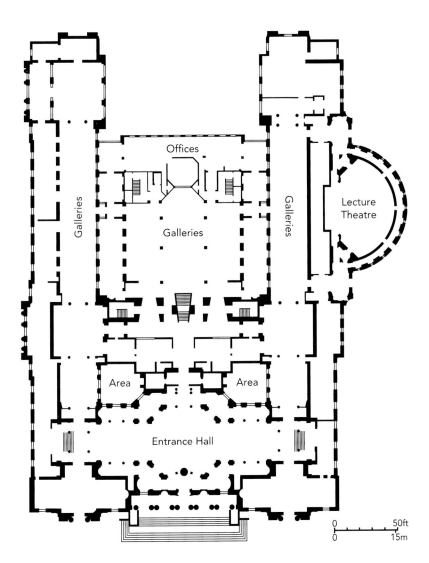

Galleries

Offices

Galleries

Galleries

Galleries

Lecture
Theatre

Area

Area

Entrance Hall

0 ————— 50ft
0 ————— 15m

Fig. 8.5. *National Museum of Wales, ground floor plan (2). In the building as completed the central courtyard and the northern public gallery have been omitted, allowing for a denser use of the site.*

the upper galleries and invite further exploration. The overall effect is stunning, and as Newman wrote 'an endlessly fascinating space in its interplay between piers and balconies, stairs and landings, high parts and low parts, light and shade'.[46]

Apart from smaller galleries on either side of the entrance, the main exhibition galleries (spacious and austere with coffered ceilings) were located in the long east and west wings. The galleries were arranged for art, archaeology, botany, folk-life, geology, industry and zoology. Archaeology, folk-life and industry have since been transferred elsewhere. The two-storey east wing was opened in 1932, and leads to a semicircular lecture theatre on the ground floor with a semicircular art gallery on the upper floor. A small section of the west wing was opened in 1927, but the major part was not completed until 1965. Externally, T. Alwyn Lloyd & Gordon – the architects for the concluding section of the west wing – were able to maintain Smith and Brewer's original design while reconfiguring the interior to provide three floors instead of two. Smith & Brewer's original design for the museum had anticipated a north wing to complete the circuit of galleries around an internal courtyard. This, however, would have presented problems of access for servicing the building. It was therefore decided in the 1960s that the north wing would eventually be built as a separate, independent building.[47] This, in turn, would have created problems of public access between different parts of the complex and in the end it was resolved to do away with the internal courtyard altogether and build instead a sequence of new galleries for Art, Natural History and the Evolution of Wales, as well as offices and a restaurant in the area. The new centre block, designed by the Alex Gordon Partnership – successor to T. Alwyn Lloyd & Gordon – was built between 1989 and 1992. While the development works well inside, the rather bland, six-storey exterior with its chessboard arrangement of windows appears somewhat at odds with the rest of the building (Fig. 8.5). Apparently, this was not intended to be a 'finished' façade, but was meant to allow for later addition.[48]

Bute Building (former Technical College)

Returning to the west side of King Edward VII Avenue, we next come to the Bute Building, which began life as a technical institute, before becoming first a Technical College, then the University of Wales Institute of Science and Technology and, finally, part of Cardiff University's wide-ranging empire. Although the aim of building a Technical Institute had been discussed on and off for two decades and a plot had been earmarked for it in the borough engineer's 1899 plan, it was not until December 1910, that an agreement was reached to construct the building at a maximum cost of £40,000.[49] An architectural competition was arranged the following year and won in October 1912, by Percy Thomas (in association with Cardiff-based Ivor Jones) out of 60 entries. In his autobiography Thomas recalled:

> that of all the Competitions I have won, this one gave me the biggest thrill, meaning, as it did, returning to Cardiff and starting in practice. After returning to Cardiff, I did the whole of the working drawings alone (we had only one pupil). As we had very little other work at that time, I was able to concentrate on the Technical College but, before the building was completed, the First World War had started.[50]

In fact, the foundation stone had been laid in April 1914, (by which time the estimated cost had risen to £50,000) and construction continued during the war. The entrance wing and the two side wings were completed in 1916 and the College was opened in March by the Lord Mayor. Two years later temporary engineering workshops were built on the ground floor of what was to become the fourth wing.

Externally, the College is a relatively straightforward instance of Neo-Greek classicism (Pl. 59). The *Architectural Review* claimed that `the elevations are reminiscent of that scholarly type of classical architecture which has distinguished the public buildings of the United States'.[51] More recent critics have been less kind, calling it 'a typical example of the institutional building of this period'[52] and 'unexciting'.[53] The five-bay centre section of the two-storey main front projects forward, enclosing a portico with giant Doric columns. Rising from behind the portico is a plain attic storey with a simple cornice and small, ornamental horns at either end. The main façade, complete with continuous cornice, extends five bays on either side of the portico. The two-storey side wings are identical, each with projecting, rusticated bays containing twin Doric columns at either the end of plain, fifteen-bay runs.

The College was planned in the form of a hollow rectangle with an assembly hall occupying a large part of the internal court. There are three floor levels, though apparently only two when seen from outside, the uppermost floor being lit from above. Entry into the building from the portico leads, via a vestibule, into a spacious but fairly low entrance hall with corridors and two sets of stairs on either side. The two-storey assembly hall, which was approached from the entrance hall by three pairs of doors, was a fine space, lit from each side by five, tall round-headed windows breaking into a segmental ceiling divided by raised bands into bays. The assembly hall has since been replaced by a nondescript cafeteria at ground-floor level and by a large lecture theatre at first-floor level.

Further work on the Technical College took place in the inter-war years. In 1927 the fourth, west wing was completed at a cost of £30,000. Finally, a two-storey extension (by Ivor Jones and Percy Thomas) was built above the assembly hall in 1934–36 with the 'walls visible from the highway' finished in Portland stone.[54] The red dragon sculpture by David Peterson above the entrance façade was added in 1984.

Pl. 59. *Technical College (now Bute Building), by Percy Thomas & Ivor Jones, 1914–36; main (east) front facing King Edward VII Avenue.* © Crown copyright: RCAHMW.

Welsh Insurance Commission

The last building planned for the Civic Centre before the First World War, but not in the end carried out, was the offices of the Welsh Insurance Commission. The Commission was set up in 1911 under the National Health Insurance Act as part of the Government's aim to decentralise departments following earlier attempts by the Cymru Fydd ('Young Wales') movement and David Lloyd George to ensure that Wales was treated as a separate national polity. As a result, it was seen at the time to be 'a very successful experiment in applied home rule'.[55] At first the Board was located in temporary offices in the City Hall.[56] Apparently a permanent building for the Commission (and Labour Exchange) was under consideration in 1913, and 'an arrangement was made with the Corporation for the free gift of a site in Cathays Park' with an agreement that the building should be completed by June, 1917.[57] By early March 1914, £6,200 had been allocated by the Government towards a total construction cost of £77,750 for erecting the building.[58] The *Western Mail* was quick to take advantage of the announcement by claiming credit for:

> inducing the corporation to offer that site [i.e., between the Technical College and the Bute reserved acre] rather than the great open space due north of Alexandra gardens, which has been definitely [*sic*] earmarked as the focus of central Government buildings when Federal Home Rule or some other general scheme of devolution assures the provision of buildings for a Welsh Parliament.[59]

In late September, 7 weeks after war had been declared, it was reported that work on the building was – in view of the current crisis – to be expedited 'to provide a certain amount of employment for unskilled labour'; the Commissioners had written to the City Council earlier, on the 18 September, stating that they were considering 'proceeding forthwith with the foundations', and 'asked the city council to convey the site over and satisfy themselves as to the plans without delay'.[60] The plans, designed by Richard Allison of the Office of Works, were approved by the Council and the town clerk was instructed to arrange the formal conveyance of the site.

The report in the *Western Mail* was accompanied by illustrations of the proposed building and a few details (Pl. 60). As far as one can tell from the elevational drawings the building was to be a rectangular block, 350 ft (107 m) long by 130 ft (40 m) wide. It was designed to be an impressive, classical style three-storey building – twenty-five bays long by fifteen bays wide – incorporating a continuous cornice between first and second floor. The main front, facing King Edward VII Avenue, would have had a projecting centre section of five bays with a three-bay portico of coupled giant Ionic columns and, rising behind that, an innovative attic storey pierced by three, large semicircular arches. The intended front to College Road would have had a slightly projecting, three-bay centre section with single giant Ionic columns all crowned by a dentilled pediment. In addition, there would have been projecting pavilions, with recessed Ionic columns facing each side, at all four corners of the building.

It is unclear whether any work on the building was actually carried out, although Chappell states that 'in 1914 work was commenced on the foundations, but was abandoned in the following year owing to the Great War'.[61] In November, 1914, the *Western Mail* illustrated a perspective of the proposed building, noting that 'these magnificent buildings will soon be in course of erection'.[62] Seven months later the matter was brought up in Parliament when a MP asked 'whether the Government intended to proceed with the construction of a Labour Exchange [*sic*] at Cardiff at a cost of £70,000 during the war'.[63] The President of the Board of Trade answered that 'it is hoped to postpone the erection of the building referred to, and negotiations to this end are now being entered into'. Presumably this referred to the letter (dated 13 July 1915) from the Office of Works asking the City Council to 'agree to a postponement of the erection of the above [Government Buildings in Cathays Park] for the duration, of which would of course be uncertain'.[64] The Council duly agreed to postpone work for 12 months. And so it continued throughout the War: the Office of Works requesting further postponements in late 1915, 1916 and 1917, and each time the Council accepting the request.[65] The last reference to anything to do with the proposed building was in December 1917 when the Board of (Welsh Insurance) Commissioners requested the City Council that 'the tenure of the site of the temporary building be extended until such time as the permanent building was ready for occupation'.[66] This, too, was accepted.

From all of the above it appears that no real work, apart from a small part of the foundations, was ever begun on the imposing offices proposed for the Welsh Insurance Commission. Instead, a temporary building was erected on part of the site at some time during the war, possibly on the foundations already completed. By December 1918, at the latest, this was in use as the offices of the National Health Insurance Commissioners (Wales).[67] It is this single-storey, rendered brick building at the northern end of the site that is the one that was optimistically marked 'Insurance Buildings' on the 1920 edition of the Ordnance Survey large scale (1: 2,500) map. The temporary building survived into the early 1950s until it was demolished to make way for the Redwood Building (see Chapter 10).

Pl. 60. *Welsh Insurance Commission offices, by Richard Allison, c.1914: a poor quality photograph (from the Western Mail of 1914) of the proposed east front facing King Edward VII Avenue.*

NOTES

1   Richard Fellows, *Edwardian Architecture: Style and Technology*, p. 93.
2   John Warren, 'Edwin Alfred Rickards', in Alastair Service, *Edwardian Architecture and Its Origins*, p. 344.
3   Fellows, *Edwardian Architecture*, p. 88.
4   Lanchester and Rickards, 'Cardiff City Hall and Law Courts', *The Architectural Review*, vol. XX, 1906, p. 233.
5   Gradidge, 'Cardiff Civic Centre', p. 15.
6   Newman, *Glamorgan*, p. 223.
7   City of Cardiff, *Welsh Historical Sculpture*, pp. 3–4.
8   Colin Cunningham, *Victorian and Edwardian Town Halls*, p. 120.
9   Newman, *Glamorgan*, p. 225.
10   Ibid., p. 225.
11   CCL: Cardiff Corporation, *Proceedings, Nov. 1902–May 1903*, p. 34.
12   Ibid., p. 241.
13   GA: BC/S/1/20917, and BC/S/1/33163.
14   *Evening Express*, 24 June 1898.
15   Dillwyn Miles, *The Royal National Eisteddfod of Wales*, pp. 19, 50, 56.
16   University College of South Wales, *New College Fund*, p. 24.
17   Ibid., p. 25.
18   *Cardiff Times*, 4 October 1902.
19   *Builder*, October 1903, vol. 85, p. 358.
20   University College of South Wales, *New College Fund*, p. 25.
21   *Cardiff Times*, 1 July 1905.
22   W. S. Purchon, 'The Public Buildings of Cardiff', *RIBA Journal*, vol. 29, p. 395.
23   Gradidge, 'Cardiff Civic Centre', p. 6.
24   University College of South Wales, *New College Fund*, p. 25.
25   Lloyd and Jenkins, *Dictionary of Welsh Biography*, pp. 1039–40.
26   Ibid., p. 54.
27   GA: GD/C/BU/4, County Hall/Buildings, 1896–97.
28   Gradidge, 'Cardiff Civic Centre', p. 10.
29   Ibid.
30   GA: Case of *Edwin Seward* v. *Corporation of Cardiff*: report on the *Scale and Cost of proposed first buildings* (c.1900).
31   NMW: Plans dated 18 Jan. 1902, included in *Stock Book of the Cardiff Museum and Art Gallery*.
32   NMW: *Minutes of Council*, 28 November 1908 – statement by Alderman W. R. Renwick, Cardiff Corporation, to the Museum Council.
33   Bassett, *The Making of a National Museum*, Part I, pp. 14–17.
34   NMW: *Minutes of Council*, 28 November 1908.
35   Douglas A. Bassett, *National Museum of Wales: A Historical Checklist*, p. 2.
36   GA: Case of *Edwin Seward* v. *Corporation of Cardiff*.
37   Bassett, *The Making of a National Museum*, Part 1, p. 18.
38   British Competitions, 'National Museum of Wales', p. 265.
39   Ibid., p. 265.
40   Bassett, *The Making of a National Museum*, Part I, pp. 22–3.
41   Ibid., p. 25.
42   Bassett, *The Making of a National Museum*, Part III, p. 13.
43   Ibid., pp. 16,18.
44   Rhiannon Mason, *Myths, Memories and Futures*, p. 29.
45   Purchon, W. S., 'National Museum of Wales', *The Architectural Review*, vol. 53, p. 45.

46   Newman, *Glamorgan*, p. 228.
47   Douglas A. Bassett, 'Wales in Miniature', *Amgueddfa*, Autumn 1993, p. 20.
48   Information from Dr Eurwyn Wiliam.
49   CCL: Cardiff Corporation, *Proceedings, Nov. 1910–May 1911*, p. 99.
50   Sir Percy Thomas, *Pupil to President*, p. 20.
51   *The Architectural Review*, May 1916, p. 105.
52   Gradidge, 'Cardiff Civic Centre', p. 8.
53   Newman, *Glamorgan*, p. 231.
54   A. Harvey, 'One Hundred Years of Technical Education in Cardiff', *Glamorgan Historian*,
        vol. 9, p. 179; GA: BC/S/1/29713.
55   Quoted by Trevor Fishlock in *A Gift of Sunlight*, p. 101.
56   Cardiff Corporation, *Cardiff 1889–1974*, pp. 34–5.
57   Chappell, *Cardiff's Civic Centre*, p. 49.
58   *Western Mail*, 5 March 1914.
59   Ibid.
60   *Western Mail*, 22 September 1914.
61   Chappell, *Cardiff's Civic Centre*, p. 49.
62   *Western Mail*, 30 November 1914.
63   *Western Mail*, 16 July 1915.
64   CCL: Cardiff Corporation, *Proceedings, May 1915–Nov. 1915*, p. 180.
65   CCL: Cardiff Corporation, *Proceedings, Nov. 1915–May 1916*, p. 133; *Nov. 1916–May 1917*,
        p. 73; *May 1917–Nov. 1917*, p. 154.
66   CCL: Cardiff Corporation, *Proceedings, Nov. 1917–Nov. 1918*, p. 119.
67   Photograph, dated December 1918, at: *cardiffparks.org.uk/cathays/info/redwood.shtml*.

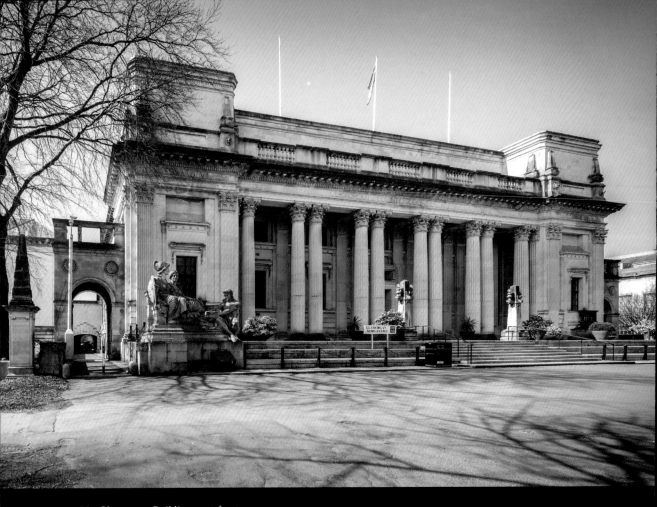

50. *Glamorgan Building, east front.*

71. *Temple of Peace and Health, Hall of Nations.*

9

DEVELOPMENT OF THE CIVIC CENTRE BETWEEN THE WARS:
BUILDINGS AND MONUMENTS

THE PERIOD THAT BEGAN after the First World War was a time of contrasts: optimism and pessimism; industry and depression; trust and tragedy. According to John Davies, 'the shipping boom that followed the war added to the wealth of Cardiff's merchant princes [but] then came the collapse of the coal trade, a disaster from which Cardiff did not recover until the later twentieth century'.[1] The halcyon days that symbolised the pre-war period for the well-off were over; instead, the coalfield valleys, which had been the basis of Cardiff's growth and wealth, were mired in poverty and unemployment.

Society and institutions throughout southern Wales were affected by the depression so that it became a difficult time in which to raise either money or morale for new developments. Nevertheless, during the couple of decades that elapsed between the end of one war and the beginning of another war, four new buildings were erected in Cathays Park, and four of those that had already been started before the war were, as noted in the previous chapter, either completed or extended (Fig. 9.1). To provide access to these developments a new road (College Road) was constructed across the northern part of the Park and Museum Avenue was extended northwards of the University College.

Pl. 61. Lord Ninian Crichton-Stuart (1883–1915), by Sir William Goscombe John, 1919.
© Crown copyright: RCAHMW.

Statue of Lord Ninian Crichton Stuart

The first sign of structural activity after the First World War came with the erection in 1919 of the bronze statue of Lord Ninian Edward Crichton Stuart (1883–1915), second son of the third Marquess of Bute (Pl. 61). After an early career in the army, and then in politics as the Member of Parliament for the Boroughs of Cardiff, Cowbridge and Llantrisant, Stuart rejoined the army in 1912. He was killed in the Battle of Loos, France, in 1915. The statue by William Goscombe John in the Gorsedd Gardens, facing the City Hall Lawn, shows him in army uniform.

Welsh National War Memorial

The War Memorial stands in a place of honour at the very heart of the Civic Centre and at midpoint within Queen Alexandra Gardens. Although not strictly a building in the sense of being a roofed structure it is, nevertheless, an elegant temple-like edifice that deserves its place among the other buildings of the Civic Centre. Newman refers to it as 'a singularly pure and beautiful classical composition',[2] and so it is.

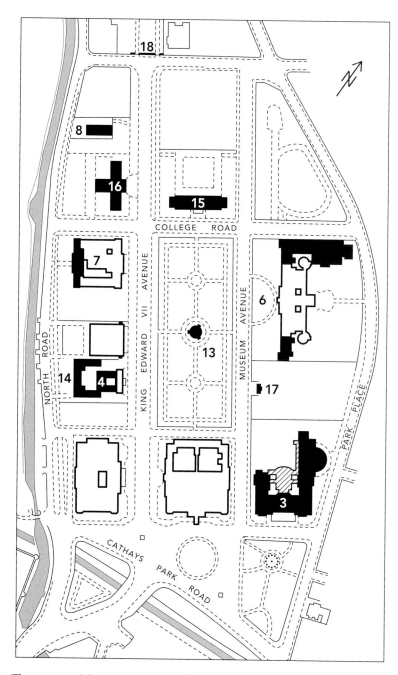

Fig. 9.1. *Development of Cathays Park between 1919 and 1940. Buildings constructed and opened before 1940 are shown solid black; buildings started but not completed before 1940 are shown with diagonal hatching;. Numbers are as follows: 3, National Museum of Wales; 4, University of Wales Registry; 6, University College (now Cardiff University); 7, Technical College; 8, Welsh Insurance Commission (temporary building); 13, Welsh National War Memorial; 14, Glamorgan County Hall extension (now part of Glamorgan Building); 15, Welsh Board of Health (now Welsh Government Offices One); 16, Temple of Peace and Health; 17, Public Conveniences; 18, Queen Anne Square Colonnade. (Based on O. S. map, 1941–2 edition.)*

The proposal for a war memorial appears to have originated in July 1917, when Councillor H. M. Thompson rekindled an earlier idea for a fountain in Queen Alexandra Gardens. The idea was transmuted to a 'national' war memorial by the City Council who, in May 1919, approached public bodies throughout Wales for assistance.[3] Support, however, was half-hearted, with many local authorities treating Cardiff's invitation 'with a mixture of indifference, suspicion and hostility'.[4] This was perhaps not surprising as a movement to commemorate the heroes of northern Wales had already been under way since January 1917, and by February 1918, nearly half the funds for a memorial in Bangor had been offered. After such a shaky start, the *Western Mail*, undaunted, took on the responsibility for raising money for a 'national' memorial in Cardiff to commemorate the fallen in the First World War – or the Great War as it was then known – by launching a fund in October 1919, and 3 months later £24,000 had been promised.[5]

The committee established to make arrangements for the war memorial had intended the monument to be in the form of a fountain located on the circular lawn in front of the City Hall and offered the commission to Sir Thomas Brock, designer of London's Victoria Memorial.[6] But his proposal was too expensive and when he died in 1922 it was decided to invite four architects to submit alternative designs. The design of J. Ninian Comper for a circular colonnade, apparently inspired by the ruins of Emperor Hadrian's buildings in Tunisia,[7] was accepted. A problem arose, however, when – after erecting a full-sized mock-up of the monument on the green circle (Pl. 62) – both the City Council and the National Museum objected to this location. Then siting the memorial in the Friary Gardens was suggested, but to this the Marquess of Bute objected. Finally, it was agreed to site the memorial in Queen Alexandra Gardens, a conspicuous position that now appears not only obvious but also admirably suited for a physical reminder of valour and abbreviated life. Construction work began in March 1926, and the completed memorial was unveiled by the then Prince of Wales in June 1928.

Pl. 62. *Welsh National War Memorial, skeletal mock-up of proposed design on Green Circle in front of City Hall.*

Pl. 63. (left) *Welsh National War Memorial, by J. Ninian Comper, 1926–8, in Queen Alexandra Gardens.*
© Crown copyright: RCAHMW

Pl. 64. (below) *National War Memorial, interior with sculpture by Bertram Pegram.*
© Crown copyright: RCAHMW.

Comper, a scholarly Gothicist, was an unusual choice for a classical war memorial. However, his design for the National War Memorial was particularly successful. It is in the shape of a circular colonnade of Corinthian columns, extended at three points to form projecting porticoes, all of them crowned with a continuous entablature with inscriptions (see below) in English and Welsh on the frieze (Pl. 63). The porticoes lead into a sunken court at the centre of which there is a circular column ringed by three shorter Corinthian columns and between these, facing the porticoes, bronze figures of a soldier, sailor and airman. Each of the warriors holds a wreath up towards a splendid winged, nude 'messenger of victory' bearing a sword at the top of the column (Pl. 64). Three leaping dolphins below the figure of victory eject water (for the memorial is also a fountain) down below, while still further down, beneath the warriors, lion heads eject more water into three overflowing basins. It is very symbolic, as well as being realistically and exquisitely carried out. All the bronze sculptures on the Memorial are by Bertram Pegram.

Note: The inscription on the outer face of the frieze reads: 'I Feibion Cymru a roddes eu Bywyd dros ei Gwlad yn Rhyfel. MCMXIV–MCMXVIII' (To the sons of Wales who gave their lives for their country in the war of 1914–1918), to which has been added on the portico facing King Edward VII Avenue, 'MCMXXXIX – Dros fôr fe droes i farw – MCMXLV' (1939 – Over sea they turned to face death – 1945); that on the inner face reads: 'Remember here in peace those who in tumult of war by sea, on land, in air, for us and for our victory endureth unto death.'

Public Conveniences

The next structure to be built in Cathays Park was a small, classically designed toilet block, situated between the National Museum and the University College and facing Museum Avenue. A plan for a 'new convenience … at a cost of £1,000' was approved on 11 July 1929.[8] A week or so later, when the scheme went before the city's Finance Committee, the estimated cost had risen to £1,800, possibly the result of upgrading to a standard suitable for the Civic Centre. Erected in or about 1930, it stands innocuously enough on its site, a symbol of civic fashion and the Welsh metropolis's wealth. It has an ornate niche between lavatories of different sexes and is clad in imitation Portland stone. Long disused, the roof and parapets have been repaired with the intention of finding a sustainable new use for the building (subject to the 1898 Act, which prohibits trading for profit).[9]

Pl. 65. *Third Marquess of Bute (John Crichton Stuart, 1847–1900), by James P. Macgillevray, 1930.*
© Crown copyright: RCAHMW.

Statue of third Marquess of Bute

The statue of John Crichton Stuart (1847–1900), third Marquess of Bute and Earl of Windsor, is the work of James Pittendrigh Macgillevray and was erected in 1930. The inheritor of enormous wealth while still an infant, the third Marquess – best known for his transformation of Cardiff Castle and Castell Coch under William Burges – was responsible for selling Cathays Park to the borough in 1898, so paving the way for the construction of the Civic Centre. Appropriately, the rather conventional standing bronze figure of the Marquess in peer's robes (Pl. 65) is sited in the Friary Gardens and backs on to the Dock Feeder that his father, the second Marquess, had had constructed.

Glamorgan Building Extension (former Glamorgan County Hall Extension)

When the original Glamorgan County Hall (see Chapter 8) was opened in 1912 the total number of staff employed in the building was 74. The Local Government Act 1929 transferred further powers to the County Council, resulting in a threefold increase in staff.[10] This necessitated erecting a new building to provide extra accommodation. There was no time to organise a competition, and instead Percy Thomas of Ivor Jones & Percy Thomas was commissioned to design a new building on an adjacent site facing North Road and immediately behind the University of Wales Registry. The new building was planned as a four-storey, square structure arranged around a central courtyard and linked by a bridge to the original building. The foundation stone was laid on 19 May 1931, and three wings of the extension were formally opened in September 1932. After acquisition by Cardiff University in 1997, the building became the home of the School of Planning and Geography.

The new building, though bulkier than Harris's earlier building, is well proportioned and sensitively handled in Italian Renaissance style (Pl. 66). Tall chimneys at the corners of the pitched roof, bold and richly detailed cornices and a heavily rusticated base and quoins recall the rear elevation of Harris's earlier building. The windows are, however, much simpler. The overall effect, though dignified, is unexciting. The fourth wing of the extension – backing on to and visually overpowering the diminutive University Registry – was not erected until the 1950s, in the post-Second World War period.

Pl. 66. *Glamorgan County Hall extension, by Percy Thomas, 1932; west front facing North Road.*
© Crown copyright: RCAHMW.

Queen Anne Square Colonnade

Although not part of Cathays Park as earlier defined, the Colonnade on the far side of Corbett Road deserves mention here because it not only veils the private housing beyond but it also demarcates the boundary between civic and private domains while at the same time allowing views through towards Nazareth House along the avenue originally planted by the third

Marquess of Bute. It was this avenue that was designed to visually connect Nazareth House with the remains of Greyfriars, and later formed the basis for King Edward VII Avenue and the spine of the Civic Centre's layout. The Colonnade, designed by Howard Williams comprises an elegant five-bay, classical style, freestone colonnade of coupled Tuscan columns supporting a moulded entablature together with red-brick gateways (vehicular and pedestrian) at either end (Pl. 67). The brick piers and entablature are topped by decorative urns. The Colonnade was built as part of the Queen Anne Square housing estate, dating from 1933, and planned by Williams for Mountjoy Estates Ltd, a company formed to administer the Bute estates in the Cardiff area.[11] Most of the thirty-one detached and semi-detached Neo-Georgian style, red-brick houses, laid out around a two-lane road, were not built until the 1950s. At the same time all the trees that had been previously (by 1941) removed were replaced.[12]

Welsh Government Offices One (former Welsh Board of Health)

The idea of erecting government buildings – especially those for devolution purposes – in Cathays Park has a long history. As early as 1913 the *Western Mail* had published an illustration of 'a prophetic view of Cathays Park when filled with public buildings already built, projected, or made possible by devolution'[13] (see Chapter 6). One of the buildings imagined was a Welsh Parliament built in grandiose style at the northern end of the Park, partly on the future site of the Welsh Board of Health offices. In 1916, in an unattributed article concerning the Technical College, it was claimed that 'the ultimate aim is to erect the Welsh Parliament House on the area on the north side',[14] and Purchon, in a 1923 article, included a site plan of Cathays Park with the 'proposed Parliament Buildings' spread across the full width of the northern part of the Park, from North Road to Park Place, and linked by a bridge across King Edward VII Avenue.[15] The scheme for building offices for the Welsh Insurance Commission – the first government building – was, as we have seen, aborted due to the First World War almost before it had begun. It was to be another twenty years before a new government building, this time for the Welsh Board of Health, was erected.

Designs for the new offices facing College Road were prepared by P. K. Hanton in 1934, the first sod was cut in March 1935 and the building finally opened 3 years later on St David's Day, 1938.[16] The Portland stone building, in a pared-down classical style, comprises a three-storey block with an attic floor and a concealed basement, cleverly disguised as a simple, but palatial two-storey building that provides a stylish backdrop to the gardens in front (Pl. 68). A strong, repetitive (fifteen-bay) pattern of tall windows extending vertically across the three lower floors and separated by pilaster-like piers, gives the impression – at least at a cursory glance – of a single high storey topped by a bold cornice. Above this, the setback attic floor, with its small, square windows and hipped slate roof, appears as a diminutive upper storey. Heraldic shields bearing the arms of the former counties and county boroughs of Wales decorate the bronze window panels, while above the pocket-sized main entrance is a stone carving of the Royal Coat of Arms. On plan the Welsh Board of Health is a long, slim building with the main entrance at mid point: the entrance vestibule gives on to a central spine corridor with a staircase of polished limestone opposite. There are secondary entrances and stairs (to first floor only) at each end of the building.

Pl. 68. *Welsh Board of Health (now Welsh Government Offices One), by P. K. Hanton, 1935–8: main (south) front facing College Road.*
© Crown copyright: RCAHMW.

Temple of Peace and Health

The last building to be erected before the Second World War was a gift from Lord David Davies of Llandinam (1880–1944), a veteran of the First World War, to the Welsh nation. It was intended to support the twin causes of peace and health, and is in two parts – the Temple of Peace itself and the administrative offices of two organisations. These were the King Edward VII Welsh National Memorial Association (founded by Lord Davies in 1912 to eliminate tuberculosis in Wales) and the Welsh Council of the League of Nations Union (founded in 1922). Significantly, the building was to be erected on the site that had been previously assigned for the offices of the Welsh Insurance Commissioners (see Chapter 8), the body that had been earlier responsible for arranging tuberculosis treatment in Wales. It is unclear when the idea for the project was first mooted but, as the architect, Percy Thomas, says that he had a direct commission from Lord Davies,[17] and Thomas' design for a Welsh National Memorial Building [*sic*] appeared in the *Builder* as early as January 1931,[18] it can be assumed that it probably happened sometime during 1930. It was not until 1934, however, that Lord Davies – brother of Gwendoline and Margaret Davies, the donators of an internationally famous art collection to the National Museum – covenanted £60,000 towards the cost (£72,000) of erecting the building.[19] The foundation stone was laid in April 1937, and the building was officially opened on 23 November 1938, by Mrs Minnie James of Dowlais, representing the war-bereaved mothers of Wales.[20] The timing was ironic for, as Thomas later noted, on 'the very day it was officially opened, workmen were digging air raid shelters on the adjoining land ready for the

Pl. 69. Temple of Peace and Health, by Percy Thomas, 1937–8; main (east) front facing King Edward VII Avenue.
© Crown copyright: RCAHMW.

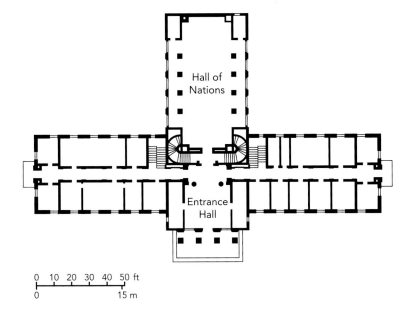

Fig. 9.2. *Temple of Peace and Health, ground floor plan. By the time that the building was constructed in 1937–8 the columns at the front and in the Temple had changed from circular to square.*

Second World War!'[21] On the demise of its original users the building became home to the Welsh Centre for International Affairs in 1973 and Public Health Wales in 2009.

One of the more interesting buildings in the Civic Centre – and certainly the most intriguing of Percy Thomas's contribution – The Temple of Peace's stark external simplicity reflects the changing mood of architecture after the First World War (Pl. 69). Unfortunately, the building has often had a bad press, its stripped-down classicism being likened to the architecture of Nazi Germany. This, however, seems to have been more to do with the inauspicious timing of its opening than of anything else. As noted above, the building, though opened in 1938, had been originally designed in 1930, 3 years before the Nazis gained power in Germany. It was during these years that Thomas was undergoing a change of heart with regard to design, as can be seen in his fine Guildhall (1930–4) at Swansea, and by the end of 1936 at the latest he had revised the Temple of Peace's exterior appearance[22] to accord more with Scandinavian Neo-Classicism – particularly the works of Asplund and Tengbom – than to any fascist rhetoric or architecture. Curiously, the central section of the main façade of the Temple of Peace bears a striking resemblance to the central part of the Eccles Building (Federal Reserve Board) in Washington, USA, opened a year earlier. However, the Eccles Building was not designed before 1935,[23] five years after Thomas's design for the Welsh National Memorial Building.

The layout is that of an elongated cross – the Temple's Hall forming the long stem, with the short, two-and-a-half storey side wings housing the administrative offices (Fig. 9.2). From the outside the contrast between the almost domestic-looking side wings, with their hipped, red-tiled roofs,

Pl. 70. *Temple of Peace and Health, low-relief sculpture 'Justice' above entrance windows.*
© Crown copyright: RCAHMW.

and the formal portico in front of a tall, boxy entrance hall could hardly be greater. The portico's four, plain and square columns reflect one of the main differences between the building as built and Thomas's 1930 scheme that had incorporated round, Ionic columns. The columns, rising from a stepped stylobate, support a plain architrave adorned with four medallions bearing the arms of England, Ireland, Scotland and Wales beneath a slab-like cornice. Behind the portico are three tall, bronze-framed windows with, above them, low relief sculptures representing Health, Justice and Peace (Pl. 70). The smooth outer walls of the entrance hall rises up to culminate in a frieze-like strip of incised squares.

After the austerity of the exterior, the interior comes as something of a surprise. First a square, low entrance hall – with walls of creamy marble and ceiling inlaid with gold rosettes along the perimeter – leading, via a short flight of steps flanked by large black marble vases, to a landing with passages on either side and the Marble Hall entrance doors in front. In the area between, curved stairs lead down to a stone-lined and vaulted Crypt that houses the Welsh Book of Remembrance bearing the names of 35,000 servicemen and women who lost their lives during the First World War. (A similar Book of Remembrance bearing the names of more than 12,000 servicemen and women killed during the Second World War is housed in the National Museum of Wales.) The walls of the Crypt are lined with shields of the thirteen old Welsh counties. The Hall of Nations, or Marble Hall as it is now known, is astonishingly rich in materials and detail, especially so if one considers that during the period when it was built southern Wales was suffering from daunting depression and devastating unemployment

(Pl. 71). The walls, broken by tall windows, are lined with creamy-grey marble symbolising peace and the floor is patterned in cream and orange Travertine. Eight great square, columns (again, round in the 1930s design) faced in ribbed black and gold marble divide the space into central nave and side aisles. Between the columns hang elegant, art-deco tubular glass light fittings. Above is a richly decorated ceiling, with geometrically patterned borders and bright green and gold coffering. While the ornate design of the Hall might seem extravagant, the effect is, all the same, remarkably effective. The Hall was originally to be known as the Hall of Nations and was intended to have a frieze between the columns and ceiling bearing the coat of arms of the various nations in the League. However, by the time that Thomas came to carry out the decorations, so many of the nations had dropped out of the League that it was decided to limit the arms to those of the British Commonwealth of Nations![24]

At the rear, almost lost between a car park and the busy North Road, is a circular Garden of Remembrance commemorating the fiftieth anniversary of the opening of the Temple of Peace and Health in 1938 and of the founding of the United Nations in 1945. Nearby on an adjoining lawn, is a distinctive memorial to the memory of victims of the Armenian genocide in 1915. The red marble stone incorporates a decorative ceramic disc and ornate cross.

Pl. 71. *Temple of Peace and Health, interior of Hall of Nations (now Marble Hall).* © Crown copyright: RCAHMW.

NOTES

1   Davies, John, *Cardiff: A Pocket Guide*, p. 117.

2   Newman, *Glamorgan*, p. 233.

3   Angela Gaffney, *Aftermath: Remembering the Great War in Wales*, p. 47.

4   Ibid., p. 51.

5   Ibid., pp. 54–5.

6   Chappell, *Cardiff's Civic Centre*, p. 27; Gaffney, *Aftermath*, p. 45.

7   Newman, *Glamorgan*, p. 233.

8   CCL: Cardiff Corporation, *Proceedings, Nov. 1928–Nov. 1929*, p. 605.

9   Information from Cardiff City Council Strategic Planning Department, 11 September 2014.

10 Chappell, *Cardiff's Civic Centre*, p. 42.

11 *Western Mail*, 1 May 1933; GA: BC/51/29154.

12 RAF aerial photograph, dated 1 March 1941.

13 *Western Mail, Industrial Supplement*, 11 June 1913.

14 *The Architectural Review*, vol. 39, May 1916, p. 105.

15 Purchon, W. S., 'The National Museum of Wales', *Architectural Review*, vol. 53, February 1923, p. 46.

16 Chappell, *Cardiff's Civic Centre*, p. 49.

17 Thomas, *Pupil to President*, p. 32.

18 *Builder*, 9 January 1931, pp. 71–3.

19 Welsh Centre for International Affairs website, *www.wcia.org.uk/history*.

20 W. R. Davies, 'Laying the Foundations', p. 15.

21 Thomas, *Pupil to President*, p. 32.

22 *Builder*, 8 January 1937, pp. 70–2.

23 Goley, Mary Anne, 'Architecture of the Eccles Building', at: *www.federalreserve.gov/generalinfo/virtualtour/architecture.cfm*.

24 Thomas, *Pupil to President*, p. 32.

10

DEVELOPMENT OF THE CIVIC CENTRE AFTER THE SECOND WORLD WAR:
BUILDINGS AND MONUMENTS

MORE THAN A DECADE was to pass after the ending of the Second World War before any further buildings were erected in Cathays Park. The immediate post-war years were, once again, to be a period of readjustment from wartime militarisation to peacetime reconstruction: lavish new public buildings were not considered to be a priority. It was during this period of recovery that the fourth Marquess of Bute died in May 1947 and his son John inherited the Glamorgan estate that, by now, had been greatly reduced to little more than Cardiff Castle and its vast park. Four months later the fifth Marquess gifted the castle and Bute Park to the people of Cardiff, thus ending nearly two centuries of the Scottish family's association with the town.

Other changes, though almost imperceptible at first, were also afoot; changes that would eventually transform Cardiff from an important provincial town to the country's centre of government. This was partly due to a gradually accumulating acknowledgement of Wales as a distinct nation with its own political existence. One aspect of this was the formal recognition, on 20 December 1955, of Cardiff as the capital of Wales, a status that would 'over the following decades … become increasingly central to [its] prosperity and identity'.[1] Nine years later the Welsh Office was established in Cardiff, and this was followed, after a referendum in 1997, by devolution for Wales,

Pl. 72. Cathays Park and the Civic Centre from the north, showing Boulevard de Nantes and termination of King Edward VII Avenue.
© Crown copyright: RCAHMW.

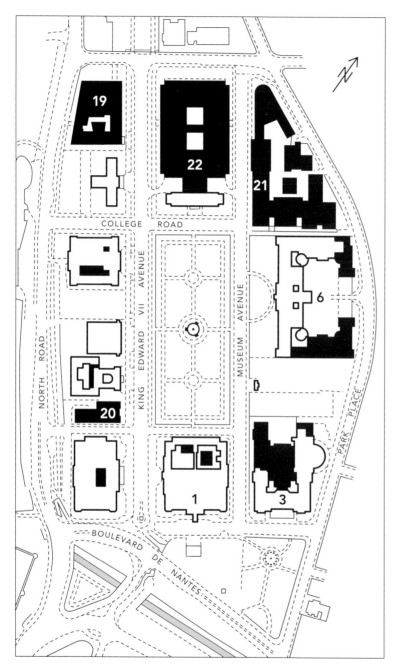

Fig. 10.1. *Development of Cathays Park since 1946. Buildings constructed since the Second World War are shown solid black. Numbers are as follows: 1, City Hall; 3, National Museum of Wales; 6, Cardiff University (main building); 19, Redwood Building; 20, Central Police Station; 21, Cardiff University Ranch Site; 22, Welsh Government Offices Two. (Based on OS map, 1969–73 and 1983–4 editions.)*

the latter helping the city 'to find a new vocation for itself in the post-coal era'.[2] During discussions dealing with the location of a home for the National Assembly of Wales, two buildings in the Civic Centre – the City Hall and the Temple of Peace – were considered as a possible base for the seat of government before it was eventually decided to erect new, purpose-made premises in Cardiff Bay.

Meanwhile, as efforts were made to complete the main building of the University College and the National Museum (see Chapter 8) and new buildings began to be erected in the Civic Centre, changes were taking place to the road layout due to re-routing of traffic following the pedestrianisation of Queen Street (Fig. 10.1). The most radical of these alterations was the replacement of the original Cathays Park Road by a new dual-carriageway (subsequently named Boulevard de Nantes) in the mid-1970s. In addition, North Road was widened and King Edward VII Avenue was terminated at its southern end with a roundabout encircling the Boer War Memorial (Pl. 72). The stopping up of the Avenue gave rise to the opportunity to redesign the area in front of the City Hall. This resulted in the enlargement of the Green Circle (already altered in the 1960s to an oval) and the coupling of it to the Gorsedd Gardens in a continuous unplanned and somewhat unsatisfactory swathe of parkland.

Redwood Building (Former New Building of Welsh College of Advanced Technology)

Pl. 73. Redwood Building, by Sir Percy Thomas & Son, 1959–60: main (east front) facing King Edward VII Avenue.
© Crown copyright: RCAHMW.

The first building to be completed in the Civic Centre after the Second World War was the New Building, in effect an extension to the old Technical College, or Welsh College of Advanced Technology as it had become known. Later, after the college had merged with Cardiff University, its name was changed to the Redwood Building after Theophilus Redwood, founding

father of the Pharmaceutical Society of Great Britain. Designed by Sir Percy Thomas & Son (the designer of the original Technical College), it was built at the end of King Edward VII Avenue, and opened in September 1960[3] (Pl. 73). As Newman has noted, 'by this time the firm had embraced modernism, though without much imagination'.[4] Revealingly, Sir Percy Thomas himself remarked that:

> I think they [Thomas's three buildings along King Edward VII Avenue] show fairly well the development of my ideas from the neo-grec of the original College, through the simplified classicism of the Temple of Peace, to the more modern treatment of … the College of Advanced Technology.[5]

Three storeys high with long rows of identical windows, almost square on plan – without any projection or indentation – and clad in Portland stone it is, apart from a large relief sculpture over the miniscule entrance, almost devoid of interest. The relief sculpture (by Bainbridge Copnall) shows an old, toga-clad man resting on a globe and a pile of books alongside figures of a younger man and woman.

Pl. 74. *Earl Lloyd George of Dwyfor (1863–1945), by Michael Rizzello, 1960.*
© Crown copyright: RCAHMW.

Statue of Earl Lloyd George

The bronze statue in the Gorsedd Gardens of David Lloyd George (1863–1945), first Earl Lloyd George of Dwyfor, by Michael Rizzello, was unveiled in July 1960. It depicts the rugged-faced, cloaked politician in defiant mood, with an arm outstretched towards the National Museum (Pl. 74). Born in Manchester, of Welsh parents, Lloyd George was brought up in Caernarfonshire before becoming a lawyer: he introduced the National Insurance Act (1911) before becoming Minister of Munitions during the First World War and then Prime Minister (1916–22).

University College – Ranch Site

With the belated completion of the main building between 1954 and 1962, further expansion of the College within the Civic Centre was confined to the old sports field, known as the Ranch Site, immediately north of Caroe's original building. As early as 1950 Sir Percy Thomas had prepared a master plan for the triangular site.[6] The design, which continued the watered-down classicism of some of Thomas's earlier buildings, took the form of a three-storey complex running along the three sides of the site with a triangular courtyard in the centre (Pl. 75). According to this scheme, there would have been slightly projecting entrance pavilions, each with a colonnaded portico, at the centre of the west and south wings and a less pronounced centre section facing Park Place. In the event only a section at the northern end was built, for the Faculty of Arts, to anything like the original concept. The high density development that followed later was entirely different, and ill at ease with everything that had gone before. Dewi-Prys Thomas rightly complained about the 'injury to the Civic Centre [by] piling on more … on the old Ranch Site with the consequent colossal pile of buildings thrusting up against the main University College building'.[7] The descriptions that follow of the Ranch Site development are in chronological order.

Law Building

This vaguely classical building by Sir Percy Thomas at the corner of Museum Avenue and Park Place was begun in 1958 for the Faculty of Arts, completed in 1962, and officially opened on February the following year (Pl. 76). Later, after reorganisation within the College, it became the Law Department. The building comprises two, three-storey wings, V-shaped on plan, with recessed attic floors. The wings meet at the northern end in a convex wall of fluted panels of Portland stone, from which arises the name 'the Bull-nose' by which the building is commonly referred to in the University. Among the fluted panels is a diminutive entrance doorway with tiny slot windows at ground level. The wings, by contrast, have continuous bands of fenestration, divided vertically by simple pilasters and horizontally by striped panels. Apparently the design needed to conform to 'city ordinances in force at the

Pl. 75. Proposed layout of new buildings for Cardiff University on the Ranch Site, by Sir Percy Thomas & Son, 1950.

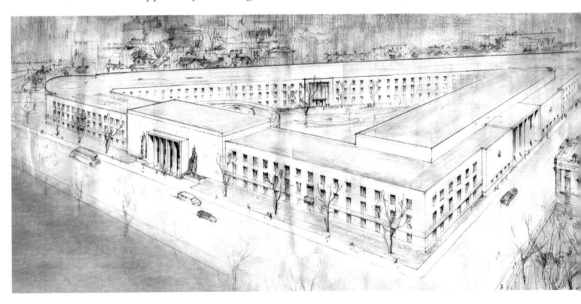

Pl. 76. *Law Building, Cardiff University, by Sir Percy Thomas & Son, 1958–62.*
© Crown copyright: RCAHMW.

time [requiring] that the building should conform to the general appearance and height of existing buildings in the Civic Centre, [so that] even the addition of a fourth floor was permitted only if it were set back from the road'.[8] A two-storey, fully-glazed extension, has since been added on the courtyard side where the two wings converge.

Sir Martin Evans Building

This, the major building on the Ranch site and built uncomfortably close to the main College building, was designed by the Percy Thomas Partnership during the late 1960s, for the Pre-Clinical Departments of the School of Medicine. It was built in three phases, the first two completed in October 1968 and third in July 1973. The building is a complex structure, imaginatively handled (Pl. 77). H-shaped on plan, it has a seven-storey centre section and four-storey wings, all constructed over an extensive, pedestrianised podium – reached by ramps – that provides cover for car parking and plant rooms. The elevations have continuous bands of windows – occasionally heightened or reduced in size to create variety – between panels of Portland stone cladding. Tall lift towers at intersections of the three wings add interest, as does the Anatomy block (facing Park Place) with its pebble-dashed walls and array of diamond shaped rooflights above the Dissecting Room. A gaudy two-storey extension in front of the centre block, designed by Rio Architects of Cardiff, was added in 2011. It is faced with multicoloured glass panels – which

does little to integrate it with other buildings of the university or the Civic Centre – and provides a new entrance and cafeteria space with a glazed honeycomb roof.

Tower Building

The Tower Building, also designed by the Percy Thomas Partnership to complement the Sir Martin Evans Building, is a case of squeezing 'a quart into a pint pot': the space on which it was built being altogether inadequate to accept such a large volume of accommodation, with the result that the skyscraper is completely at odds with the rest of the university buildings and the Civic Centre (Pl. 78). Although begun after the Sir Martin Evans Building it was completed earlier, in 1967. Built for the Faculty of Economics and Social Studies and the Department of Mathematics, it is now occupied by the Department of Psychology and by Administration. It comprises a tall, twelve-storey, 150 ft (46 m) high main block with ribbon windows and Portland stone panels, a dark grey, shaft-like lift tower and a projecting box-like lecture theatre block over a dark grey base. Later additions include an entrance canopy at the front and a three-storey extension at the rear; the ground floor cafeteria, by Powell Dobson Architects of Cardiff, was added in 1999, and the two upper floors, by the Welsh School of Architecture Project Office, in 2003. In a curious attempt to reflect the building's educational purpose, hundreds of orange-coloured ceramic discs – 'Mind's Eye', by Peter Randall-Page – were fixed to the external walls of the lecture-theatre block in 2007.

Life Sciences Building

This building facing Museum Avenue – designed by Boyes Rees Architects of Cardiff – was squeezed in between the west wing of the Sir Martin Evans Building and the Law Building in 2003 (Pl. 79). Of all buildings on the Ranch Site it is the only one, apart from the Law Building, in which the design appears to have made any concession to the earlier mood of the Civic Centre, although in this case more in spirit than any precise way. Dignified and elegant, it rises seven, fully glazed floors – with horizontal slats to deflect sunlight – between slim, bookend towers of Portland stone. In an informal nod to its classical environment it incorporates residual reminders of an entablature at the top and a (sloping) stylobate to the base.

Cubric Building

This black, two-storey glass box inserted in the courtyard area between the Sir Martin Evans Building and the Tower was, until 2016, the home of the

Pl. 77. (opposite, top)
Sir Martin Evans Building, Cardiff University, by Percy Thomas Partnership, c. 1966–73.
© Crown copyright: RCAHMW.

Pl. 78. (opposite, bottom)
Tower Building, Cardiff University, by Percy Thomas Partnership, 1966–7. The view is from the rear, showing additions by Powell Dobson Architects, 1999, and Welsh School of Architecture Project Office, 2003.
© Crown copyright: RCAHMW.

Pl. 79. (below) *Life Sciences Building, Cardiff University, by Boyes Rees Architects, 2003: main (west) front facing Museum Avenue.*
© Crown copyright: RCAHMW.

Brain Research Imaging Centre that formed part of the Psychology Department. Designed by Noel Architects of Cardiff and completed in 2006, it makes a strange contrast to the white Portland stone buildings all around it. It offers no concessions to classicism, the only articulation being narrow gaps between the sheer glass walls and the only decoration being ventilation louvres at high level, above the second floor.

Temporary Laboratories

A prefabricated building, popularly known as the 'Black Box', was erected for the University College in 1965 on the area earmarked for a future north wing of the National Museum of Wales. It was intended to provide temporary accommodation for the Chemistry and Physics departments for at least 10 years. Designed by Alex Gordon & Partners for easy assembly, the building was severely utilitarian in form and appearance and erected within 8 months.[9] At 200 ft (61 m) long by 89 ft (27 m) wide on plan, it fitted exactly over the footprint of the Museum's intended north wing. The two-storey building was clad in black and transparent glazed panels throughout, and by its extreme simplicity provided an intriguing contrast with the remainder of the Civic Centre's white buildings. When the laboratories were dismantled in the early 1990s the Museum's plans had changed and the site later became a visitor car park.

Pl. 80. Central Police Station, by John Dryburgh, 1966–8: main (east) front facing King Edward VII Avenue.
© Crown copyright: RCAHMW.

Central Police Station

The Police Headquarters, erected immediately to the north of the Law Courts in 1966–8, is outspokenly modern in its design and very much of its time. Nevertheless, it manages to blend with the classical buildings

Pl. 81. *Welsh Government Offices Two (former Crown Building), by Alex Gordon & Partners, 1976–80.* © Crown copyright: RCAHMW.

around it by virtue of its proportions, careful modelling and, of course, an extensive use of Portland stone. Designed by the city architect John Dryburgh to accommodate the police department, until then housed in the Law Courts, the building is L-shaped on plan – with one of the short ends facing King Edward VII Avenue – and five storeys high (Pl. 80). It stands on a low podium, broken by steps in front of the main entrance, and is divided into two layers, vertically. The lower two floors are set well back, as though to form a perimeter colonnade, but without the columns. Off-centre entrances with trough-like concrete canopies and a projecting Coroner's Court on the south side provide points of interest. The three floors above are cantilevered forward – the third and fourth with continuous bands of windows accented by close-set concrete mullions, and the fifth floor (containing a gymnasium and rifle range) mostly solid. The basement houses cells for detainees and car parking.

Welsh Government Offices Two

The last major building to be erected in Cathays Park was an enormous block designed by Alex Gordon & Partners, and built between 1976 and 1980 as government offices (Crown Building) at the rear of the former Welsh Board of Health (now known as Welsh Government Offices One). The city planning department had, apparently in 1968, 'expressed a preference that the site should be completed with high-rise buildings "which

Pl. 82. *Welsh Government Offices Two, interior of Entrance Hall.*

would form a backcloth to Cathays Park"'.[10] Fortunately, this proposal was not accepted by the Royal Fine Art Commission at the time, and the architects were then asked to prepare a scheme for a low-rise building. Even so, this unimaginatively named building, with five storeys above ground and a two-storey car park below, still dominates the northern end of the Civic Centre (Pl. 81). Its somewhat forbidding exterior has caused considerable criticism, so that it has been called a 'fortress in the park' and 'a perversely appropriate symbol of closed, inaccessible government'.[11]

Nevertheless, although the building may seem remote and inappropriately bulky, the designers do seem to have striven – more perhaps than with any other post-war building in the Park – to relate it to its civic surroundings. To begin with, it is a symmetrically planned building, precisely aligned on an axis running though the centres of the former Welsh Board of Health, National War Memorial and City Hall. Then there are the colonnades of tall, angular piers – apparently rising from sloping sills – that surround the building on all four sides, suggestive at least of a classical temple with columns standing on a low podium. Cantilevered forward above the colonnades, a slab-like projection (actually the fourth storey) pierced with a regular pattern of narrow windows, suggests a possible surrogate entablature. The four lower floors are all faced in Portland stone, while the setback fifth storey is clad in bronze-coloured aluminium as though part of a contrasting roof. A wide, solid-looking bridge at first floor level connects the new building to the former Welsh Board of Health. The entrance is tucked away beneath the bridge, so that it is almost hidden from the road.

Inside, the 'public' areas appear luxurious in contrast to the stern exterior. First, a spacious, two-storey entrance hall with travertine-clad walls (Pl. 82). From this an axially positioned, grand staircase, again travertine-clad, leads up to the first floor with its carpet-covered corridors. Here, the internal layout of the building becomes clearer, with the centre zone occupied by a pair of back-to-back glass-roofed atria, or garden courts, and around these the individual and open-plan offices. Each atrium is stepped vertically, gradually increasing in size with each succeeding floor.

Queen Alexandra Gardens – Monuments

During the last quarter of the twentieth century the Gardens became the favoured location in Cardiff for a variety of monuments commemorating people and events. Unfortunately, they are scattered across the Gardens in an ill-considered and uncoordinated way, the only unifying thread being a slab of crude rock as an integral part of each design. The monuments are, in the order of erection, as follows:

City of Cardiff Falklands Conflict Memorial

The earliest monument commemorates Cardiff men who were killed in action during the Falklands Conflict in 1982. It was laid out in 1983 as an informal and shady retreat, almost within the shadow of the Welsh National War Memorial. It is lined with conifers, bushes and low shrubs and is paved with flagstones (Pl. 83). At the inner end there is a large standing stone with a plaque inscribed with the names of the seven men who gave their lives. Although pleasant enough in itself, it, nonetheless, seems like a visual intrusion – a visual intervention at variance with the otherwise open and formal layout of the Gardens.

Pl. 83. *City of Cardiff Falklands Conflict Memorial, 1983, Queen Alexandra Gardens.*
© Crown copyright: RCAHMW.

Raoul Wallenberg

This is a simple affair comprising a tree and a small, pointed rock with a plaque dated 1985 commemorating the life of Raoul Wallenberg (1912–47), a Swedish diplomat who is said to have saved the lives of up to 100,000 Jews in Hungary during the Second World War. Wallenberg was arrested in 1945 and died in Russian captivity.

Spanish Civil War Memorial

A large, standing stone erected in 1992 has a plaque 'dedicated to the Welsh volunteers for Liberty who defended democracy in the Spanish Civil War 1936–1938'. On another face of the stone there is a plaque inscribed with a quotation by the Spanish Republican propagandist 'La Pasionara' and decorated with an olive branch and a dove.

Welsh National Falklands Conflict Memorial

This takes the form of a large, rectangular pedestal approached by steps on each side, and surmounted by a large rock that had been brought 8000 miles (12,800 km) from one of the battlefield sites (Pl. 84). It was erected in 2007. Each face of the pedestal has a polished, black marble insert. Two of these inserts are inscribed with a map of the Falkland Islands and a text relating to the conflict. The remaining faces are inscribed with the names of the 255 British soldiers, sailors and airmen who gave their lives during the hostilities.

Gift of Life Stone

A kind of grave-slab with, at one end, a tall boulder sliced in half. A bilingual plaque states that it was erected by the Kidney Wales Foundation in 2007, 'In remembrance of all organ and tissue donors'.

Pl. 84. *Welsh National Falklands Conflict Memorial, 2007, Queen Alexandra Gardens.*
© Crown copyright: RCAHMW.

NOTES

1   Davies, *Cardiff: A Pocket Guide*, p. 122.
2   A. Hooper and J. Punter, *Capital Cardiff 1975–2020*, p. 298.
3   Harvey, 'One Hundred Years of Technical Education in Cardiff', p. 185.
4   Newman, *Glamorgan*, p. 232.
5   Thomas, *Pupil to President*, p. 52.
6   Drawing by R. F. Buckley, Sir Percy Thomas & Son, dated April 1950.
7   Thomas, 'A Quiet Dignity …', p. 69.
8   Official Opening brochure, p. 7.
9   *Architects' Journal*, 8 February 1967, p. 372.
10 'Long Life Low Energy Loose Fit', *Building*, 13 March 1981.
11 A. Lipman, 'The fortress in the park', *Architects' Journal*, 4 June 1980.

CARDIFF'S CIVIC CENTRE
IN CONTEXT

T HE PUBLIC BUILDINGS of Cathays Park were largely constructed during the twentieth century. The ideas that shaped most of them and the Civic Centre's layout were, however, largely derived from nineteenth-century thinking. It was during the nineteenth century, too, that many formally planned groups of public buildings were erected elsewhere in Britain and on the European mainland. In order to understand how Cardiff's Civic Centre relates to these precedents, it might be useful look at some of the more interesting civic groups here and abroad.

In Britain the most comprehensive examples of early nineteenth-century urban planning had taken place in Edinburgh, London and Newcastle-upon-Tyne. Edinburgh is notable for its New Town, which had been planned by James Craig as far back as 1766, though it was not completed until 1820.[1] The scheme comprised five long, parallel streets – with squares at either end of the broad, central street – and a grid of rectangular blocks in between. Development was slow, and it was not until the 1780s that an attempt was made to impose some uniformity by limiting the height of the principal streets to three storeys and others to two storeys;[2] later still, in 1791, Robert Adam was commissioned to design Charlotte Square at the western end. A church was intended to terminate the vista at each end, but only St George's (by Robert Reid), facing Charlotte Square, was built in 1811–14. The success of the New Town led to further extensions in similar grand style to the north (1802 onwards) and to the west (1808 onwards).[3]

Glasgow should also be mentioned here, for its George Square development appears, at first, to be equally promising. Appearances, however, can be deceptive for the Square began life as part of an unimaginative grid of streets, and it was not until the 1820s that it was fully developed with Georgian town-houses and hotels. Later, after the opening of a railway station on its northern side in 1842, George Square became a centre for mercantile activity and home for the Chambers of Commerce (1874), the General Post Office (1878), and the ornate City Chambers (1888).

In London the most far-reaching example of integrated planning was John Nash's scheme to link Regent's Park with the centre by a processional way, via Regent Street, Piccadilly Circus, Waterloo Place and The Mall.[4] It was built from 1811 onwards with extensive blocks of stuccoed three- and four-storey terraces on three sides of the park and along the connecting streets. Sometimes the buildings were embellished with giant Ionic columns as on the palatial Cumberland Terrace. Nash's terraces were in Regency style that, like the forms adopted in Edinburgh's New Town, was based on classical prototypes.

Newcastle's Grainger Town, built between 1834 and 1839 by the builder–developer Richard Grainger (aided by various architects), was different to the above in that it mixed commercial development with housing. It 'brought a new sophistication to the town, and a classical grandeur combined with Picturesque planning influenced by Nash's London developments'.[5] The scheme comprised a series of streets built in freestone with ashlar façades

– again in classical style, this time Greek Revival – near the town centre, and included a theatre, many shops and a market. At the centre, Grey Street, a gently curving thoroughfare sweeping down a slight hill, was said to be 'a finer piece of urbanism than Nash's Regent Street'.[6]

While enlightened, the above examples were, at least when first built, mainly exercises in residential planning. In fact, apart from a lone example from Devon, little effort was made during the early nineteenth century to organise public buildings into civic groups. However, at Devonport, now a suburb of Plymouth, John Foulston was responsible for a colourful grouping that included an austere Guildhall (1821) with a bold Greek Doric portico, an Egyptian-style Institution (1823) and a Greek Doric commemorative column (1824).[7] The Guildhall was on an island site at the end of a street lined with classical terraces, with the Institution, column and a couple of chapels (one designed in exotic 'Hindoo' style) assembled on the north side. Although on paper the group appears organised, on site it looked curiously lopsided and eclectic (and even more so since the 1960s when the classical terraces were replaced by unsympathetic flats).

One might have expected to find an attempt at civic grouping in some of the planned industrial towns that arose in the nineteenth century, but being tied towns they had, by their very nature, little need for public buildings. At Tredegar (laid out between 1800 and 1820), for instance, the only public building was the market hall (1811), which fronted a circular piazza or market place at the junction of four cross-roads.[8] Saltaire, in Yorkshire, built 50 years later (1853–75), was an exception to the trend and a brave attempt at both social and town planning. It was the result of a philanthropic approach to the welfare of the inhabitants who worked in the mills that dominated the town. Public buildings were introduced gradually, and 'in most cases followed the chronological development of the street plan'[9] (Fig. 11.1). The earliest were two chapels, followed by the works' school in 1867 and a large, imposing Institute in 1869. The building of these symmetrically planned buildings, which faced each other across an open square bisected by the main road leading to the gigantic mills, 'reinforced the presence of formal, axial planning for this part of the village'.[10]

These were relatively small-scale developments. For larger groups of public buildings it is necessary to go to Birmingham or Liverpool, though in neither case does it appear that the layout was planned from the outset. In Birmingham, a memorable collection of public buildings gradually developed around the Town Hall that had been largely built between 1832 and 1834 following a competition won by Joseph Hansom and Edward Welch.[11] For more than 20 years the Town Hall remained in isolation until a number of other public buildings – Midland Institute (1855), Central Free Library (1864–65; rebuilt 1882 after a fire), Council House (1874–85), Mason College (1875), and City Museum and Art

Fig. 11.1. *Plan of Saltaire, c.1910. Public buildings are shown in black. The two central buildings on either side of the central street are the Institute (right) and the Work's School (left); the other buildings are Nonconformist chapels. (Based on OS map, 1908 edition.)*

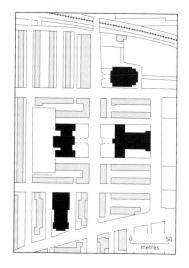

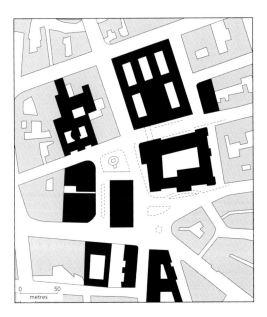

Fig. 11.2. (above) *Plan of central Birmingham, c.1914. In the centre is the Chamberlain Memorial, and below that the rectangular Town Hall. Surrounding these are the Council House, Corporation Art Gallery, Central Free Library, University and College buildings and the main Post Office. (Based on OS map, 1912 edition.)*

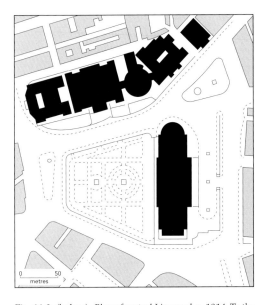

Fig. 11.3. (below) *Plan of central Liverpool, c. 1914. To the right of St John's Garden is the bulky mass of St. George's Hall. To the north, from left to right, are the Technical School, Free Library and Museum, Walker Art Gallery and Sessions House. (Based on OS map, 1908 edition.)*

Gallery (1880s) – were erected nearby (Fig. 11.2). All of these buildings were to take account of the Town Hall's classical design in the architectural treatment of their elevations, so that there was a unity of expression if not in layout. By 1914 a School of Art, government offices and a main Post Office had been added to the group. The Library, Institute and Mason College were subsequently demolished in redevelopment after the Second World War.

Liverpool has been more fortunate in retaining its own impressive group of public buildings (Fig. 11.3). This notable collection began with the erection, between 1841 and 1856, of the immense St George's Hall at the top of a sloping site next to St John's Church and its triangular cemetery. At the time the cemetery was still surrounded by terrace housing and commercial properties, including Lime Street Station. Later, the properties in William Brown Street were demolished and a noble line of neo-classical buildings – Library and Museum (1860); Art Gallery (1877); Reading Room (1879); Sessions House (1882) – erected in their place. Later still, in 1898, the church was demolished and the cemetery landscaped to create a kind of (Roman) 'forum' partly surrounded by public buildings.[12] Together, St George's Hall and the William Brown Street buildings form a majestic assemblage. Yet, for all that, the group remains unbalanced, suggesting that it came into being more by opportunistic circumstances than as the result of visionary planning.

At much the same time as St George's Hall was being built a bold scheme for public buildings was being planned in London following the advice of Prince Albert. Here, in South Kensington, a large area of land was purchased with profits from the 1851 Great Exhibition to erect a group of educational and cultural buildings. A number of schematic plans were drawn up for what was to become known as 'Albertopolis', including one prepared by C. R. Cockerell at the Prince's request. Ultimately the simplistic layout that was finally used appears to have been based on a sketch made by the Prince himself.[13] For many years the central area was occupied by the Royal Horticultural Society Garden (opened in 1861) that the Prince hoped would eventually 'form … the inner court of a vast quadrangle of public buildings'.[14] An International Exhibition was held in 1862 in a purpose-made building immediately south of the gardens. Later, the Albert Hall was erected (1867–71) at the northern end of the site, and the exhibition building was demolished to make way for the Natural History Museum (1873–81). Later still, the Horticultural Garden was closed

Fig. 11.4. *Plan of 'Albertopolis', South Kensington, London, c.1914. At approximately 53 acres (21 hectares) in extent the site is slightly smaller than Cathays Park. The Albert Memorial and Royal Albert Hall are at the top of the plan and the Natural History Museum at the bottom, with the Imperial Institute and the Royal College of Science in between. (Based on OS map, 1916 edition.)*

and virtually all vestiges of the Prince's vision of a central garden surrounded by public buildings was lost as various educational, cultural and domestic buildings were erected on the site.

According to John Physick and Michael Darby, 'the disintegration of the Kensington estate began in 1886', when 'a large plot of land … north of the just completed Natural History Museum was selected for the Imperial Institute … thus effectively to destroy the north-south axis upon which the estate had developed'[15] (Fig. 11.4). Visually the buildings – mostly designed in a Neo-Renaissance manner, or 'Mid-Victorian eclecticism'[16] – blended well together, though built in a variety of materials (red brick, buff and yellow terracotta, white Portland stone). However, by 1914 – with buildings crammed uncomfortably together into a confined area – there was little open space left for greenery. By now Cardiff's Civic Centre was beginning to surpass Albertopolis, both in its architecture and as an exemplar of the Prince's visionary idea. The overcrowded situation at South Kensington was made still worse by later developments which included the Science Museum (1913–28) and 'mediocre Modernistic boxes'[17] that were erected in the 1950s to replace the Imperial Institute.

While there were relatively few examples of good urban planning in Victorian Britain there was no lack of large civic buildings. This was especially the case with town halls that represented not only 'a place's political development' but also symbolised `the vigour, and spirit, of a place' and its 'cultural aspirations, wealth and self-worth'.[18] Both Birmingham's Town Hall and Liverpool's St George's Hall stand out as striking mid-nineteenth century examples of Neo-Classical architecture. Hansom and Welch's Town Hall in Birmingham – in fact, a large hall for concerts and public meetings – was modelled on a Roman temple and encircled by giant Corinthian columns raised on a high podium (Pl. 85). The original plan by H. L. Elmes for Liverpool's St George's Hall was for two separate structures, with one containing a concert hall and the other the law courts. This was then revised to combine hall and courts in a single, grandiose building enveloped with porticoes screened by giant Corinthian columns. The Town Hall (1853–8) in Leeds, though less austere than the two already noted, is also primarily a public hall and is again encircled by giant Corinthian columns and pilasters, and has a tall tower topped by a dome. Public buildings were invariably erected as one-off ventures rather than components of a pre-planned group, although later there were occasional attempts to form civic groups by assembling additional public buildings close to an existing one. Tellingly, Ian Morley – in his survey of 125 civic buildings built in Britain between 1880 and 1914 – was only able to find one scheme, that of the City Hall and Law Courts in Cardiff, that included more than one building in a single project.[19]

Following the success of the new Houses of Parliament in London, which had been built (1837–67) in Perpendicular Gothic style, there was a return to Gothicism for the architecture of many public buildings. Indeed, from the

Pl. 85. *Birmingham Town Hall, by J. Hansom & E. Welch, 1832–34.*

1860s onwards 'Gothic town halls outnumbered classical'.[20] Of these, the most outstanding was that built at Manchester (1868–77). An article in the *Builder* in 1878 even suggested 'that Gothic is more suitable than Classical for a building with a multiplicity of functions'.[21] Another well-known example of a Neo-Gothic public building was the Law Courts, London, erected in 1874–82. As the nineteenth century wore on the 'battle' between classical and Gothic architecture became less pronounced and gradually freer styles began to appear. One example of this more relaxed attitude is Sheffield's Town Hall (1890–7), which was built in Free Renaissance, a style ultimately derived from classical architecture. Though the building combined English, French and Flemish details, the final result, with its tall tower, gables and spiky pinnacles looks almost more Gothic than classical.

Towards the end of the nineteenth century the exuberant Neo-Baroque style, again derived from classical architecture, came into vogue, first with the Battersea Town Hall (1891–3), followed by the Dock Office (1897–1900), Barry (Pl. 86), and Colchester Town Hall (1898–1902). These were colourful buildings with white Portland stone podiums and bright red brick upper floors enlivened by Portland stone columns, pilasters and curved, segmental pediments. They were showy, flamboyant structures, to say the least, and the style soon became neglected in favour of something less ostentatious and more in accord with the kind of Baroque favoured in mainland Europe. This

Pl. 86. *Dock Office, Barry, by Arthur E. Bell, 1897–1900, with statue of David Davies, founder of the Barry Docks, in front.*

was especially the case in Cardiff, where the Beaux-Arts inspired designs for the Town Hall (later City Hall) and Law Courts introduced a nobler and more assured version of classical architecture. According to C. H. Reilly, Professor of Architecture at Liverpool University, 'Every student was full of it. When the building [City Hall] was finished in 1905, everyone who could afford it flocked to Cardiff and came back enthralled.'[22] Together, the two white edifices 'set a pattern which was widely imitated in public buildings up to the First World War'.[23]

Individually, the buildings of Cathays Park may not be internationally groundbreaking in terms of originality and design. Nevertheless, as a collection of fine public buildings in a park-like setting, they are outstanding and quite without equal in Britain.

While the arrangement of Cathays Park in its final form appears to have been at least partly fortuitous, there had been European precursors for planned, formal layouts. Indeed, when Edwin Seward gave his address on 'The Architectural Growth of Cities, and the Future of Cardiff' in 1894, he argued that authorities on the Continent often 'had a high appreciation of the beautiful in architecture' and that their towns were therefore worth looking at.[24] During the first half of the 19th-century public buildings were occasionally planned around a square, 'the most distinct element of the urban structure [and] the most easily imageable', according to Christian Norberg-Schulz.[25] 'The square,' he goes on, 'is determined by … the buildings [which] should form a continuity *around* the space.' One of the earliest examples of such a formally planned group of public buildings was at Karlsruhe, the newly founded capital of the Grand Duchy of Baden (Fig. 11.5). Here Friedrich Weinbrenner planned a radial town with its main axial road leading to the palace. The Marktplatz at the centre of the town, and on the main axis, is a double piazza. The larger piazza, where the markets are held, was surrounded by three-storey houses and had a plain pyramidical monument in the centre.[26] On the lesser piazza the classical porticoes of the church (1807–16) and city hall (1804–24) face each other across a narrower space.

More sophisticated in its regularity and elegance, was the Königsplatz in Munich, capital of Bavaria (Fig. 11.6). The square here was laid out with free-standing buildings on three sides. Two of the buildings – the Glyptothek, a sculpture museum (by L. von Kenze, 1816–30), and the Antikensammlungen, a picture gallery (by G. F. Ziebland, 1838–42) – face each other on opposite sides of the square. Almost identical in shape and size – one with Ionic columns, the other with Corinthian columns – each stands as a solitary Greek Revival cube surrounded by greenery.[27] The square itself is broken up by a regular series of grassed parterres and divided symmetrically by an axial boulevard, closed at one end by an imposing gateway (also by von Kenze, 1862) that was inspired by the Propylaea of the Acropolis at Athens.

Similar in scale and grandeur, but less clinical, is an early example from Finland where in 1812, 3 years after the country had become an autonomous Grand Duchy, Helsinki was made the new capital. A few years later a splendid town plan consistent with the town's raised status was drawn up by Johan Ehrenstrom. Integral to his plan was Senate Square, which was intended as 'a symbolic centre for the whole Grand Duchy, with all the major institutions arranged around it in accordance with a precise classical hierarchy'[28] (Fig. 11.7). Although Ehrenstrom had planned the square with surrounding buildings to be 'erected in a noble style, with the Lutheran Church on the high terrace',[29] it was to be a German architect, Carl

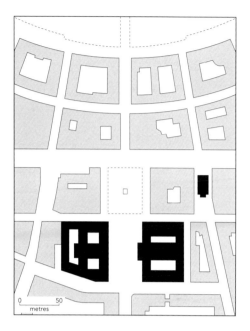

Fig. 11.5. *Plan of Marktplatz, Karlsruhe, Germany The church (right) and city hall (left) face each other across the lesser square.*

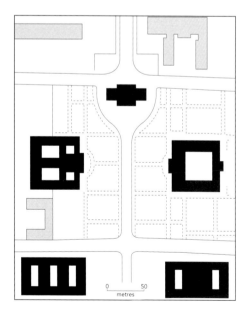

Fig. 11.6. *Plan of Konigsplatz Quarter, Munich, Germany. The Glyptothek (right) and the Antikkensmmlugen (left) face each other across formal gardens with triumphal gateway to the north.*

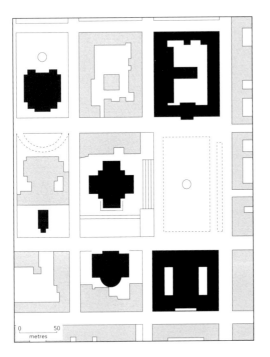

Fig. 11.7. Plan of Senate Square, Helsinki, Finland. The cruciform Lutheran cathedral is in the centre, facing the square, with university buildings at the bottom and state buildings at the top.

Ludwig Engel, who designed the buildings around the square. These were the Senate (1820–2) on the east side, the University (1828–32) and University Library (1836–40) on the west side and the tall, green-domed Lutheran cathedral (1830–52) raised high above a monumental flight of steps on the northern side. The overall effect is stunning, making it 'one of the great set-pieces of European neo-classicism'[30] (Pl. 87). A similar kind of public group around a rectangular piazza was planned for Oslo, Norway, by Hans D. F. Linstow in 1835.[31] The piazza was to constructed on both sides of the main thorough-fare (Karl John Gate) leading up to the Royal Palace with the University on the north side and the Stort-ing (parliament) on the south side. Unfortunately, only the University (with two side wings) was built (1840–52) according to the plan.

Finland and Norway would have seemed faraway and off the beaten track to most educated people in Britain during the nineteenth century, and therefore of little architectural consequence. France and Austria, on the other hand, were nearer, and the architectural development of their capital cities was therefore of greater influence. Seward had referred, in his 1894 lecture, to 'the recent improvements of Paris and Vienna', probably with Haussmann's boulevards and Förster's Ringstrasse in mind. Georges-Eugene Haussmann was respon-sible for dramatically remodelling much of Paris on Beaux-Arts lines between 1854 and 1870 with grand boulevards lined with unified façades. The wide, new streets, often cutting through existing development, created major axes across the city with squares or traffic circles at intersections. The project was, more than anything, a planning exercise that resulted in elegant, but dense, blocks of development. Later, parks and green spaces were added and trees planted along the avenues. The overall transformation was on an enormous scale and 'it exerted tremendous influence, throughout Europe and beyond, on the development of major cities'.[32]

Ludwig von Förster's prize-winning Ringstrasse development in Vienna was equally influential but in quite a different form. Here a grand, sem-icircular, tree-lined boulevard, two and a half miles (4 km) long by 185 ft (57 m) wide, was laid out on the site of the city's fortifications and protec-tive banks between 1858 and 1865. The Ringstrasse formed a garland around the old town, with parks and public buildings placed at irregular intervals along either side of the boulevard like bright jewels on a green necklace. Many of the public buildings (mostly built in the 1870s) were erected inde-pendently; others were arranged in formal groups around parks, such as the Fine Arts Museum and Natural History Museum facing each other across

Pl. 87. Senate Square, Helsinki, designed by Johan Ehrenstrom, 1812–17, with Lutheran cathedral (1830–52), left, and Senate (1820–2), right, by Carl ludwig Engel.

the Maria-Theresien-Platz.[33] However, 'the grandest assembly [of public buildings in late nineteenth-century Europe], and the most incongruous,' according to Nikolaus Pevsner,[34] surrounds the Rathaus Park where a Greek Revival Parliament, a stylised, symmetrical Gothic Rathaus (City Hall), and a late Renaissance – almost Neo-Baroque – National Theatre and University occupy four separate sides of an extensive open space (Fig. 11.8). Incongruous they may be, but the spaciousness of the park and its abundant trees and greenery goes far to alleviate the uneasy clash of architectural styles.

One last European example should be noted, as outwardly at least it has certain similarities to Cathays Park in its size and Beaux-Arts design. This is the Jubilee Park in Brussels, first constructed under the patronage of King Leopold II for the 1880 National Exhibition to commemorate the 50th anniversary of Belgian independence. Here, a 74-acre (30-hectare) park was laid out on the site of a military training ground and a row of temporary, glass-fronted exhibition pavilions erected across the eastern end. The site was then used for the 1897 International Fair, after which the pavilions were gradually replaced by a permanent U-shaped complex of Neo-Baroque museum buildings (c.1890–1910) connected at the centre by a triumphal arch (1904–5). Most of the site, however, is given over to open parkland.

Fig. 11.8. *Plan of Rathauspark on the Ringstrasse, Vienna, Austria. Located around the central park are the Parliament (bottom), Rathaus (left), University (top) and Burgtheater (right).*

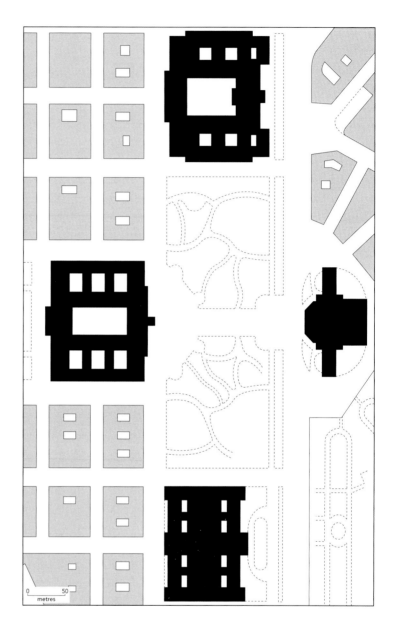

Each of the Continental examples that have been mentioned had the benefit, at least in the early stages, of Royal patronage. In Cardiff the nearest thing to such a patron was the third Marquess of Bute, a Scottish aristocrat who not only extended, reconstructed and restored the castle but also laid down conditions that were to greatly influence the layout of the Civic Centre in Cathays Park. Fortuitously, the layout of the Civic Centre bears more than a slight resemblance to Helsinki's Senate Square and to parts of Vienna's Ringstrasse. More than either of these projects, however, Cardiff's venture in architectural town-planning is, or appears to be, reminiscent of what was taking place in the United States of America at about the same time. Here, there had been a profound change in architectural and town planning attitudes, a change that was reflected in an unexpected return to classicism.

The change began with the 15th World's Fair, held in Chicago in 1893 to commemorate the 400th anniversary of Columbus' 'discovery' of America. The main site, Jackson Park on the shore of Lake Michigan, was planned by Daniel Burnham on a vast scale and generally along Beaux-Arts lines, with landscape and lakes laid out by Frederick Olmsted and numerous buildings designed by different architects. Between the two main entrances (one for visitors entering by rail and another for visitors coming across the lake by boat) was a large piazza, or Court of Honor, at the end of a formal lagoon flanked by a collection of monumental, neo-classical pavilions. A further group of pavilions was arranged more informally around a second, irregularly shaped and more picturesque lake. Nearly all of the buildings in the Fair were temporary structures constructed with steel or timber frames and clad in a mixture of plaster, cement and jute fibre. They were painted white, so that the Fair became known as the White City. The only permanent structure was Charles Atwood's Palace of Fine Arts, an imposing building with a large dome rising behind a central portico and long side-wings adorned with multitudes of Ionic columns. Despite the temporary nature of its buildings, the Fair was, according to Hitchcock, 'the most complete new urbanistic concept to be realized since the replanning of Paris and Vienna'.[35] Giedion, on the other hand, disparagingly called it 'the beginning of "mercantile classicism"', referring to 'the influence of its plaster architecture [as being] widespread and tenacious'.[36] Nevertheless, the *Western Mail* editor, Lascelles Carr, had been impressed and wrote admiringly of it (see Chapter 4). So too had many architects and planners, for with its integrated design of landscape and buildings the Fair seemed to provide a vision of what might be possible.

Soon, the Chicago Fair became the inspiration for the City Beautiful movement, which began as a response to overcrowding in the tenement areas of large towns in the United States. While many reformers concentrated on improving sanitary conditions, the leaders of the City Beautiful movement were more interested in creating beautiful cities that followed Beaux-Arts ideas, believing that this would lead to the sweeping away of social ills and inspire moral and civic virtue.

The first large-scale attempt to incorporate the movement's ideals was incorporated in the McMillan Plan (1901) for Washington, which aimed to redesign the monumental core of the capital. Although Peter Price had enthusiastically commented on the 'beautifully laid out' city on his visit in 1884 (see Chapter 4) the 'grand avenue' that Charles L'Enfant had envisioned in 1791 in his scheme for the city was, in reality, a disorderly mixture of uses that included naturalistic parks, botanical greenhouses and a railway station with rail tracks crossing from one side to the other. The McMillan Plan included a proposal to extend the grand avenue as far as the George Washington statue.

It also envisioned reconstructing the National Mall, as it came to be called, with a central expanse of grass 300 ft (91 m) wide by 1.2 miles (1.8 km) long lined on either side with four rows of elms and beyond those groups of classically designed buildings. It was to provide a monumental, dignified and symbolic setting for government buildings, museums and national memorials as well as being a stage for national events and public gatherings free from commercial advertising. The plan was largely carried out – with museums built mostly during the 1930s – in what Pevsner unflatteringly called 'Washingtonian Classical Re-Revival',[37] though not finally complete until the 1970s.

Richard Fellows, in his book *Edwardian Architecture*, refers to Cathays Park as 'in some ways like a miniature Washington'.[38] This is certainly true in respect to some of the founders' aims for architectural dignity and civic identity, as well as in the Park's overall layout and the developers' old-fashioned perseverance with historic architectural styles. Washington's National Mall was, of course, built on a much grander and more elaborate scale. But that should not diminish the importance of Cardiff's Civic Centre. After all, William Harpur's 1899 development plan designating a 'grand avenue' and specific sites for specific buildings, and the architectural competition that followed for the design of the [then] Town Hall and Law Courts, had already preceded Washington's McMillan Plan by more than two years!

More importantly, Cardiff's Civic Centre can be seen not only as the result of an increasing awareness of developments elsewhere but also as the consequence of a growing cultural and patriotic movement in Wales, a movement that had been set alight in the 1880s by the *Cymru Fydd* ('Young Wales') crusade and continued until the First World War. As an indirect response to that remarkable Welsh flowering of artistic endeavour – made up of works by architects, artists, sculptors, writers and musicians, and a growing affirmation of national identity by the public – the Civic Centre in Cathays Park represents a most impressive cultural and creative achievement.

NOTES

1   J. Gifford *et al.*, *The Buildings of Scotland: Edinburgh*, pp. 271–333.

2   C. and R. Bell, *City Fathers*, pp. 101–3.

3   Gifford *et al.*, *Edinburgh*, pp. 335–54, 358–83.

4   H. R. Hitchcock, *Architecture: Nineteenth and Twentieth Centuries*, pp. 102–6.

5   J. Grundy *et al.*, *The Buildings of England: Northumberland*, p. 107.

6   Hitchcock, *Architecture: Nineteenth and Twentieth Centuries*, p. 111.

7   Bridget Cherry and Niklaus Pevsner, *The Buildings of England: Devon*, pp. 675–6.

8   John B. Hilling, 'The Development of Tredegar, 1800–1820', *Gwent Local History*, 94 (2003), pp. 62–7.

9   N. Jackson *et al.*, *Saltaire*, pp. 39–40.

10 Ibid., p. 98.

11 Anthony Peers, 'The Pride of Birmingham and an Ornament to England', *Transactions of the Ancient Monuments Society*, vol. 58, pp. 9–27.

12 R. Dixon and S. Muthesius, *Victorian Architecture*, p. 172.

13 E. H. W. Sheppard (gen. ed.), *Survey of London*, vol. 38: *South Kensington Museums Area*, p. 55.

14 Ibid., p. 56.

15 John Physick and Michael Darby, *Marble Halls: Drawings and Models for Victorian Secular Buildings*, p. 197.

16 Dixon and Muthesius, *Victorian Architecture*, p. 172.

17 Gavin Stamp, 'What Did We Do for the Victorians?' in *Victorians Revealed*, p. 9.

18 Morley, 'Representing a City and Nation', p. 64.

19 Ibid., p. 69.

20 Cunningham, C., *Victorian and Edwardian Town Halls*, p. 132.

21 Quoted by Dixon and Muthesius, in *Victorian Architecture*, p. 168.

22 C. H. Reilly, *Representative British Architects of the Present Day*, p. 119.

23 David Watkin, *A History of Western Architecture*, p. 558.

24 *Western Mail*, 21 February 1894.

25 Christian Norberg-Schulz, *Existence, Space and Architecture*, pp. 84–5.

26 Hitchcock, *Architecture: Nineteenth and Twentieth Centuries*, pp. 43–4.

27 Ibid., pp. 51–2.

28 Riita Nikula, *Wood, Stone and Steel*, p. 65.

29 Nils Erik Wickberg, *The Senate Square, Helsinki*, p. 122.

30 Watkin, *Western Architecture*, p. 432.

31 Marian C. Donnelly, *Architecture in the Scandinavian Countries*, pp. 206–7.

32 Watkin, *Western Architecture*, p. 391.

33 Hitchcock, *Architecture: Nineteenth and Twentieth Centuries*, pp. 214–16.

34 Pevsner, *An Outline of European Architecture*, p. 214.

35 Hitchcock, *Architecture: Nineteenth and Twentieth Centuries*, p. 323.

36 Sigfried Giedion, *Space, Time and Architecture*, p. 273.

37 Niklaus Pevsner, *A History of Building Types*, p. 134.

38 Fellows, *Edwardian Architecture*, p. 88.

12

CONCLUSION

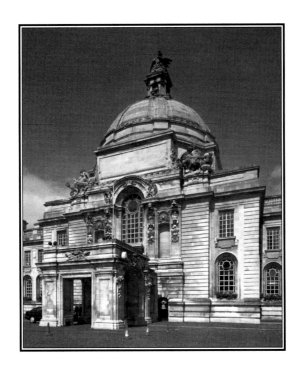

IN DRAWING TO A CLOSE this history of Cathays Park and its evolution from waste land to iconic Civic Centre, it is the intention here to draw attention to some aspects of its development not considered elsewhere. These include a quick look at attitudes to the Civic Centre as built, an enquiry as to whether the hopes of its originators have been realised, and a brief examination of the state of the Civic Centre as it is today.

The history of the area known as Cathays Park covers two, more or less equal, periods. The first of these, lasting from about 1790 to 1898, was that of a gentleman's private park that had been established by the fabulously rich Bute family. The second period, from 1898 to the present, saw the area develop in an entirely different way to become a national Civic Centre, full of white buildings. Despite an intrinsic disparity between the two periods, there is an ongoing, physical link, namely a splendid avenue of trees. It is to this avenue that the third Marquess of Bute's thoughts were directed when he made his final visit to Cardiff. Bute had met up with Andrew Pettigrew, his head gardener, and, as they strolled together through the Castle grounds and into Cathays Park and along the avenue that Pettigrew had planted for him in 1879–80, the Marquess pointed to the trees and said,'There, Pettigrew, there's something that will stand as our monument, yours and mine for many generations after we have departed.'[1] And 115 years later, the avenue still survives – at least in substance, if not with all of its original trees – as King Edward VII Avenue.

Architectural attitudes to the Civic Centre have varied over the years. Edgar Chappell noted in 1946 that'Cardiff is renowned throughout the world for its fine assemblage of public buildings … grouped together on a single well-planned site.'[2] He, being local, was naturally biased in favour. John Newman, a respected architectural historian with no reason to be partisan, writing in 1995, called Cathays Park'the finest civic centre in the British Isles'.[3] Most people would, I think, agree with this sentiment. Ian Nairn, on the other hand, likened the Civic Centre to'a stone zoo, one weary neo-Classical hulk after another, lumped together on a regular grid … an utterly alien model for urban improvement'.[4] Harsh words, indeed! But then Nairn was, in the series of articles for *The Listener* in which the above comment first appeared in 1964, desperately seeking out what he called'proper modern architecture'in British towns. Clearly, Cathays Park was not the obvious place to look for futuristic, technologically advanced buildings.

These opposing views raise the question of what should a Civic Centre look like. Ought a Civic Centre be a realisation of a single vision with every building in the same architectural style? Or ought each building bear witness to its own individual purpose and its designer's preference? There is no indisputable answer, but much must depend on the size of the overall project (if, indeed, it be a single, planned scheme) and the length of time taken to construct it. Bearing in mind the extensive nature of Cardiff's Civic Centre and the fact that its twenty or so buildings were brought about by at least eight different agencies over a period of more than a century, it would be foolish to expect all parts to have materialised from the same or similar mould. At the same time, would a Civic Centre in which every building was different in style, form and materials, and ignored its neighbours and setting, have made much sense?

As it happens, the Civic Centre, which is the subject of this book, has avoided both of these extremes. Instead it is an amalgam of different buildings whose overt individuality has been largely kept in check by three overriding factors. These factors, or constraints, can be summarised as:

1. The employment of architectural styles loosely based on Classical precedents.
2. The use of a single material, Portland stone, to face elevations.
3. The close relationship of each building to the regular framework of roads that form the site's infrastructure.

Within these constraints the buildings are varied – with a lessening of detail as one proceeds 'in time' from south to north through the Park – yet still (for the most part) have a sense of belonging to the overall scheme of things. A colourful landscape of trees and other planting provides a soft background that adds a cohesive element to the whole. As a complete, or near complete (for who can know the future?) collection of public buildings within an organised landscape, Cathays Park is without doubt exceptional.

How, then, does the Civic Centre live up to its founders' aspirations? To answer this question it is necessary to refer to the ambitions of some of the original enthusiasts, Peter Price, Lascelles Carr and Edwin Seward. Price, an early advocate of building in Cathays Park, and Carr, a later convert, had both been impressed by architectural schemes they had seen in North America and both wished to see similar ventures in Cardiff. Furthermore, Price had, as far back as 1892, suggested grouping public buildings 'around a central park', and, a year later, Carr had argued for Cardiff's public buildings to be 'placed on a worthy site, dignified in design, ample in extent, and creditable in execution'. Seward had been impressed, in his 1894 lecture on the future of Cardiff, by what was taking place in Paris and Vienna and, as well as recommending similar wide new thoroughfares and open spaces embellished with fountains and statues for Cardiff, had suggested Cathays Park as a possible location for 'the town's institutions now seeking homes'. To a large extent all of these wishes were incorporated in the subsequent development of the Park.

Another person who had high hopes for the future of Cathays Park was the third Marquess of Bute. Having invested heavily in its landscaping, Bute was keen – once the park was to be acquired for public buildings – to ensure that as much as possible of the landscaping be retained for the benefit of all, and it is for this reason that he laid down stringent conditions before selling the land to the corporation. Fortunately, for today's users these conditions have been generally complied with, with the result that the great avenue has survived, the Friary and Gorsedd Gardens remain as green oases, and commercialism (apart from the annual 'Winter Wonderland') is noticeable by its absence.

And what of the expectations of the town's councillors? Evidently, from what has been noted in earlier chapters, they also had high hopes – hopes national in scale and of the highest artistic standards. These hopes, too, have been achieved in large measure. For instance, five buildings, or groups of buildings, in the Park are of national status: National Museum of Wales, University of Wales Registry, Temple of Peace and Health, Welsh National War Memorial, and the Welsh Government Offices. In addition a number of the statues in the Park can be considered as of national importance. As for artistic standards, the very fact that the designers of many of the buildings in the Park were chosen by way of architectural competition surely indicates a desire on the part of their proponents to use the best talent available. This way of thinking resulted in a number of excellent buildings that received wide acclaim at the time when they were constructed.

Taking into consideration the above observations, I think it is safe to say that generally speaking the Civic Centre has been a success and that it has, in contrast to London's 'Albertopolis' in South Kensington, largely validated its founders' original aspirations. Indeed, one can go further and argue – along the lines of UNESCO's criteria for heritage listing – that Cardiff's Civic Centre is 'an outstanding example of an architectural ensemble which illustrates a significant stage in [Welsh] history'.

Finally, what of the situation today? Is all well, apart from the interminable rows of cars that line the avenues, or are there environmental matters that need to be taken in hand? Unfortunately, the answer has to be a negative one for in truth the late twentieth century and the early twenty-first century have not been kind to Cathays Park. This is perhaps surprising as the Park has enjoyed 'conservation area' status since 1975 and all of its buildings are listed, apart from those built since the Second World War.

Despite the Park's conservation area status, many trees are missing or have been replaced with inappropriate species – such as at the northern end of King Edward VII Avenue – while paving materials have been allowed to deteriorate or be replaced with unsuitable substitutes. In addition, there has been loss of original features (such as at the Gorsedd Circle), an unsightly paraphernalia of alien objects has appeared on roofs, and memorials have been erected in an uncoordinated way. To this list could be added the questionable layout of the space in front of the City Hall as a grassed area together with its utilisation each winter as a fairground, resulting in a visual blight for more than 4 months each year.

In fairness, it should be pointed out that a forward-looking *Appraisal* of the Cathays Park Conservation Area was published (on the Web) by the City Council in 2009. However, despite a positive proposal 'to prepare and implement a restoration and development plan for Cathays Park … in line with the Parks Partnership Programme',[5] there has been little sign of progress on the ground since then.

All of this suggests that a new, updated conservation plan is needed for the Civic Centre, and one that carries with it sufficient authority and power to enforce its recommendations. Only in this way can Cardiff's remarkable Civic Centre receive the care it deserves and thus justify the vision of its founders. More than that, it would be some recognition of the debt we owe to those who laboured so painfully in the nearby Valleys to dig out the 'black gold' that produced the wealth needed to create the Civic Centre.

NOTES

1   CCL: Pettigrew, *Public Parks of Cardiff*, vol. 2.
2   Chappell, *Cardiff's Civic Centre*, p. xiii.
3   Newman, *Buildings of Wales: Glamorgan*, p. 220.
4   Ian Nairn, *Britain's Changing Towns*, p. 139.
5   City of Cardiff Council, *Conservation Area Appraisals*, p. 28.

Brief Biographies
of Architects

Allison, Sir Richard John (1869–1958): Born in London, of Scottish descent, Allison entered H. M. Office of Works, London, in 1889, becoming Assistant Architect in 1901, Architect in 1911 and Principal Architect in 1914. He was responsible for the Science Museum, London (1919–28), and ambassadors' residences in Stockholm (1915) and Tokyo (1928). Allison was knighted in 1927.

Boyes Rees Architects: Architectural practice established in 1961, with offices in Cardiff and London.

Brewer, Cecil Claude: See under **Smith, Arnold Dunbar**.

Caroe, William Douglas (1857–1938): The son of a Danish consul, Caroe was born in Liverpool and educated at Ruabon and Cambridge. After working with J. H. Christian and later with Herbert Passmore he founded his own practice, which was mainly concerned with ecclesiastical buildings and their conservation. Caroe was also responsible for a number of country houses and some educational buildings. The practice was continued by his son **Alban Caroe** (1904–91).

Comper, Sir John Ninian (1864–1960): Comper was born in Aberdeen. After moving to London, he was taken into partnership with William Bucknall from 1888 to 1905. He was one of the last of the great Gothic Revival architects and his practice was mostly of an ecclesiastical nature, covering new buildings, restoration and church furnishings, much of it in Scotland. Comper was knighted in 1950.

Dryburgh, John (1918–91): Born in Berwick-upon-Tweed, Dryburgh worked in Coventry, Liverpool, Portsmouth and Swansea before becoming Cardiff's first City Architect from 1956 to 1974. He was responsible for the design of the Empire Swimming Pool in the 1950s (since demolished), as well as carrying out a large programme of local authority housing and school building in the city.

Gordon, Sir Alex (1917–99): Gordon was born in Ayr, Scotland, and moved to Wales in 1925 to work in Swansea. He became a partner with T. Alwyn Lloyd (q.v.) in 1946 and, on the latter's death in 1960, established the practice of Alex Gordon and Partners, with offices in Cardiff and London. He became President of the RIBA in 1971, and was knighted in 1988.

Hanton, Peter Kydd (1884–1963): Hanton was a Scottish architect. After working in Edinburgh for a brief period he moved to London in 1905. He joined H. M. Office of Works in 1909, and was promoted to Senior Architect in 1920.

Harris, E. Vincent (1876–1971): Harris set up in practice with Thomas A. Moodie (1874–1948) after winning the Glamorgan County Hall competition in 1908. The practice was, however, short-lived for, apart from designing Cardiff's now demolished Central Fire Station (1910), in Westgate Street, work ran out and the practice was dissolved in 1913. Later, Harris won a number of important competitions and became an established architect of public buildings. He was awarded the RIBA Royal Gold Medal in 1951.

Lanchester, Henry Vaughan (1863–1953): The son of an architect, Lanchester was born in London. In 1896 he formed a partnership with James Stewart and Edwin Rickards, with the express purpose of entering competitions, of which the Cardiff Town Hall and Law Courts was their first major success in 1897. After the deaths of Stewart and Rickards, Lanchester was joined by G. Lucas and T. A. Lodge. He was a founder member of the Town Planning Institute, became editor of the *Builder* and was awarded the RIBA's Royal Gold Medal in 1934.

Lloyd, Thomas Alwyn (1881–1960): Lloyd, who was born in Liverpool, worked with Raymond Unwin on Hampstead Garden Suburb before becoming architect to the Welsh Town Planning and Housing Trust. Later, Lloyd set up an architectural practice in Cardiff, planned a number of garden village developments in Wales, and wrote *Planning in Town and Country* (1935), and, with Herbert Jackson, *South Wales Outline Plan* (1947). He became President of the Royal Town Planning Institute in 1933.

Moodie, Thomas A.: See under **Harris, E. Vincent**.

Noel Architects: Architectural practice established *c*.1990, with office in Cardiff.

Powell Dobson: Architectural practice established in 1966, with offices in Cardiff, London and Swansea.

Price, Peter (1825–92): Price was born in Builth. He became a master builder before joining his brother-in-law, W. P. James, in Cardiff in the early 1850s. Price was responsible for the Royal Arcade, Cardiff, in 1858. The partnership was dissolved in 1867 and Price began practising as an architect. Price's designs included a board school in Roath (1882) and David Morgan's shop in the Hayes (1891).

Rickards, Edwin Alfred (1872–1920): Born in London, he was one of the original partners of the firm Lanchester, Stewart and Rickards. He was a brilliant draughtsman with a flair for Baroque detailing.

Rio Architects: Architectural practice established *c.*2008, with office in Cardiff.

Seward, Edwin (1853–1924): Seward, who was a native of Yeovil, came to Cardiff at the age of 16. He joined Walter Parry James & George Thomas in 1875, and helped to make the firm (James, Seward and Thomas) one of Cardiff's leading architectural practices. Seward was responsible for many local buildings, including the Free Library, the Royal Infirmary (1883), the Coal & Shipping Exchange (1888 and 1912), and Turner House, Penarth (1888).

Smith, Arnold Dunbar (1866–1933): Smith joined Cecil Claude Brewer (1871–1918) in partnership in 1895 and together they won the competition for the Passmore Edwards Settlement, London, the following year. With their National Museum of Wales competition entry in 1910 they effectively became pioneers of a revival of Neo-Classicism in Britain, following an earlier return to classicism in the USA. One of their best-known buildings was Heal's shop (1916), Tottenham Court Road, London.

Stewart, James A. (1865–1904): Born in Scotland, he was one of the original partners in the firm Lanchester, Stewart and Rickards. Although he was involved in the design of the Cardiff Town Hall and Law Courts he withdrew from the practice in 1901.

Thomas, Sir Percy Edward (1883–1969): Thomas, the son of a sea captain from Narberth, worked in various offices before winning the Cardiff Technical College competition and setting up in practice with Ivor Jones. This was the beginning of a practice that eventually became the largest in Wales and included civic buildings in Bristol, Cardiff and Swansea as well as many university buildings. Twice elected president of the Royal Institution of British Architects, Thomas was awarded their Royal Gold Medal in 1939, and was knighted in 1946.

Williams, Howard (1892–1964): Williams was born in Cardiff, and became responsible for the design of a chain of cinemas between the wars in Wales and the West of England. His most influential client was the fourth Marquess of Bute who commissioned him to carry out extensive works in the Cardiff area as well as at Rothesay, Scotland.

Wills, Herbert W. (1864–1937): Wills began in practice with a Mr Hannaford, Swansea, about 1892. A brother-in-law of J. Viriamu Jones, Principal of the University College of South Wales and Monmouthshire, Wills was chosen as architect for Aberdare Hall, Cardiff, in 1893. He was also architect for Swansea's unsuccessful bid for the University of Wales' Registry in 1896. In 1900 Wills moved to London to join John Anderson, and was editor of the *Builder* from 1913 to 1918.

Architectural Glossary

The following is not a full glossary of architectural terms but, rather, provides brief definitions of some of the terms found in the main text.

Arcade: A line of arches supported by columns or piers.

Architrave: The lowest part of an **Entablature**, or the decorated frame of a door or window.

Ashlar: Masonry using large blocks of regularly faced stone with thin pointing in between.

Attic storey: A small top storey built above the main façade and often set back.

Baroque: Decorative style of 17th and early 18th century, derived from **Classical** architecture of the **Renaissance**.

Beaux-Arts: Decorative style associated with the Ecole des Beaux Arts in Paris, marked by axial planning and grandiose use of the **Orders**.

Capital: The top part or head of a column belonging to one of the **Orders**.

Classical: In architecture a term used for the buildings of Ancient Greece and Rome largely based on the use of **Orders** or columns with fixed proportions and elements.

Coffer: Decorative sunken panel in ceiling, dome or **Vault**; **Coffering**, an arrangement of the same.

Colonnade: A line of columns supporting, without arches, an **Entablature**, lintels or upper structure.

Colonnette: A small column.

Composite (Order): One of the **Classical Orders**, characterised by a **Capital** which combines **Corinthian** foliage and Ionic volutes.

Corinthian (Order): One of the **Classical Orders**, characterised by an elaborate **Capital** decorated with formalised leaf ornament.

Cornice: The projecting, uppermost part of an **Entablature**.

Cupola: A small dome crowning a larger dome, or **Turret**.

Dentil: A small, square block arranged at closely spaced intervals on the lower side of a **Cornice**.

Doric (Order): One of the **Classical Orders**, with a simple round **Capital**.

Entablature: In Classical architecture the assemblage of horizontal parts, comprising **Architrave**, **Frieze** and **Cornice**, carried on a wall or columns.

Freestone: A softish stone that can be readily cut in all directions.

Frieze: A horizontal band forming the middle section of an **Entablature**; alternatively a horizontal band of decoration.

Georgian: A **Classically** based style from 1714 to 1830.

Gothic: A medieval style of building, characterised by the use of pointed arches and vaulting.

Gothic Revival: A conscious movement to use Gothic forms, particularly for religious and educational buildings, during the 18th and 19th centuries

Greek Revival: A conscious movement from the mid-18th century onwards to use ancient Greek forms and motifs.

Ionic (Order): One of the **Classical Orders**, characterised by the use of inward curling **Volutes** on the **Capital**.

Jacobean: A style belonging to early 17th century England and Wales, in essence a mixture of styles with densely applied **Classical** ornament and traces of Perpendicular Gothic.

Loggia: A space or gallery open to one side, often with the roof on the open side supported by free-standing columns.

Neo-Baroque: A revival of the **Baroque** style, particularly in early 20th century Britain; also known as Edwardian Baroque.

Neo-Classicism: A conscious return during the late 18th and early 19th centuries to a purer imitation of the ancient architecture of Greece and Rome.

Orders: Different versions of the column and **Entablature** (or post and lintel) system of **Classical** architecture. The main Greek orders are **Corinthian**, **Doric** and **Ionic**, to which were added the Roman **Tuscan** and **Composite** orders. Different types of orders can be seen in the colonnaded porticoes of the National Museum (**Doric**) and the former Glamorgan County Hall (**Corinthian**).

Pediment: A triangular gable to the roof ends of **Classical** temples; on a smaller scale, they are often used above door and window openings.

Piano Nobile: The principal floor in a **Classical** building, above the ground floor or basement.

Picturesque: The aesthetic quality defined as between the 'sublime' and the 'beautiful', and characterised in architecture and landscape by irregular forms and textures. It formed the basis of the Picturesque Movement, which arose in the Welsh Marches and Wales at the end of the 18th century.

Pilaster: A flat column against a wall, sometimes quasi-structural, sometimes purely ornamental.

Podium: A continuous raised platform on which stands a building.

Porte-cochère: A porch large enough to allow wheeled vehicles to enter.

Portico: A projecting porch – usually in front of an entrance – with its roof supported by columns.

Quoin: An external corner of a building, or part of building, often using dressed stones to emphasise the corner.

Regency: A term used for late **Georgian** architecture at the beginning of the 19th century.

Renaissance: A style based on the revival of **Classical** architecture, beginning in Italy during the 15th century and spreading further afield during the 16th and 17th centuries.

Rock-faced: Masonry struck to produce a rough, natural surface.

Rustication: Masonry treated with deep, recessed joints or chamfered or decorative quoin-stones to produce an exaggerated effect of strength.

Stylobate: The steps to a raised platform under a **Colonnade**.

Terracotta: Hard, unglazed clay tiles

Turret: A small tower usually forming part of a larger structure.

Tuscan (Order): One of the **Classical Orders**, derived from an ancient type of Roman (Etruscan) temple and similar to the **Doric** order.

Vault: An arched (usually stone) ceiling or roof.

Venetian Window: A three-light window with a taller, arched central light flanked by lower, flat-headed lights.

Volute: A spiral scroll.

Bibliography

Archives

Aberystwyth: National Library of Wales (NLW)
1. Undated [*c*.1820s] and unsigned map of area between Crockherbtown and Blackweir, Cardiff, showing proposed canal and roads. [Bute A24]

Cardiff: Cardiff Central Library (CCL)
1. Cardiff Corporation, *Proceedings of the Council and of the Several Committees of the Council*, various annual volumes.
2. Cardiff Corporation, *Cathays Park: Conditions as to Grants of Land*, dated 1 Aug. 1901 [Q948.2(543)CAR].
3. Cardiff Corporation, *Cardiff New Town Hall and Law Courts: Conditions and Instructions for Competing Architects and Epitome of Requirements with Plan of Site, 14 August, 1897* [948.2(628)CAR].
4. *Cardiff Corporation Bill, 1898: Statement as to the Principal Objects of the Proposed Bill for the Information of Owners and Ratepayers* [948.2(566)CAR].
5. Pettigrew, A. A., *The Public Parks and Recreation Grounds of Cardiff*, 5 typescript volumes, Cardiff, 1929.
6. The Bute Collection, Box XI.
7. *Tithe Apportionment Award, St John's Parish, Cardiff, 1844.*
8. Undated 25 inch to mile map of Cardiff, *c*.1851, based on a survey by Ordnance Survey.
9. Waring, Thomas, *Map of Cardiff and District*, 1869.

Cardiff: Glamorgan Archives (formerly Glamorgan Record Office) (GA)
1. Stewart, David, *Atlas and terrier of the Bute estate, 1824* [D/DB].
2. Case of Edwin Seward *v.* Corporation of Cardiff, 1919-11 (documents relating to proposed Welsh National Museum in Park Place, Cardiff, in 3 parts) [BC/C/43].
3. Glamorgan County Council, County Hall/Buildings, 1896–1897 [GD/C/BU/4].

4.   Glamorgan County Council, *Proposed New County Hall and Offices at Cardiff – Conditions and Instructions for Competing Architects* (Cardiff, 1908).

Cardiff: National Museum of Wales (NMW)
1.   Bassett, Douglas A., 'National Museum of Wales: A Historical Checklist or Inventory', unpublished paper, *c*.1980.
2.   Minutes of General Purposes & Building Committee.
3.   Minutes of National Museum of Wales Council, 1907 to 1909.
4.   Stock Book of the Cardiff Museum and Art Gallery.

Official Documents

Cadw, *Register of Landscaped, Parks and Gardens of Special Historic Interest, Part 1: Parks and Gardens: Glamorgan* (Cardiff, 2000).
Cardiff City Council, *Cardiff City Centre Conservation Area Appraisals*, 2009.
Cardiff Corporation Act, 1898 (61 and 62 Vict. c. CXXVIII.), London, 1898.
Ordnance Survey, 1 inch to a mile map, sheet 36, dated 1833; 25 inches to a mile County Series' maps dated, 1880–82, 1901, 1920 and 1941–42; 1:1,250 scale National Grid maps dated 1952–54, 1962–66, 1983–84 and 1992–94.

Books, Journals and Pamphlets

Anon., 'Cardiff', *Picture Post*, 18 March 1939, pp. 21–9.
Anon., *Illustrated Guide to Cardiff* (1882).
Architectural Design & Construction, 'Architecture of State: The Welsh Board of Health, Cardiff', January 1940, pp. 8–9.
Architects' Journal, The, 'Temporary Laboratories at Cardiff', 8 February 1967, pp. 367–71.
Architectural Review, The, 'Cardiff City Hall and Law Courts', vol. 20, November 1906, pp. 233–64.
Architectural Review, The, 'The Glamorgan County Hall', vol. 32, December 1912, pp. 343–51.
Architectural Review, The, 'Cardiff Technical College', vol. 39, May 1916, pp. 105–10.
Atkins, T., *A Catalogue of Household Furniture, Fixtures and Other Effects … Which Will Be Sold by Auction, on the Premises, at Cathayes, Near Cardiff, Glamorganshire, on Wednesday, the 30th Day of June, 1824.*
Axon, Mary, 'Mr McConnochie's House, Cardiff.' in J. M. Crook (ed.), *The Strange Genius of William Burges, Art-Architect, 1827–1881* (Cardiff, 1981).
Barrie, D. S. M., *The Taff Vale Railway* (Headington, 1962).

Bassett, Douglas A., *The Making of a National Museum*, Parts I, II, III and IV, reprinted by Gee & Son (Denbigh) Ltd., 1982, 1983, 1984, and 1992 from articles originally published in *The Transactions of the Honourable Society of Cymmrodorion.*

Bassett, Douglas A., 'Wales in Miniature', special issue of *Amgueddfa*, Autumn 1993, pp. 3–35.

Bell, C., & R., *City Fathers: The Early History of Town Planning in Britain* (London, 1969).

British Competitions, 'Glamorgan County Council Hall at Cardiff', No. 21 [vol. II, Part 9], 1909, pp. 269–310, Academy Architecture (London, 1909).

British Competitions, 'National Museum of Wales', No. 34/35 [Vol. III, Part 10/11], 1910, pp. 265–80, Academy Architecture (London, 1910).

Builder, 'Competitions: University College, Cardiff', vol. 85, October 1903, p. 358.

Builder, 'University of Wales Registry', vol. 96, 27 February 1909, pp. 248–9

Builder, 'Proposed Welsh National Memorial Buildings, Cardiff', 9 January, 1931, pp. 71–3.

Builder, 'Temple of Peace Building Now Being Erected', 8 January 1937, pp. 70–2.

Building, 'Police Headquarters, Cardiff', 15 November1968, pp. 135–7.

Building, 'Long Life Low Energy Loose Fit', 13 March 1981, pp. 39–46.

Cardiff City Council, *Illustrated Catalogue of Welsh Historical Sculpture Presented to the City of Cardiff by the Rt. Hon. Lord Rhondda of Llanwern, M.A. 27th October, 1916* (Cardiff, nd., *c*.1916).

Cardiff Corporation, *Cardiff 1889–1974: the story of the county borough* (Cardiff, 1974).

Cardiff Corporation, *Pettigrews: the family who created Cardiff's parks* (Cardiff, *c*.2006).

Carr, Lascelles, *Yankee Land and the Yankees* (Cardiff, 1893).

Carter, Harold, *The Towns of Wales* (Cardiff, 1965).

Chapman, John, *A Guide to Parliamentary Enclosures in Wales* (Cardiff, 1992).

Chappell, Edgar L., *History of the Port of Cardiff* (Cardiff, 1939; 2nd edn, 1994).

Chappell, Edgar L., *Cardiff's Civic Centre: A Historical Guide* (Cardiff , 1946).

Cherry, Bridget and Pevsner, Nikolaus, *The Buildings of England: Devon* (London, 1989).

Collett, John Kyte, *New Municipal Buildings for Cardiff, a Fresh Scheme by Mr J K Collett: How the Town May Secure Half a Million* (Cardiff, 1897).

Colvin, Howard, *A Biographical Dictionary of British Architects 1600–1840* (London, 1978).

Cronin, Revd J. M., *Cardiff Grey Friars* (Cardiff, 2nd edn 1928).

Crook, J. Mordaunt (ed.), *The Strange Genius of William Burges, 'Art-Architect', 1827–1881. A Catalogue to a Centenary Exhibition* (Cardiff, 1981).

Crook, J. Mordaunt, *William Burges and the High Victorian Dream* (London, 2nd edn, 2013).

Cunningham, Colin, *Victorian and Edwardian Town Halls* (London, 1981).

Daunton, M. J., *Coal Metropolis: Cardiff 1870–1914* (Leicester, 1977).

Daunton, M. J., 'Coal to Capital: Cardiff since 1839', *Glamorgan County History*, vol. VI (1988), pp. 203–23.

Davies, John, *Cardiff and the Marquesses of Bute* (Cardiff, 1981).

Davies, John, *Cardiff: A Pocket Guide* (Cardiff, 2002).

Davies, Wayne K. D., 'Towns and Villages', in David Thomas (ed.), *Wales: A New Study* (Newton Abbot, 1977).

Davies, W. R., 'Laying the Foundations: The Contribution of Lord Davies of Llandinam', in *The United Nations at Fifty: The Welsh Contribution* (Cardiff, 1995).

Dixon, R. & Muthesius, S., *Victorian Architecture* (London, 1978).

Donnelly, Marian C., *Architecture in the Scandinavian Countries* (Cambridge, Mass., 1992).

Edwards, E. W., 'Cardiff Becomes a City', *Morgannwg*, ix (1965).

Evans, M. and Fairclough, O., *The National Museum of Wales: A Companion Guide to the National Art Gallery* (Cardiff and London, 1993).

Fellows, Richard, *Edwardian Architecture: Style and Technology* (London, 1995).

Fishlock, Trevor, *A Gift of Sunlight* (Llandysul, 2014).

Frampton, Kenneth, *Modern Architecture: A Critical History* (London, 4th edn, 2007).

Freeman, J. M., *W. D. Caroe: His Architectural Achievements* (Manchester, 1990).

Gaffney, Angela, *Aftermath: Remembering the Great War in Wales* (Cardiff, 1998).

Geddes, Patrick, *Cities in Evolution: An Introduction to the Town Planning Movement and the Study of Civics* (London, 1915).

Giedion, S., *Space, Time and Architecture* (London, 3rd edn, 1954).

Gifford, J., McWilliam, C. and Walker, D., *The Buildings of Scotland: Edinburgh* (London, 1984).

Gilpin, William, *Observations on the River Wye and Several Parts of South Wales, etc. Made in the Summer of the Year 1770* (rev. copy of 5th edn, 1800) (London, 2005).

Gladwin, D. D. and J. M., *The Canals of the Welsh Valleys and Their Tramroads* (Headington, 1991).

Gorst, Thom, 'Crown Offices, Cardiff', in *The Buildings Around Us*, pp. 143–6 (London, 1995).

Gradidge, R., 'Tour of Cardiff Civic Centre' (unpublished lecture notes for Victorian Society Meeting, Penarth, 1969).

Gray, A. Stuart, *Edwardian Architecture: a Biographical Dictionary* (London, 1985).

Green, Simon, *Dumfries House*, RCAHMS (Edinburgh, 2014).

Grundy, J., McCombie, G., Ryder, P., Welfare, H. and Pevsner, N., *The Buildings of England: Northumberland*, London, 1992 (repr. 1999).

Guest, Revel and John, Angela V., *Lady Charlotte Guest: An Extraordinary Life* (Stroud, 2nd edn, 2007).

Hannah, Rosemary, *The Grand Designer: Third Marquess of Bute* (Edinburgh, 2012).

Harding, Joan N. (ed.), *Aberdare Hall, 1885–1985* (Cardiff, 1986).

Harvey, A., 'One Hundred Years of Technical Education in Cardiff', *Glamorgan Historian*, vol. 9, pp. 173–90 (Barry, 1973).

Hilling, John B., *Cardiff and the Valleys: Architecture and Townscape* (London, 1973).

Hilling, John B., *Plans and Prospects: Architecture in Wales 1780–1914* (Cardiff, 1975).

Hilling, J. B., 'The Development of Tredegar, 1800–1820', *Gwent Local History*, 94 (2003), pp. 55–76.

Hitchcock, H. R., *Architecture: Nineteenth and Twentieth Centuries* (London, 3rd edn, 1969).

Hooper, A. and Punter, J., *Capital Cardiff 1975–2020* (Cardiff, 2006).

Ince, Laurence, *The South Wales Iron Industry 1750–1885* (Birmingham, 1993).

Jackson, N., Lintonbon, J. and Staples, B., *Saltaire* (Reading, 2010).

James, B. Ll., *A Bibliography of the History of Cardiff, Survey of Cardiff Occasional Paper No. 1* (Cardiff, 1989).

Jones, Gwyn & Quinn, Michael (eds), *Fountains of Praise: University College, Cardiff, 1883–1983* (Cardiff, 1983).

Jones, Stephen K., *Brunel in South Wales*, Volume 1 (Stroud, 2005).

Jones, Thomas, *Rhymney Memories* (Llandysul, centenary edn 1970).

Kidner, R. W., *The Rhymney Railway* (Oxford, 1995).

Lee, Brian, *Cardiff Remembered* (Stroud, 1997).

Lipman, Alan, 'The Fortress in the Park', *The Architect's Journal*, 4 June 1980.

Lloyd, Sir John Edward and Jenkins, R. T., *The Dictionary of Welsh Biography down to 1940* (London, 1959).

Lord, Peter, *The Visual Culture of Wales: Imaging the Nation* (Cardiff, 1998, 2000).

Lord, Peter, *The Visual Culture of Wales: Industrial Society* (Cardiff, 1998).

Malkin, B. H., *The Scenery, Antiquities, and Biography of South Wales* (London, 1804).

Matthews, J. H. (ed.), *Cardiff Records*, 6 vols (Cardiff, 1898–1911).

McLees, David, *Castell Coch* (Cardiff, 2005).

Mason, Rhiannon, 'Representing the Nation', in *Myths, Memories and Futures: The National Library and the National Museum in the Story of Wales* (Cardiff, 2007).

Miles, Dillwyn, *The Royal National Eisteddfod of Wales* (Swansea, 1978).

Morgan, Dennis, *Memories of Cardiff's Past* (Derby, 2006).

Morley, Ian, 'Representing a City and Nation: Wales's matchless Civic Centre', *Welsh History Review*, XXIV, 3 (2009), pp. 56–81.

Morris, J. H. and Williams, L. J., *The South Wales Coal Industry 1841–1875* (Cardiff, 1958).

Nairn, Ian, *Britain's Changing Towns,* BBC (London, 1967).

National Museum of Wales, *An Illustrated Guide* (Cardiff, 1948).

Newman, John, *The Buildings of Wales: Glamorgan* (London, 1995).

Nikula, Riita, *Wood, Stone and Steel: Contours of Finnish Architecture* (Helsinki, 2005).

Norberg-Schulz, *Christian, Existence, Space and Architecture* (London, 1971).

Paterson, D. R., *Early Cardiff – A Short Account of Its Street-names and Surrounding Place-names* (Exeter, 1926).

Pearson, Fiona, *Goscombe John at the National Museum of Wales* (Cardiff, 1979).

Peers, Anthony, 'The Pride of Birmingham and an Ornament to England', *Transactions of the Ancient Monument Society,* Vol. 58 (2014), pp. 9–27.

Perkins, John W., *The Building Stones of Cardiff – Geological Trail Guides* (Cardiff, 1984).

Pevsner, Nikolaus, *An Outline of European Architecture* (London, 7th edn, 1963).

Pevsner, Nikolaus, *A History of Building Types* (London, 1976).

Pevsner, Nikolaus, *Pioneers of Modern Design* (originally *Pioneers of the Modern Movement*) (New Haven and London, 4th edn, 2005).

Physick, John, and Darby, Michael, *Marble Halls: Drawings and Models for Victorian Secular Buildings* (Victoria and Albert Museum exhibition catalogue) (London, 1973).

Price, Peter, 'Notes of a Trip to Canada and the United States with the British Association in 1884', *Cardiff Naturalists' Society Report and Transactions*, vol. XVII (1895), pp. 35–48.

Purchon, W. S., 'The Public Buildings of Cardiff', *RIBA Journal,* vol. 29 (1922), no. 13, pp. 385–95.

Purchon, W. S., 'The National Museum of Wales', *The Architectural Review*, vol. 53, February 1923, pp. 45–51.

RCAHMW, *Glamorgan*, vol. IV, Part 1: *The Greater Houses* (Cardiff, 1981).

Rees, D. Morgan, *Mines, Mills and Furnaces* (London, 1969).

Rees, William, *Cardiff – A History of the City* (Cardiff, 2nd edn, 1969).

Reilly, C. H., *Representative British Architects of the Present Day* (London, 1931).

Rowson, S. and Wright, I. L., *The Glamorganshire & Aberdare Canals*, vol. 1 (Lydney, 2001), vol. 2 (Lydney, 2004).

Seward, Edwin, *The Architectural Growth of Cities and the Future of Cardiff – Presidential Address to the Cardiff, South Wales and Monmouthshire Architects' Society*, reprinted from *Western Mail*, Cardiff, 21, 22, 23 February 1894.

Sheppard, F. H. W. (gen. ed.), *Survey of London*: vol. 38: *South Kensington Museums Area* (London, 1975).

Speed, John, *The Theatre of Great Britain, Part II: The Principality of Wales* (London, 1676).

Stamp, Gavin, 'What Did We Do for the Victorians?', in *Victorians Revealed* (Studies in Victorian Architecture and Design, vol. 2), Victorian Society (London, 2010).

Summerson, John, *The Classical Language of Architecture* (London, 1980).

Thomas, Dewi-Prys, 'A Quiet Dignity… – William Douglas Caroe and the Visual Presence', in Jones and Quinn (eds), *Fountains of Praise: University College, Cardiff, 1883–1983*, pp. 53–71.

Thomas, Hilary M., *A Catalogue of Glamorgan Estate Maps* (Cardiff, 1992).

Thomas, Hilary M. (ed.), *Diaries of John Bird, Clerk to the Frst Marquess of Bute 1790–1803* (Cardiff, 1987).

Thomas, Sir Percy, *Pupil to President: Memoirs of an Architect* (Leigh-on-Sea, 1963).

Trow, A. H. and Brown, D. J. A., *A Short History of the College, 1883 to 1933* (Cardiff, 1933).

Turner & Sons, Ltd., *Superb Buildings, Erected by E. Turner and Sons, Ltd Builders and Contractors* (London, 1929).

University College of South Wales and Monmouthshire, *New Buildings – Explanatory Statements by the Competing Architects Regarding the Plans Forwarded by Them* (Cardiff, August 1903).

University College of South Wales and Monmouthshire, *New College Fund – Statement and Appeal* (Cardiff, May 1905).

Vining, Jonathan, *Cathays Park: A Landscape Analysis of Cardiff's Civic Centre*, Welsh School of Architecture (unpublished thesis) (Cardiff, 1983).

Wakelin, P. and Griffiths, R. A., *Hidden Histories: Discovering the Heritage of Wales*, RCAHMW (Aberystwyth, 2008).

Wales and the Marches Catholic History Society, *The Early History of Nazareth House, Cardiff* (Cardiff, 2005).

Walker, Diane A., *A Guide to the Parish Church of St Margaret, Roath* (Cardiff, nd).

Warren, John, 'Edwin Alfred Rickards', in Alastair Service (ed.), *Edwardian Architecture and Its Origins* (London, 1975).

Watkin, David, *English Architecture: A Concise History* (London, 1979).

Watkin, David, *A History of Western Architecture* (London, 1986).

Wickberg, Nils Erik, *The Senate Square, Helsinki* (Rungsted Kyst, Denmark, 1981).

Williams, Matthew, '"A most magnificent House near Cardiff": The mystery of Cathays Park', in *Friends* [of National Museum of Wales] *Newsletter and Magazine*, Aug. 2002 [unpaginated].

Williams, Moelwyn I., 'Cardiff – Its People and Its Trade, 1600–1720', *Morgannwg*, vol. 7 (1963).

Wilson, John, 'The Chicago of Wales: Cardiff in the Nineteenth Century', in *Planet* 115 (Aberystwyth, 1996).

Wilson, John R., *Memorializing History: Public Sculpture in Industrial South Wales*, The University of Wales Centre for Advanced Welsh and Celtic Studies' Research Paper no. 5 (Aberystwyth, 1996).

Winks, Revd W. E., *Cardiff Exhibition, 1896 – Illustrated Official Guide to the Town and Exhibition* (Cardiff, 1896).

Yates, George, *A Map of the County of Glamorgan; From an Actual Survey* (London, 1799). (Facsimile edn, South Wales Record Society and Glamorgan Archive Service, Cardiff, 1984).

Websites

British History Online: *www.british-history-ac.uk/catalogue*

Cardiff County Council – Public Art Register: *www.cardiff.gov.uk/publicart*

Cardiff Parks: *cardiffparks.org.uk/cathays/info/index.shtml*

19th Century British Newspapers: *www.bl.uk/reshelp/findhelprestype/news*

RIBA Library: *www.architecture.com/RIBA/Visitus/Library*

Welsh Newspapers Online: *welshnewspapers.llgc.org.uk/en/home*

City Beautiful Movement: *en.wikipedia.org/wiki/City_Beautiful_movement; xroads.virginia.edu/~CAP/CITYBEAUTIFUL/*

Index

Abercynon 8, 9, 14
Aberdare 6, 8, 14, Fig. 2.1
Aberdare Hall 45, 53, 94, Fig. 3.4, Pl. 16
Aberystwyth 81
'Albertopolis' *see* London, South
    Kensington
architects
    Allison, Sir Richard John 136, 193,
        Pl. 60
    Anderson, Sir Rowand 117
    Boyes Rees Architects 163, 193, Pl. 79
    Brewer, Cecil Claude 128, 130, 193
    Burges, William 38, 39, 40, 41, 146,
        Pls. 12, 13, 14
    Caroe, Alban 121, 193
    Caroe, William Douglas 117, 119,
        193
    Collett, John Kyte 70, Pl. 21
    Comper, Sir John Ninian 98, 144,
        145, 193, Pl. 63
    Corbett, E. W. M. 42, 60
    Dryburgh, John 165, 193, Pl. 80
    Fowler, C. B. 43
    Frame, William 45
    Gordon, Sir Alex 194
    Gordon, Alex & Partners 164
    Gordon, Alex, Partnership 134
    Grant, J. P. 44
    Hanton, Peter Kydd 149, 194, Pl. 68
    Harris, E. Vincent 124, 125, 126, 194,
        Pl. 50
    Hughes Harold 114
    James, Seward & Thomas 22
    Jones, Horace 16, Pl. 8
    Jones, Ivor 134
    Jones, Ivor, & Percy Thomas 135,
        147
    Jones, J. P., Richards & Budgen 68
    Kempson & Fowler 44

Lanchester, Henry Vaughan 77, 83,
    194
Lanchester, Stewart & Rickards 77,
    80, 83, 106, Pls. 29, 36
Lloyd, Thomas Alwyn 115, 194
Lloyd, T. Alwyn, & Gordon 133, 134
McKim, Mead & White 131
Moodie, Thomas A. 124, 194
Mylne, Robert 32
Mylne, William 32
Noel Architects 164, 194
Powell Dobson Architects 163, 194,
    Pl. 78
Price, Peter 50, 51, 52, 57, 67, 189, 195
Pritchard, John 42
Pugin & Pugin 44
Rickards, Edwin Alfred 106, 110,
    114, 195, Pl. 34
Rio Architects 161, 195
Seward, Edwin 23, 54, 56, 58, 59,
    60, 64, 66, 127, 128, 178, 180,
    189, 195, Pls. 9, 17, 18, 19, 20,
    54
Smith & Brewer 128, 134, Figs. 8.4,
    8.5, Pls. 55, 56
Smith, Arnold Dunbar 128, 130, 195
Smith, Arnold Dunbar 128, 130, 195
Stewart, James A. 195
Tanner, Sir Henry 55
Thomas, (Sir) Percy Edward 134,
    135, 147, 150, 151, 52, 153, 159,
    160, 195, Fig. 9.2, Pls. 66, 69, 75
Thomas, Sir Percy, & Son 159,
    Pl. 73
Thomas, Percy, Partnership 161, 161,
    Pls. 77, 78
Waterhouse, Sir Alfred 70, 72
Welsh School of Architecture
    Project Office 163, Pl. 78
Williams, Howard 148, 196, Pl. 67

Wills, Herbert W. 45, 67, 114, 115, 196, Pl. 16, 38
architectural competitions 105, 106, 117, 124, 128, 134
Assembly of Wales, National 157
Avenue, The 42, 45, 77, 78, 79, 80, 84, 188

Balfour, Arthur, prime minister 82
Barry, Docks Office 177, Pl. 86
Bather, Dr F. A. 128, 130, 132
Battersea, Town Hall 177
Bird, John, Bute's clerk 6, 30, 31, 32
Birmingham 64, 95, 173–4, Fig. 11.2
Town Hall 173, 176, Pl. 85
Blackfriars friary 43
Boulevard de Nantes (formerly Cathays Park Road) 77, 90, 91, 92, 99, 158
Bridgend 123
Bristol 64
British Association for Science, annual conference 52
Brussels (Belgium), Jubilee Park 181
builders
    Davies, Charles 81
    Turner, E., & Sons 80, 106
Buist, councillor 68
Bute, 4th Earl of *see* Bute, 1st Marquess
Bute, 1st Marquess xx, 9, 28–33
Bute, 2nd Marquess xx, 9, 14, 33–4, 36–7, 146, Pl. 11
Bute, 3rd Marquess xx, 16, 17, 19, 20, 21, 22, 23, 24, 37–45, 50, 53, 55, 56, 57, 59, 60, 64, 67, 68, 69, 71, 72, 76, 77, 80, 91, 96, 142, 146, 148, 182, 188, 189, Pl. 65
Bute, 4th Marquess xx, 44, 45, 80, 83, 84, 106, 144
Bute, 5th Marquess xx, 156
Bute, Charlotte Jane (nee Windsor), wife of 1st Marquess of Bute 28–9, 30, 32
Bute, Frances (nee Coutts), 2nd wife of 1st Marquess of Bute 32, 33
Bute, Gwendolen Mary (nee Fitzalan-Howard), wife of 3rd Marquess of Bute 42
Bute Building *see* Technical College
Bute Docks Company 22
Bute estate 5, 17, 22, 34, 36, 40, 56, 69, 72, Fig, 2.2

Bute family xx, 24
Bute Ironworks, Rhymney 33
Bute Park 91, 156
Bute Reservation 72, Figs. 6.1, 8.1
Bute trustees 17, 20
Butetown, Cardiff 17

Caernarfon 81
Caerphilly 16
Caerphilly Mountain 17
Cambrian, The, newspaper 8
Cambridge 119, 121, 125
Canal, project in Cathays Park 9, 35
Canal, proposed in Canton 36
Canton, Cardiff 16, 18, 23, 66
Canton Bridge 54, 55
Capital, of Wales 58, 82, 156
Cardiff
    Blackweir 35
    Borough 18, 42, Fig. 2.2
    City 70, 83
    Coal & Shipping Exchange 104
    Corporation 32, 94
    Council 45, 50, 52, 53, 60, 68, 69, 97, 143, 144
    County Borough 22
    County Court Offices 55
    Fine Art and Industrial Exhibition (1870) 19, 21
    Guild Hall 4, 16 Pl. 2
    in the seventeenth century 3, Pl. 1
    in the eighteenth century 5, Pl. 3
    Library 19, 21, 23, 50, Pl. 9
    Mayor (and Lord Mayor) 70, 76, 83, 84, 134
    municipal buildings, site for 51, 55, 59, 72, Fig. 4.1
    Museum 21, 23, 50, 77
    Museum (proposed) 59, 70, 80, 127, Pl. 54
    New Theatre 59
    Park Hotel 71
    Parks Department 83, 98, 100
    Police Station 59
    population 50, 80
    Post office, new 54
    St Mary's Church 3, 4, Pl. 3
    Theatre Royal 19
    Town Hall (New) 4, 16, 20, 23, 24, 52, 54, 79, Pl. 8
    Town Hall (Old) *see* Guild Hall

Town Hall (proposed) 50, 54, 56, 59, 60, 70, 77, Pls. 17, 19, 21
  see also City Hall
Town Hall committee 53, 54, 55, 56, 59, 60, 67, 68, 70, 79
Quay (Town) 3, 5
Cardiff Arms Park 21, 50, 54, 56, 59, 64, 71
Cardiff Castle 3, 19, 28, 29, 30, 32, 33, 35, 36, 37, 39–40, 42, 43, 45, 91, 93, 146, 156, Fig.
 3.2, Pls. 10, 12
Cardiff Corporation Act (1898) 72, 76, 96
Cardiff-Dowlais Iron and Steel Works 23
Cardiff Exhibition (1896) 60, 64–7, Fig. 5.1, Pl. 20
Cardiff Times 20, 52, 82, 83
Cardiff University *see* University College of South Wales and Monmouthshire, and University College, Ranch Site
Cardigan Castle 115
Carno 7
Carr, Lacelles, editor *Western Mail* 53, 56, 57, 58, 59, 69, 71, 183, 189
Castell Coch 40, 146
Castle Stables 41, 42, Fig. 3.4, Pl. 13
Cathays, Cardiff 30, 76
Cathays, derivation of name 28
Cathays House 30, 32–4, 36, 37, 72, Figs. 3.1, 3.2, Pl. 11
Cathays Nursery 37
Cathays Park 9, 21, 28–46, 50–9, 64, 67, 71, 76, 77, 80, 81, 85–7, 90–101, 104, 142, 146, 172, Pls. 23, 24, 28, 72
Cathays Park, attempt to acquire 19, 22, 24, 53, 68, 69
Cathays Park, layout 77, 143, 148, 178, 182, 184, Figs. 6.1, 8.1, 9.1, 10.1
Cathays Park Conservation Area 190
Cathays Park Road 76, 77, 99, 158
  see also Boulevard de Nantes
Cathedral Road, Cardiff 68
Chicago (USA) 56, 57, 64, 93, 183
Childs, George Pl. 4
City Beautiful movement 93, 183
City Hall (Town Hall until 1905) 77, 80, 83, 84, 85, 92, 94, 95, 96, 104, 105, 106–12, 128, 136, 156, 157, 176,

178, 184, Figs. 8.1, 8.2, 10.1, Pls. 22, 29, 30, 31
  Assembly Hall 111–12, 114, Pl. 35
  Clock tower 107, Pl. 32
  Council Chamber 106, 107, 110, Pls. 30, 34
  Marble Hall 85, 108, 111, Pl. 33
City Hall Lawn (formerly Green Circle) 96, 98, 99, 144, 158
Clutterbuck, Thomas, tenant of Cathays House 30, 31
Colchester, Town Hall 177
Competition, architectural 105, 106, 117, 124, 128, 134
Corbett Road, Cardiff 36, 37, 45, 46, 66, 68, 77, 96
Crawshay, Richard, ironworks owner 30
Crimean War 122
Crokerton, Cardiff 3, 4, 6, 19, 37, Pl. 3
Crocherbton *see* Crokerton
Crown Building *see* Welsh Governemnt Offices Two
Crown Gardens 100
Crystal Palace, London (1851 Exhibition) 64
Cubric Building (Cardiff University) 163-4,
Cyfarthfa Ironworks 5, 23
Cymru Fydd (Young Wales) 136, 184

Davies, Lord David (of Llandinam) 150
Devonport, Devon 173
Dobbin Pits farm, Cathays 28, 37, Fig. 3.3
Dock Feeder 36, 37, 45, 72, 76, 77, 81, 92, 96, 99, 115, Fig. 3.3
Docks
  Bute docks 19, 20, 22, 23, 36, 41, 104
  Bute East 16
  Bute West 10, 14, 15, 16, 36, Pl. 6
  Roath 22
  Roath Basin 20, 40
Dowlais 14
Dowlais Ironworks (later Steelworks) 5, 22, 23 Pl. 4
Drill Hall 77
Druidical Gardens 98
Dublin 121
Duncan, David, editor *Cardiff Times* 20, 42
Dutch Elm disease 96

Eccles Building, Washington (USA) 151
École des Beaux Arts, Paris 95
Edinburgh, New Town 172
Edinburgh, Duke of 121
Eisteddfod, National (1899) 76, 83, 115
engineers
    Brunel, Sir Isambard Kingdom 14,
      Pl. 7
    Green, James 9
    Harpur, William 77, 79, 184
    McConnochie, John 41
    Rose, Mr 64
    Trevithick, Richard 8
Evening Express, newspaper 69, 70, 71

Feeder (Dock), bridge 45, 46
Forman, Mr 33
Friars, The 30, 36, 69
Friary Gardens 68, 83, 96, 99–100, 144,
    190, Fig. 8.1, Pl. 27

Geddes, Patrick, town planner 87
Germany, Nazi, architecture of 151
Gilpin, William 2
Glamorgan Building *see* Glamorgan
    County Hall
Glamorgan County Council 67, 76,
    123
Glamorgan County Hall 77, 85, 87,
    94, 123–6, 147, Figs. 8.1, 8.3, 9.1,
    Pls. 50, 51, 52, 53
Council Chamber 126, Pl. 53
Glamorgan County Hall extension
    147, Pl. 66
Glamorgan County Council Offices *see*
    Glamorgan County Hall
Glamorganshire Canal 3, 5, 7, 14, 16,
    23, 30, 32, 36, 91, Figs. 1.1, 3.1, Pl. 5
Glamorganshire Canal Company 36
Glasgow 64, (George Square) 172
Gloucester 16
Gorsedd Circle 76, 98, 115–16, 190,
    Pls. 26, 39
Gorsedd Gardens 83, 96, 98, 99, 158,
    190, Fig. 8.1, Pl. 26
Gorsedd Gardens Road 77
Government Offices 86, 92, 94, 100,
    137, 190, Fig. 10.1, Pl. 23
    see also Welsh Board of Health;
      Welsh Government Offices Two
Grangetown, Cardiff 18, 64
Great Heath, Cardiff 28, 32

Great Western Railway 70
Green Circle *see* City Hall Lawn
Greyfriars (Dominican) friary 30, 42,
    45, 69, 91, 148, Fig. 3.4, Pl. 15

Helsinki (Finland), Senate Square
    179–80, 182, Fig. 11.7, Pl. 87
Herbert, Sir Ivor, MP 85
Herbert family 29
Herbert House 3, 30, 42, 44–5 Fig. 3.4,
    Pl. 15
Hollier, Henry, Bute's steward 30
Homfray, Samuel, ironworks owner 8
Howells, Hon. Anthony, USA consul 57

James, Mrs Minnie (of Dowlais) 150
Jones, A. Garth, glass designer 110, 111
Jones, Alderman David 52, 67

Karlesruhe (Germany), Marktplatz
    179, Fig. 11.5
King Edward VII 85
King Edward VII Avenue 64, 84, 91,
    92, 96, 99, 158, 188, 190, Pl. 24
King Edward VII National Memorial
    Association 150
King George V 86, 117, 130
Kingsway 76, 77, 81, 83

Law Building (Cardiff University)
    160–1, Pl. 75
Law Courts 77, 80, 83, 84, 85, 92, 95,
    96, 105, 112–14, 128, 176, 178, 184,
    Fig. 8.1, Pl. 36
    Courts Hall 113–14, Pl. 37
Leeds, Town Hall 176
Lewis, Sir William T., Bute's agent 50,
    52, 53, 54, 55, 56, 60, 67, 68, 72
Life Sciences Building (Cardiff
    University) 163, Pl. 79
Little Heath, Cardiff 28, 32
Liverpool 22, 37, 64, 95, 173, 174,
    Fig. 11.3
    St George's Hall 174
Llandaf 123
Llandaf Cathedral 42, 91
Lloyd George, Earl David 110, 136,
    159, Pl. 74
London 16, 22, 31, 70, 172, 177
    South Kensington 174–6, 190,
      Fig. 11.4
Luton 33

Malkin, Benjamin 2, 3
Manchester 64, 70, 177
memorials and statues
    Aberdare, Lord 98, 123, Pl. 49
    Boer (South African War) 84, 99
        121–2, Pl. 46
    Bute, 3rd Marquess 100, 146, Pls.
        27, 65
    Falklands Conflict (City of Cardiff)
        167, Pl. 83
    Falklands Conflict (Welsh national)
        168, Pl. 84
    Cory, John 98, 116, Pl. 40
    Crichton-Stuart, Lord Ninian 98,
        142, Pl. 61
    Gift of Life 168
    Lloyd George of Dwyfor, Earl David
        98, 159, Pl. 74
    Raoul Wallenberg 168
    Spanish Civil War 168
    Tredegar, 1st Viscount 99, 122,
        Pl. 47
    Welch Regiment 2/7th (Cyclists)
        Battalion 99
    Welsh National War 87, 92, 98,
        142–6, Fig. 9.1, Pls. 25, 62, 63,
        64
    Williams, Judge Gwilym 123,
        Pl. 48
Merthyr Tydfil 2, 6, 7, 9, 14, 23, 30, 34,
    35, 123, Figs. 1.1, 2.1
Mid-Glamorgan County Council 125
Mountjoy Estates Ltd 148
Mount Stuart, Scotland 33
Munich (Germany), Königsplatz 179,
    Fig. 11.6
Museum Avenue 80, 84, 92

Napoleonic Wars 6, 9
National Library 81
National Museum of Wales 21, 77, 80,
    81, 86, 87, 92, 94, 98, 100, 127–34,
    190, Figs. 8.1, 8.4, 8.5, 9.1, 10.1,
    Pls. 26, 55, 56, 57, 58
Nazareth House 41–2, 45, 68, 91, 92,
    147, 148, Fig. 3.4, Pl. 24
Neath 2, 123
Newcastle-upon-Tyne, Grainger Town
    172–3
Newport 16
North Road, Cardiff 30, 32, 37, 41, 54,
    76, 77, 81, 83, 158, Fig. 3.1

Oslo (Norway) 180
Ottawa (Canada) 52

Paris (France) 58, 180, 183
Park House 41, Pl. 14
Park Place, Cardiff 35, 37, 45, 46, 54,
    59, 70, 76, 81, 96, 98, Fig. 3.3
Parks Department 98, 100
Parliament, Welsh 136, 148
Penarth 2
Penarth Dock 23
Penydarren Ironworks 5, 8, 23
Penydarren Tramroad 14, Fig. 1.1
Peoples' Palace 58, Pl. 18
Pettigrew, A. A., gardener to Butes 30,
    37, 72, 77, 87, 188
Philidelphia (USA) 52, 57
Pierhead, Cardiff Pl. 6
Plymouth, Earl of 117
Plymouth Ironworks 5, 23
Police Station, Central 164–5, Fig. 10.1,
    Pl. 80
Pontypridd 123
Poor Sisters of Nazareth 42
Portland stone, use of 93–4
public conveniences 146, Fig. 9.1

Queen Alexandra Gardens 84, 85, 92,
    97, 143, 144, 167, Fig. 8.1, Pl. 25
Queen Anne Square 91, 95, 148
Queen Anne Square Colonnade 147–8,
    Fig. 9.1, Pl. 67

Ramsdale, councillor 68
Ranch Site see University College,
    Ranch Site
Ratepayers Committee 70, 71
Redwood Building 137, 158–9,
    Fig. 10.1, Pl. 73
Rhondda, Lord 110
Rhondda Fach 15
Rhondda Fawr 15
Rhymney 33
Rhymney Ironworks 16, 33
Rhymney Railway 16, 17, Fig. 2.1
Rhymney Valley 7
Roath, Cardiff 18, 16, 23, 30, 32
Roman Catholic cathedral (proposed) 44
Roman remains 45
Royal Welsh College of Music and
    Drama 41, Pl. 13
Royal Fine Art Commission 166

St David's Cathedral, Charles Street 44
St Margaret's Church, Roath 31, 33
Saltaire, Yorkshire 173, Fig. 11.1
Sandby, Paul, painter 4, Pl. 3
Scandinavian Neo-Classicism 151
Scotland 33, 40
sculptors
    Bankart, G. P. 111
    Bayes, Gilbert 131
    Brock, Thomas 144
    Clapperton, Thomas J. 110, 131
    Copnall, Bainbridge 159
    Crook, T. Mewburn 110
    Evans, David 131
    Fehr, H. C., 106, 107, Pl. 32
    Garbe, Richard L. 131
    Gillick, Ernest G. 110
    Hampton, Herbert 123, Pl. 49
    Hodge, Albert 112, 125, Pl. 51
    John, Sir William Goscombe 96,
        110, 115, 116, 122, 123, 142,
        Pls. 40, 47, 48
    Macgillevray, James Pittendrigh 146,
        Pl. 65
    McGill, Donald 112
    Merrifield, Leonard S.,110
    Montford, Paul 107, 112, Pl. 31
    Pegram, Alfred Bertram 131, 145,
        Pls. 57, 64
    Pegram, Henry Alfred 110
    Peterson, David 135
    Pomeroy, F. W. 110
    Poole, Henry 107, 110
    Rizzello, Michael 159, Pl. 74
    Thomas, J. Harvard 110
    Toft, Albert 122, Pl. 46
    Turner, Alfred 110
    Wagstaff, W. Wheatley 110
Sheffield, Town Hall 177
Short, Robert, Bute's gardener 36
Shrewsbury 70
Sir Martin Evans Building (Cardiff
    University) 161–2, Pl. 77
Sophia Gardens, Cardiff 19, 64, 68
South African War (1899–1902) 121
South Kensington, London 174–6,
    Fig. 11.4
South Wales Daily News, newspaper 68,
    69, 76, 85
South Wales Railway 16
Speed, John, map-maker 3, 5
statues see memorials and statues

Stewart, David, surveyor 36
Swansea 2, 7, 16, 81, 151

Taff , river 3, 14, 28, 36
Taffs Well 16
Taff Vale Railway 8, 10, 14, 15, 16, 37,
    64, Figs. 2.1, 3.3, Pl. 7
Technical College (former Technical
    Institute) 86, 87, 134–5, Figs. 8.1, 9.1
technical schools (proposed) 50, 77
Temperance Town, Cardiff 18, 56, 70,
    71, Pl. 21
Temple of Peace and Health 87, 100,
    150–3, 157, 190, Fig. 9.1, Pls. 69,
    70, 71
    Hall of Nations 152–3, Pl. 71
    Garden of Remembrance 153
Times, The, newspaper 82
Thomas, T. H. 85
Thompson, Herbert 53
Thompson, H. M., councillor 143
Toronto (Canada) 52
Tower Building (Cardiff University)
    162–3, Pl. 78
Tredegar 173
Tredegar, Lord 30, Fig. 3.1
Turnpike road see North Road

University College, Newport Road 22,
    23, 24, 50, 54, 116
University College of South Wales and
    Monmouthshire 21, 76, 82, 84, 85,
    87, 92, 93, 100, 116–21, 147, 158,
    Figs. 8.1, 9.1, 10.1, Pls. 41, 42, 43,
    44, 45
    Drapers' Library 119, 121, Pls. 43,
        44, 45
    Great Hall 117, Pl. 41
University College (proposed) 50, 51,
    68, 77, 79
University College, Ranch Site 159–64,
    Figs. 10.1
    see also Law Building; Sir Martin
        Evans Building; Tower Building;
        Life Science Building; Cubric
        Building
University College, temporary
    laboratories 164
University of Wales 67, 76
University of Wales Registry 67, 68, 69,
    81, 93, 94, 114–15, 190, Figs. 8.1,
    9.1, Pl. 38

Valhalla (Welsh) 84–5
Vienna (Austria) 58, 183
    Ringstrasse 180–1, 182, Fig. 11.8

Wales, Prince of 82, 99, 117, 121, 144
Ward, John, museum curator 127
Washington (USA) 52, 183–4
Weekly Mail, newspaper 82
Welsh Board of Health 87, 100, 148–9,
    166, Fig. 9.1, Pl. 68
Welsh Book of Remembrance 152
Welsh College of Advanced
    Technology *see* Technical College;
    Redwood Building
Welsh Council of the League of
    Nations Union 150
Welsh Government Offices One
    see Welsh Board of Health

Welsh Government Offices Two 165–6,
    Fig. 10.1, Pls. 81, 82
Welsh Insurance Commission Offices
    87, 136–7, 149, 150, Figs. 8.1, 9.1,
    Pl. 60
Welsh Museum of Natural History,
    Arts and Antiquities 127
Welsh National Museum, movement
    for 58
Western Mail, newspaper 24, 53, 55, 56,
    59, 68, 69, 72, 82, 136, 137, 148
Westminster 58
Windsor, Lord 66
World's Fair 56, 57, 64, 93, 183

Yates, George, map-maker 28